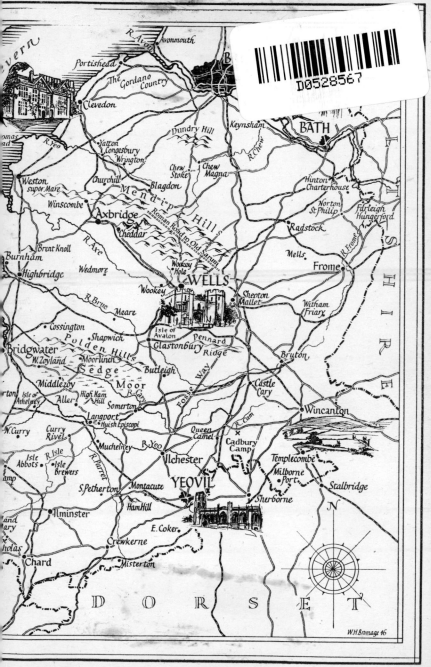

R. Avon
Avonmouth
Portishead
The Gordano Country
Clevedon
B
BATH
Dundry Hill
Keynsham
R. Chew
Yatton
Congesbury
Wrington
Chew Stoke
Chew Magna
Churchill
Blagdon
Weston super Mare
Mend-ip Hills
Hinton Charterhouse
Norton St. Philip
Farleigh Hungerford
Winscombe
Axbridge
Radstock
Cheddar
Roman Road to Old Sarum
Mells
R. Frome
Frome
Brent Knoll
R. Axe
Burnham
Wedmore
Wookey Hole
WELLS
Highbridge
Wookey
Shepton Mallet
R. Brue
Meare
Witham Friary
Cossington
Shapwich
Isle of Avalon
Pennard Ridge
Poldern Hills
Glastonbury
Bridgwater
W. Zoyland
Moorlinch
Sedge
Butleigh
Bruton
Middlezoy
Moor
Fosse Way
Castle Cary
ton Isle of Athelney
Aller
High Ham Hill
R. Cary
Somerton
Wincanton
N. Curry
Curry Rivel
Langport
Huish Episcopi
R. Cam
Queen Camel
Cadbury Camp
Isle Abbots
R. Isle
Isle Brewers
Muchelney
R. Yeo
Ilchester
Templecombe
Milborne Port
Stalbridge
amp
R. Parrett
S. Petherton
Montacute
YEOVIL
Sherborne
and ary e holas
Ham Hill
E. Coker
N
Ilminster
Crewkerne
Chard
Misterton

D   O   R   S   E   T

W. H. Bromage 46

COMPANION INTO SOMERSET

The Abbot's Kitchen, from Glastonbury Abbey

COMPANION INTO
SOMERSET

By MAXWELL FRASER

WITH FIFTEEN PLATES
AND A MAP

METHUEN & CO. LTD. LONDON
36 Essex Street, Strand, W.C.2

First published in 1947

CATALOGUE NO. 3144/U

THIS BOOK IS PRODUCED IN COMPLETE
CONFORMITY WITH THE AUTHORIZED
ECONOMY STANDARDS

PRINTED IN GREAT BRITAIN

TO

MY MOTHER

CONTENTS

ILLUSTRATIONS

ACKNOWLEDGMENTS

SOMERSET is a county of kindly people, and since the earliest days of my childhood I have had help and friendship from all sorts and conditions of people, in all parts of the county. Many of its traditions were told me years ago, by the country folk who cherished them, and everywhere my interest in Somerset's beautiful old buildings has been fostered by the pride of local people in their great inheritance, but among those who have contributed to my knowledge of the "crooked shire" I owe special thanks to Mr. A. S. Macmillan, of Yeovil; Mr. D. Macmillan, and Mr. E. Brewser, of Castle Cary; Mr. H. Balch, and the late Mr. Robert King, of Wells; Mr. Geoffrey Luttrell, of Dunster, and the late Mr. Arthur Fownes Luttrell, of East Quantoxhead; Mr. W. E. Murley, Headmaster of the East Coker schools; Mr. John Hatton, of Bath; the late Mr. Maurice Page, of Bridgwater; the late Mr. Arthur Clayton of Glastonbury; Mr. W. J. E. Lee, and Mr. V. Danby, of Watchet; the Rev. Cecil B. Hunt, of Chedzoy; Mr. W. Marston Acres, of Wedmore; Wing-Commander G. W. Hodgkinson, of Wookey Hole; Mr. Havilland Hoskyns, of South Petherton; Mr. A. W. Vivian-Neal, of Poundisford Park; and Mr. H. St. George Gray, of Taunton, Secretary of the Somersetshire Archaeological Society.

The editors and staffs of Somerset's excellent local newspapers have always been of the greatest assistance, and I gladly acknowledge my special debt to Mr. John Goodchild, Editor of the *Western Gazette* of Yeovil, for permission to quote from his article on Martin Strong, published in the *Proceedings of the Somersetshire Archaeological Society* in 1932.

I am also indebted to the *Proceedings* of the Society generally for archaeological particulars, and to the invaluable

Year Books of the Society of Somerset Folk, and the publications of the Folk Press, for many little-known facts about the county.

In conclusion, I should like to say I am fully conscious of the wealth of interesting details I have been obliged to omit, but Somerset is a very large county, and so richly endowed with history and legend, prehistoric and Roman remains, and splendid buildings, that it has been impossible to do more than act as a good companion, pointing the way to fresh discoveries in this most fascinating county, whose scenery is more varied than that of any other English shire, and whose interest is inexhaustible.

The constant activity of the Somersetshire Archaeological Society is continually bringing new facts and sites to light, and since this book was written several Roman sites have been uncovered, notably the beautiful mosaic floor in a field near Low Ham church; whilst the remote Exmoor village of Luccombe was chosen by Mass-Observation for their factual account of life in an English village.

M. F.

Chapter One: BATH—"THE QUEEN ENCHANTED"

Bath before and after Beau Nash—Neighbouring villages

EVER since the third century A.D., when Solinus Caius Julius, writing of the world's wonders, described Bath, this lovely city beside the Avon has been more praised, berated, and minutely described, in every age, than any other city of Britain but London.

Although Bath to-day is almost purely Georgian, and still looks, as a Frenchman wrote in 1811, "like a city that has been cast in a mould all at once, and turned out of it perfectly fresh and youthful", the magnificent Roman Baths, twenty feet below the present city level, make even the far-distant past seem curiously real, but to most visitors the characters of fiction seem even more vividly alive than those of history. Bath's streets teem with memories of irascible Captain Absolute; Squire Bramble; lovable Catherine Morland, sedate Anne Elliot, Henry Tilney, Captain Wentworth and all their acquaintance; amiable Mr. Pickwick, embarrassed Winkle, and the incomparable Sam Weller, pronouncing the waters to taste of "warm flat-irons"—what a peerless crowd of humanity, real and imagined, makes the background of Bath!

"Like a Queen enchanted", sang Swinburne in his *Ballad of Bath*, and truly Bath is enchanted—for what other city in the world with so long a history has so little that is tragic, and so much that is gay and good to record? Kings and saints, nuns, monks, abbots, bishops, Nonconformists, soldiers and politicians, authors and fashionables, have ranged its streets in turn, many of them fanatical, yet not one story of religious persecution mars its history. Although it was laid waste by Saxons, and later by Danes, no later

I

wars ravaged it, and for nearly two thousand years it has restored the sick, or soothed the dying.

Bath's origin is picturesquely accounted for by legends in which the names of King Lud, Prince Bladud, and Shakespeare's King Lear, are interwoven. The full story was set down by John Wood and "attested by prominent citizens of Bath" in 1741, in a document preserved in the British Museum, and has been told in more or less identical terms by later writers, until it is almost as familiar as the legend of Alfred and the burnt cakes.

Conjecture is on surer ground with the coming of the Romans, for they not only left behind them the magnificent baths, but coins and jewellery, dropped everywhere with their usual carelessness; inscriptions from grateful invalids, giving thanks for their recovery; and monuments to those who were buried in the Roman cemetery. Roman Bath, founded about A.D. 54, was for 200 years a pleasure city, but with the withdrawal of the legions, the peace and safety of Bath fled, but how or when it was devastated, no man knows, although a fragment of a contemporary Chronicle preserved at Exeter described its desolation.

Gradually, however, the city was rebuilt, and Christianity came to Saxon Bath about the middle of the seventh century. The first church was built on the site of the present abbey church, and was the setting for the coronation of King Edgar in the tenth century. The Saxons learned to appreciate the value of the hot springs, and small hospitals for poor and leprous pilgrims were founded.

With the coming of the Normans, John de Villula, Bishop of Wells, rebuilt the abbey on a magnificent scale, and made it the seat of his bishopric, fixing the essential character of Bath for over four centuries, although its fortunes fluctuated greatly.

In 1499, when the monastery founded by the Saxons had fallen to a very low ebb, Bishop King rebuilt the abbey church, inspired by the dream of angels ascending and descending a ladder between heaven and earth, which is commemorated on the West front of the Abbey to this day. It was the last pre-Reformation church built in England, and had hardly been completed when the Abbey was dissolved.

In the sixteenth century the abbey church was again in a terrible state of dilapidation, the streets of the town were narrow, and sanitation deficient. When Queen Elizabeth visited Bath in 1574, strenuous efforts were made to disguise the state of the city. Garlands of green were hung on the abbey church to hide its ruinous condition, "quiresters" were brought over from Wells, the windows were mended, the bellman given a new coat of "black frise at XV pence the yard", and rubbish was cleared away from the foot of the town walls, where it was customarily thrown.

In 1590, Elizabeth gave Bath a new charter, confirming all its ancient rights, but in the following year, when she passed through on her way to visit her godson, Sir John Harington, at Kelston, the smell of the city proved too much for her, and she drove on after expressing her displeasure forcibly. Although it is not on record what she said, the Queen certainly expressed herself to some purpose, and eleven years later, the memory of her royal indignation was such that when the citizens heard she intended to visit Bath again, they sent in a panic to Bristol, Frome, and even further afield, to get "Paviors against the Queen's comynge", and were probably mightily relieved when her health prevented the visit. It is a curious sidelight on sixteenth-century mentality that, judging by the Municipal Records, after they heard the Queen would not come, nothing whatever was done beyond claiming their expenses to date!

Bath escaped destruction in the Civil War, due, possibly, to the fact that it was represented in Parliament by that queer, tortuous character, William Prynne, and that the great fight in 1643 took place on Lansdown Hill, then outside the town boundary.

John Evelyn, who visited Bath in 1654, described the city under the Commonwealth " ... The King's Bath is esteemed the fairest in Europe. The town is entirely built of stone, but the streets, narrow, uneven and unpleasant."

Great rejoicings followed the accession of Charles II, who visited the city in 1663. Pepys was at Bath five years later, and gives one of his usual vivid pictures of life in the city.

II

Bath at the opening of the eighteenth century gave no sign of its future glory, but when Richard Nash was appointed Master of Ceremonies in 1708, its greatest days began. He immediately started the much-needed work of reforming Bath society, but it was not until 1742, at the very height of his power as uncrowned King of Bath, that his famous rules were posted in the Pump Room. He found an uncouth society where even the highest circles were uneasily conscious of the superior elegance of the French, and by banishing swords, preventing duels with all the rigour of the law, and enforcing elegance, taste and courtesy, he inaugurated a new conception of social intercourse, which gradually spread all over the country.

Whilst Beau Nash was raising the tone of Bath society, two men were providing a fitting background for the elegance he introduced, when Ralph Allen's enormous wealth, joined with John Wood's architectural genius, swept away the medieval city and "town planned" the splendid, dignified streets and crescents we see to-day.

Ralph Allen, who began life as an obscure assistant in the post office of a remote Cornish town, rose by sheer merit to the enjoyment of a prodigious fortune, and remained to the end of his life the pattern of a true gentleman, modest, simple and generous. When he died, William Pitt wrote to Mrs. Allen "Mankind has lost in him such a benevolent and tender friend as I fear the example of his virtues will not have power to raise up to the world again." Allen figured in many books and memoirs of his day, but his truly lovable character is most happily delineated by Fielding, who described him under the name of Squire Allworthy in *Tom Jones*, in a passage too long to be quoted here, but worth reading as an example of eighteenth-century virtues, which comes as a welcome antidote to the too-familiar story of eighteenth-century vices.

When Ralph Allen came to Bath as assistant postmaster, his attention was frequently drawn to the great inconveniences of the postal system, and at the age of twenty-six he devised a system of cross-country posts for England and Wales, which he inaugurated at his own expense—an hazardous speculation which brought him a rich harvest. It has been estimated that his receipts averaged £12,000 a year between 1720 and 1764, and further riches accrued when he acquired and exploited the quarries of Bath stone at Combe Down.

It was in order to overcome the objections of many contemporary architects and builders that he built his splendid house, Prior Park, where such diverse celebrities as Princess Amelia, Pope, Fielding, Warburton, Pitt, Garrick, Quin, Sterne, John Wesley, and others, enjoyed his princely hospitality. The mansion was designed by John Wood the elder, "Not only to see all Bath, but for all Bath to see", and it is still a magnificent sight from every viewpoint.

The most astonishing thing about John Wood and his son and namesake is that so little is known of them. Although the elder Wood settled in Bath in 1727, and remained there until his death in 1754, and his son lived in the city until 1782, and although between them they reconstructed Bath on the lines followed by succeeding architects, all through a period when so many famous writers were recording almost every action and trait of individual members of Bath society, the two Woods remain unrecorded and unknown to fame, apart from their splendid creations.

Under Beau Nash, the neglected roads were relaid and lit, a regular tariff for lodgings was enforced, and the unruly chairmen controlled, the Pump Room built, and Assembly Rooms opened. The orchestra was instituted, and became famous under the Linleys and the Herschels. The Bath theatre was opened and achieved well-deserved fame under the Palmers, who set Mrs. Siddons and other famous people on the road to success, and the younger John Palmer devised the mail-coach which not only revolutionized the conveyance of letters, but travelling generally. All the famous products bearing the name of Bath also made their first appearance—Bath Chairs, Bath Buns, Bath Chaps, Bath Olivers not to mention Bath "Cats"—and Sally Lunn opened her famous shop.

Dr. Oliver developed the healing waters, and invented the biscuit which bears his name, and with Ralph Allen and the two Woods providing the background and accommodation, the whole aspect of the city was changed.

Eighteenth-century planning can be seen to perfection in Bath, for in addition to the many supreme individual examples of architecture, it has been triumphantly adapted to the difficulties of its hilly site. Dickensians will remember Mr. Pickwick and his friends "came to the unanimous conclusion that Park Street was very much like the perpendicular streets a man sees in a dream which he cannot get up for the life of him", and Defoe tells us Queen Anne, when Princess, had an alarming demonstration of the steepness of the streets, for the horses dragging the royal carriage slipped on Lansdown Hill and ran backwards downhill, until the footmen and bystanders succeeded in arresting its progress.

So far from being intimidated by the difficulties of the site, the two Woods were inspired to create the famous Circus and Royal Crescent, in addition to composing many beautiful streets and groups of houses. The lovely honey-colour of the beautiful Bath stone, and its general effect in the superb setting of green hills and trees beside the River Avon, makes Bath the loveliest of Georgian towns, and the most perfect eighteenth-century survival in the world.

Fortunately, in spite of the damage done by the air-raids, and the major disaster of the destruction of all but the outer walls of the Assembly Rooms, Georgian Bath was so well-built that its character, and the greater part of its actual fabric, has survived, and all who are planning for its future, however much they disagree on other points, are unanimous in insisting upon preserving its integrity.

III

It was against this background that Bath became the centre of wit and fashion. The writers who frequented eighteenth-century Bath are still widely read, quoted, and deservedly admired as classics. The correspondence of its visitors is read and discussed, and their diaries are known far and wide. What a company they are—inimitable Jane Austen; Fanny Burney; charming Mrs. Elizabeth Montague, "Queen of the Blue Stockings", and her sister Mrs. Scott; Lord Chesterfield; Walpole with his peevishness dissolving into laughter over Anstey's rhymed Bath Guide; Caroline Herschel, chronicling the doings of her beloved brother William; Johnson and his Boswell; and countless others, who have so minutely chronicled every incident of life in eighteenth-century Bath that we can follow them through every hour of the day, from their breakfast in Spring Gardens to their evenings at the Assembly Rooms and card tables.

2

Gay as they were, the social round was usually a little stereotyped, although sometimes there are curious incidents like the "frolic" proposed by her Bath friends, when Mrs. Thrale and Fanny Burney visited Mr. Ferry, the Bath alderman, and Fanny says, with her tongue in her cheek: ". . . we perceived through a glass a perspective view of ships, boats and water. This raree-show over, the maid who officiated as show-woman had a hint given her, and presently a trap-door opened and up jumped a covered table, ornamented with various devices. When we had expressed our delight at this long enough to satisfy Mr. Ferry, another hint was given, and presently down dropped an eagle from the ceiling, whose talons were put into a certain hook at the top of the covering of the table, and when the admiration at this was over, up again flew the eagle, conveying in his talons the cover, and leaving under it a repast of cakes, sweetmeats, oranges, and jellies.

"When our raptures upon this feat subsided, the maid received another signal, and then seated herself in an armchair which presently sank down underground, and up in its room came a barber's block, with a vast quantity of black wool on it, and a high head-dress.

"This, you may be sure, was more applauded than all the rest; we were *en extase*, and having properly expressed our gratitude, were soon after suffered to decamp."

On the other side of the picture are the pious and earnest citizens who flocked to the Countess of Huntingdon's chapel, and listened to the exhortations of Wesley and Whitfield, and the prodigious industry of William Herschel, who brought the Bath orchestra to the highest pitch of perfection whilst also studying astronomy and burnishing lenses for his telescopes, and studying the heavens on every clear night.

IV

Early in the nineteenth century, the great public functions so carefully built up by Beau Nash began to decline, and exclusive private parties began to take their place. Celebrities still flocked there, but by 1830 it had become largely populated by retired admirals, generals, civil servants and clergymen, depicted in the later novels of Jane Austen, whose own father retired from the rectory at Steventon to live in Bath.

V

In the twentieth century, Bath, still famous and beautiful beyond compare, has many celebrated visitors and residents, but has an equally warm welcome for the less famous, entertaining them so royally that many find all their pleasure in the City itself, but Bath's surroundings are well worth exploring. There are delightful villages among the neighbouring hills and valleys, and the city is a perfect introduction to the rich and varied beauty and interest of Somerset, where age-old traditions and customs still flourish, and beauty is paramount.

Among the places within easy reach are Batheaston, with the villa made famous by Sir John and Lady Miller; Swainswick, birthplace of William Prynne; Bathford, on a hill sloping to the Avon, above the old Fosse Way, and St. Catherine's Court, a lovely old manor-house in its terraced gardens, close to the Gloucestershire border.

Langridge, in a deep hollow, has an ancient manor-house unique in the West Country for its fortified thirteenth-century peel tower, surviving from sixteenth-century alterations. There is a diminutive church with brasses to the Walsh family, who owned the manor in the fifteenth century. Charlcombe also has a diminutive church with considerable Norman work, and a monument to Sarah Fielding, which says she was worthy of a nobler monument, but her name will be written in the Book of Life.

Loveliest of all the villages round Bath are Bathampton, with its monuments to Admiral Phillip, founder of the Australian Commonwealth, Sir Roderick Murchison, the distinguished geologist, and members of Ralph Allen's family; Claverton, with the curious tomb of Ralph Allen himself, and memories of his friend Richard Graves, who was rector there for fifty-five years; and Widcombe, where Walter Savage Landor wanted to be buried. Widcombe Manor, an exquisite gem of eighteenth-century architecture, is neighboured by the house in which Fielding wrote part of *Tom Jones*, and the attractive and interesting old church.

Moving southward along the Somerset bank of the Avon, we can climb Combe Down, past Prior Park, to Monkton Combe, beside the Midford Brook; or go by way of Bathwick, where Clark Russell, famous author of sea stories, is buried; or we can go by the road past the sham Midford Castle to South Stoke with its small church and great tithe barn, and Combe Hay, beside the Cam Brook. Combe Hay Manor House is set in wooded hills, with lawns sloping down to the village, and the church where the poet Noel Carrington is buried. The fiery Cavalier, Sir Lewis Dyves, was also buried at Combe Hay. He defended Sherborne Castle gallantly, and Evelyn said that he was "indeed a valiant gentleman, but not a little given to romance when he spake of himself".

In the hills north of Combe Hay is English Combe, so called because it lay on the English side of the Wansdyke, the line of which can be traced in an orchard by the church. This very retired and pretty village was once the residence of Saxon Kings, and afterwards a seat of the Bishops of

Coutances, and of the De Gourneys, of whose castle a fosse and mound survives. The church has a considerable amount of Norman work, and is neighboured by a large barn which once belonged to the Priors of Bath.

South of Combe Hay is Wellow, with a station on the Somerset and Dorset Railway. The remarkably fine church was largely rebuilt by Sir Walter Hungerford in 1372, and the old manor-house of the Hungerfords was rebuilt in the seventeenth century. There is a local tradition that when any evil threatened the house of Hungerford a white lady appeared beside the holy well of St. Julian, which can be found in a cottage garden near by.

Dr. John Bull, long reputed the author of our National Anthem, although modern research tends to show it was the work of many hands, was born at Wellow in 1562. Whether he composed the National Anthem or not, his ingenuity as a composer for the virginals caused him to rank as one of the founders of the modern pianoforte repertory, and his fame in his own day is shown by an anecdote of his travels abroad, related by Wood: "Hearing of a famous musician belonging to a certain cathedral (at St. Omer's, as I have heard), he applied himself as a novice to him to learn something of his faculty, and to see and admire his works. This musician, after some discourse had passed between them, conducted Bull to a vestry, or music school, joyning to the cathedral, and shew'd to him a lesson or song of forty parts, and then made a vaunting challenge to any person in the world to add one more part to them, supposing it to be so compleat and full that it was impossible for any mortal man to correct, or add to it. Bull thereupon desiring the use of ink and rul'd paper (such as we call musical paper), prayed the musician to lock him up in the said school for two or three hours; which being done, not without great disdain by the musician, Bull in that time, or less, added forty more parts to the said lesson, or song. The musician thereupon being called in, he viewed it, tried it, and re-try'd it. At length he burst out into a great ecstasy, and swore by the great God that he that added those forty parts must either be the devil or Dr. Bull, &c., Whereupon, Bull making himself known, the musician fell down and ador'd him."

*Down the Avon—The Way to Wells—Roads to Bath—Dundry
and the Chew Valley—The Vale of Wrington—The Gordano
Country—Around Congresbury*

A JOURNEY down the Avon was almost obligatory in
eighteenth-century Bath; Princess Amelia went all the way
to Bristol and back by wherry in 1728, the year after the
river was made navigable to the sea, and there are still boating parties, particularly on the fine stretch to Saltford, the
most popular boating station on the river.

The Avon leaves Bath by way of Twerton, where Fielding once lived, and below Weston, which was the birthplace
of the lovable St. Elphege, Archbishop of Canterbury in
1006, who allowed himself to be murdered by the Danes
rather than raise a ransom at the expense of his diocese.
Weston is beautifully placed in the shelter of Lansdown Hill,
below the ornate tower where William Beckford, whose
own life was nearly as fantastic as his fantasy *Vathek*, lies
buried.

Newton St. Loe, on the south bank, is a trim and pretty
little village on a hill, with a restored church, an eighteenth-
century mansion, and the remains of a castle where King
John took refuge from his justly incensed barons. Near by is
Corston Manor, now a farmhouse, where seven-years-old
Robert Southey spent the unhappy school-days described
in *The Retrospect*.

Kelston Park is set on a wooded bluff rising sheer from the
north bank of the river. The house built in 1587 by Barozzi,
for Sir John Harington, the wit, poet, and favourite of his
godmother Queen Elizabeth, was damaged during the Civil
War, and later pulled down, but we can still read his

Diaries, and accounts of the splendid entertainment he gave his loving but exacting godmother, which cost so much he had to sell beautiful St. Catherine's Court to pay for it. Kelston Church has a unique musical epitaph to his descendant, Henry Harington, who founded the Bath Harmonic Society.

There is a particularly delightful walk from Kelston to Prospect Stile, near the race-course on Lansdown Hill, and the monument to Sir Bevil Grenville, the gallant grandson of the immortal Sir Richard Grenville. He was killed at the Battle of Lansdown in 1643, a battle which Fuller says "was disputed rather by parcels or piecemeals, and seemed not so much one entire battle as a heap of skirmishes huddled together".

The restored church of Saltford has a curiosity in memorial stones, where a mason of Charles Stuart's days has resorted to a quaint device to crowd in all his inscription, on a seventeenth-century monument to Robert and Lamorock Flower:

"Flowers they war,
    Nipt in ye springe,
  But flourishing now
    With Christ their king."

After leaving Saltford and its boats, the Avon becomes the boundary between Gloucestershire and Somersetshire. There is a ferry and bridge at Keynsham, where the River Chew joins the Avon. Many legends cling to the town, which takes its name from St. Keyne, who changed the reptiles into stone, and left so many ammonites in the district to prove the story; whilst Bath itself is a testimony to the truth of the tale of Prince Bladud and his pigs. A monastery of Austin Canons was founded at Keynsham in 1170 on a magnificent scale, but the Reformation and the Brydges family between them made a clean sweep, the abbey being used as a quarry for the Brydges' mansion, which in its turn disappeared, and furnished the monastic odds and ends incorporated in many of the local houses and garden walls. The church has some elaborate monuments to the Brydges family.

It was at Keynsham that indecision and delay robbed the luckless Monmouth of any chance of capturing Bristol, and turned him back to Norton St. Philip on his fatal march to Sedgemoor.

The river takes a great bend round the meadows of Keynsham Hams to meet the tide at Hanham Lock and flow through wooded banks past Brislington, which is now a suburb of Bristol. Close by St. Anne's Park Station is the tree-filled valley where the ruined well and chapel of St. Anne can be found. The ferry which conveyed pilgrims over the Avon is still in existence. The chapel was founded by Roger, first Earl de la Warr, in the thirteenth century, and was visited by Henry VII and his Queen, and only the foundations remain, but the well has been restored by the City of Bristol.

II

Bristol was constituted a county in itself as far back as the fourteenth century, but its history is so bound up with that of the West Country that it is dear to every Somerset heart. Its Merchant Venturers made its fame international, and its history a part of the Empire and of the United States.

Happily, the Abbey and the great parish church of St. Mary Redcliff, with its memories of Handel and Chatterton, have survived the devastating air raids of 1940 and 1941, in which so many of the city's beautiful old buildings perished. Bristol is still a superb centre for touring north Somerset.

III

Probably the most popular of all excursions from Bristol are to Bath and Wells—either direct, or on one of the many delightful "round trips" which give such a comprehensive view of the charming countryside of North Somerset, with its hills and valleys and surprisingly remote and unspoiled villages, completely different in surroundings and appearance from those of West Somerset, for here are many limestone hills with great gorges and caves, and houses of stone with slate roofs, as beautiful in their own way as the red earth, rich woods and cob-walled cottages topped with deep thatch, which are found in West Somerset.

The Wells Road leaves Bristol by way of Whitchurch, now joined up with the city, and drops down Pensford Hill to the deep valley in which Pensford lies, with the church of Publow showing on the skyline.

A huge railway viaduct of sixteen arches, a hundred feet high, bestrides the valley like a Roman aqueduct. Pensford is an attractive little place, even without its viaduct, for it is gathered round an imposing church beside the little River Chew, a happy little river that only knows beautiful scenery and picturesque villages in all its journey to join the Avon at Keynsham.

South of Pensford the road continues through Temple Cloud, high up on a hill giving wonderful views of the surrounding country. It is said to have been the site of a Roman encampment and a temple in honour of Claudius Caesar, the name of which, Templum Claudii, has been corrupted to Temple Cloud. In the valley below the village of Clutton can be seen, on the edge of the colliery country, but the main road continues through Farrington Gurney, a large village whose church is on the Midsomer Norton road, beside an old manor-house, and although rebuilt occupies an

Cheddar Gorge

Evening, Watchet Harbour

Clevedon

ancient ecclesiastical site, and has a quaint Norman effigy over the west doorway, locally known as "old Farrington", and believed to be Thomas Gourney, who was lord of the manor in the thirteenth century.

South of Farrington Gurney, the road reaches Wells through Chewton Mendip. Another road runs to Midsomer Norton, and there is a choice of ways to Bath, or back to Bristol.

IV

The Midsomer Norton road reaches Bath by way of Paulton, a mining village in flourishing coal fields, but with charming surroundings.

Camerton, also in the coal-mining district, has memories of a Somerset rector who is familiarized to us by his *Journal of a Somerset Rector*, although his life and outlook were very different from those of the earlier Somerset diarist, James Woodforde. The Rev. John Skinner was rector of Camerton from 1800 to 1839, working for his parishioners with all the zeal of his conscientious and ardent nature, although saddened by the early loss of his devoted wife, his daughter, and other members of his family, which preyed on his affectionate nature, and eventually contributed to his tragic end by his own hand.

Widely read, intellectual, and keenly interested in Somerset archaeology, he played a leading part in preserving the fine chambered tumulus at Stoney Littleton, which is now scheduled as an Ancient Monument. His goodness, and his sense of the responsibilities of his office, shine through all the entries of his journal, and he gives a great insight into the life of all classes, from the colliers of the district to the distinguished friends with whom he stayed, or made archaeological tours, and the quarterly clerical meetings he attended. It is interesting to find him complaining of rainy summers, scarcity of servants, strikes, empty churches and all the other ills we are inclined to think modern afflictions unknown to "the good old days". His comment on the French insurrection of 1830 is almost startlingly applicable to-day: "Kings are out of fashion, and all authority is now kicked against unless it proceeds from the People."

The Fosse Way passes through the parish, and the old rector found many Roman remains in the district.

Another way to Bath from Farrington Gurney is through High Littleton, with a church 500 feet above sea level. Timsbury also stands high, with charming views towards Camerton. Timsbury House is a fine old timbered mansion, and the church has an effigy of the Elizabethan Sir Barnaby Samborne, "who lived all his days faithful to his prince".

North of Timsbury is Marksbury, where there are memorials to several of the Pophams, who were long seated at the neighbouring Hunstrete Manor, including the eccentric lady for whose midnight funeral in 1797 the road from Hunstrete to Marksbury church was lined with torches.

v

Yet another delightful trip from Bristol would be to explore the villages of Dundry Hill and the Chew Valley.

Leaving Bristol by the Bedminster road, we reach Dundry church, one of the finest landmarks of north Somerset. Built by Bristol's Merchant Venturers in the reign of Edward VI, its great tower is crowned by an elaborate parapet, and is set on a hill nearly 800 feet above sea level, commanding one of the most famous and extensive views in Somerset. There is a steep road down to Winford, on a tributary of the Chew, in a semicircle of hills, where a road climbs south over Crown Hill to Nempnett Thrubwell, whose queer name has puzzled the learned, who have never quite agreed upon its derivation. The village is on high ground overlooking a deep valley, and commands views of the Wrington Valley, Blagdon Lake and the Mendips, and Lansdown and Bath.

There is a network of tiny streams all round Nempnett Thrubwell, and we shall find the source of the Chew if we follow the road along the foot of the Mendips to Chewton Mendip. There is a little group of villages in the hills which lie north and instead of following the course of the River to Chew Stoke, we can go by way of Stowey, a charming haunt of peace which has a quaint and interesting old church, the remains of an old manor-house and beautiful Sutton Court, where John Locke loved to stay with his friend John Strachey and Bishop Hooper took refuge from the Marian persecutions. Part of the house dates back to the time of Edward II and a chapel and great parlour were added in 1558 by the famous Bess of Hardwick, who married Sir William St. Loe as her third husband, and inherited all his wide estates. There is a lane running north-westward from Stowey to Chew Stoke, with its graceful restored church and the old rectory, a quaint building with small octagonal turrets and a brave display of heraldic devices.

Beyond Chew Stoke is Chew Magna, which was originally called Bishop's Chew. The main street has a raised causeway and several old houses, and the church was built or restored by Bishop Beckington. It has a very fine gilded Perpendicular screen, a Norman font, and numerous interesting monuments, including the gigantic effigy of Sir John St. Loe, measuring 7 feet 4 inches in length and 2 feet 4 inches across the breast, with his wife looking very diminutive beside him. There is also a gaudily painted wooden figure, said to be Sir John Hautville, of the time of Henry III, with whom many local legends are associated. He once carried three men at once to the top of Norton Hautville Church, and took a great stone from the summit of neighbouring Maes Knoll and threw it to its present site, half buried under a hedge by the Pensford Road, where it is known as Haut-ville's Coit.

The Stanton Drew Circle is near the church, and consists of three circles. The circles are believed to have served a similar purpose to those at Stonehenge and Avebury. There is, of course, a local legend that the stones represent a bridal party turned to stone for dancing on Sunday. The fine old parsonage near the bridge has the arms of Bishop Beckington over one of the windows, and there is an old farm near the church with interesting features. The parents of John Locke lived near by at Belluton Farm and among the tombs in the church is one to Sir Michael Foster, a Judge of the King's Bench in the eighteenth century, who had such a high character for learning and integrity that Lord Chief Justice De Grey called him ". . . the Magna Charta of liberty of persons as well as fortunes". North of Stanton Drew, under Maes Knoll, is Norton Malreward, which Chatterton alleged to be the birthplace of his supposititious monk Rowley. Eastward is Pensford with the Chew winding to Publow beyond, with its beautiful church tower and its quaint old cylindrical lock-up, and to Compton Dando with its pleasant fourteenth-century church and an ancient bridge across the Chew. Both villages are near the line of the old Wansdyke, that great fortified Saxon earthwork which stretched for miles across the county and can still be traced in some districts.

VI

Next we will leave Bristol by Long Ashton, with its hills and woods and lovely views, of which Collinson the eight-eenth-century historian of Somerset was vicar, and is buried in the church, which also has a marvellous painted tomb with the effigies of Sir Richard Choke, one of the Justices of the Common Pleas, who died in 1483, and of his wife. A wall five miles in length encloses the well-wooded park of Ashton Court, which was enclosed in 1391, by Thomas de Lyons, and is perhaps the oldest deer park in England. The splendid front of the house was designed by Inigo Jones, the greater part of the rest of the house dating from a considerably earlier period. The property came to the Smyths in Elizabethan days, and Thomas Smyth, a Stuart M.P., is said to have been one of the last people to keep a jester.

A little detour on the way to Brockley takes us to Chelvey with a wonderful old group of manor-house, church, rectory, and barn. Chelvey Court, now a farm, is an extraordinary house more like a fortress, with the arms of the Tynte family, who owned it, and the date 1600 over the porch, and a horseshoe nailed on the bottom stair of the splendid Jacobean staircase to prevent witches walking up it.

Brockley is best known for its wooded hills and combe, which Coleridge climbed in May 1795, and was inspired to write a poem on the "Enchanting Spot" with its "luxury of landscape . . . Elm-shadowed fields, and prospect-bounding sea". The village, too, is worth more than a passing glance, with its fine church in the park of Brockley Court.

Wrington has many memories of Hannah More, who lived at Barley Wood near by, where she was visited by many of the greatest people of the day. It was there Lord Macaulay learned to love the West-Country scenery, and his letters from Clifton tell how well he remembered every feature of the scenery. Hannah More first built herself a cottage at Cowslip Green, the other side of Wrington, and built Barley Wood about 1802. William Wilberforce persuaded Hannah and her sister Patty to do their great work for the poor people of the district, undertaking to be responsible for the necessary funds. Their first venture was a Sunday School at Cheddar, which they established in spite of considerable opposition. One rich farmer assured them that religion was a most dangerous thing, especially to agriculture, and had done the greatest mischief ever since it was introduced by the monks at Glastonbury!

The people themselves were so ignorant that they opposed the kindly sisters even more fiercely than the farmers, and Hannah More once wrote ". . . they thought we wanted to sell their children for slaves". Eventually schools were opened at many places in the neighbourhood, and Friendly Benefit Societies were instituted. They found such a great need for sound secular literature that they began to write simple tracts, and they further brightened the lives of the children by the first Sunday School Treat, where 517 children from the rural schools they set up were entertained on Callow Hill in 1791—and were condemned by several of the local clergy for their "Methodistical and revolutionary undermining of the distinction of rank and the British constitution itself".

The cottage in which John Locke was born in 1632 has been pulled down, but a memorial hall has been built in the village to commemorate its association with the great philosopher, although his birth there was purely accidental. His parents lived in the Chew Valley, and his mother was on a visit to Wrington, and being taken ill in the church, was hurriedly conveyed to the nearest cottage. When he visited Holland he became acquainted with William of Orange, who, on landing in England to become William III, requested Locke to draw up a new Constitution of England. Locke held weekly conferences with the Government to advise them how to save the financial situation of the country. His great *Essay concerning Human Understanding*, which transformed European philosophy, has been studied by thinkers of all countries ever since its publication.

The Rev. William Leeves, poet and composer, chiefly remembered for the music he wrote to the song *Auld Robin Gray*, was rector of Wrington from 1779 to his death in 1828, and was a frequent and welcome visitor at the home of Hannah More.

There are memorials of all three of Wrington's celebrities in the church and busts to their memory in the church porch. The tower of the church is a grand example of the Perpendicular towers for which Somerset churches are so justly famous.

The return to Bristol can be made along the main road to Bedminster, or by pretty and devious lanes which might include a visit to Butcombe, above the Blagdon Lake, or by Barrow Gurney, in a valley between hills covered with orchards and rich pastureland.

VII

The last of our trips from Bristol will take us to the Gordano country and the coast, through Leigh Woods and the Nightingale Valley. It was at Leigh Court that Sir George Norton sheltered Charles II after his flight from the Battle of Worcester, travelling postilion with Jane Lane. There is an elaborate monument to Sir George in the church, and lovely views of the Avon Gorge from the churchyard.

There is a ferry across the Avon at the quaint little pilot village of Pill, long the nursery of Bristol Channel pilots. At one time there were thirteen inns in Pill, swarming with the crews of vessels waiting the tide to dock at Bristol, and when the first steam-tug tried to get up the river, it was seized by the men of Pill, taken back to King road, and turned adrift after her crew had been put ashore. The United Kingdom Pilots Association was started among the men of Pill, and the village is still the pilot station for the Port of Bristol.

The curious name of the Gordano country dates back to the thirteenth century, when it was spelled "Gordene", and is believed to refer to the triangular shape of this country-

3

side of smiling pastures, woods, and fine old manor-houses wedged in between two long, low ranges of hills.

Easton-in-Gordano is a pleasant little village, whose church has a Perpendicular tower. An inscription dated 1633 records the wish of Samuel Sturmy, who wrote a *Mariner's Guide to Knowledge*, that a copy of his book should be kept in the church, but the Guide is now in the Bristol Public Library. Portbury, a delightful little place, was an old Roman station. Its church has a Norman south door, and the parochial schools are held in an ancient building which belonged to the Augustinian abbey at Bristol.

Clapton church has a curious wooden screen which was probably brought from Clapton Court, and is a remarkable example of an early domestic screen. The old manor-house is partly modern, but incorporates a square embattled tower built in 1440, and a great entrance arch.

There are also Weston-in-Gordano and Walton-in-Gordano, on the road between Portishead and Clevedon, both attractive little villages, Weston with the oldest and most-interesting church, and Walton with cliffs overlooking the Bristol Channel and a queer sham castle which is a great landmark, built in the reign of James I on the plan of a medieval fortress.

Portishead is inclined to straggle so much that its attractions are not always realized on a fleeting visit. Although it has extensive and important docks, they are well hidden behind a wooded hill, and there are woodland walks, fine sands and cliff paths by the coast, some really lovely old houses, and the loveliest of unspoiled woodlands in another Nightingale Valley, not to be confused with the one near Leigh. There is Norman work in the parish church, which has the finest Perpendicular tower in the Gordano country, and some interesting and unusual features, including the old musicians' gallery. Victor Halliwell, the engineer who was drowned at Windermere, in company with Sir Henry

Seagrave, is buried in the churchyard. Near by is a mellow Elizabethan mansion, with a distinctive hexagonal turret, and a pleasant walk over the fields leads to the Tudor farmhouse of Capenore Court, and the picturesque thatched Grange. Portishead House, overlooking the sea, is traditionally believed to have harboured French spies during the Napoleonic wars, and even to have been visited by the French Emperor himself!

Portishead has the highest tides in the world, except for the Bay of Fundy on the Canadian coast of the Atlantic. The tide at Portishead rises as much as 45 feet in March.

Six miles through the delightful Gordano country brings us from Portishead to Clevedon, whose charms as a holiday resort are only matched by the importance of its literary associations. Here, too, the town straggles in every conceivable direction, and needs exploring to realize its attraction to the full. The old village is still gathered under the ancient church, much as in the days when Arthur Hallam, Tennyson's beloved friend, was laid there to rest. Full of bright promise, he died at Vienna, whilst touring Europe with his father, Henry Hallam, the historian, at the early age of twenty-two, and it is a tragic circumstance that his brother Henry, another delightful and brilliant boy, also died abroad, seventeen years later, at the age of twenty-six. Both were brought home to be buried in the family vault at Clevedon church, and here, too, are their young cousins, Abraham Elton, aged fourteen, who was drowned attempting the rescue of his brother Charles, aged thirteen, whilst bathing, in 1819, the bodies being found locked in each other's arms.

It was not until after the publication of *In Memoriam* that Tennyson visited Clevedon Court, the home of his friend's grandfather, but Thackeray knew it well and wrote parts of *Vanity Fair* whilst staying there, and described it as "Castlewood" in *Henry Esmond*. Many of his sketches of the Court and its inmates are preserved in the library. Thackeray's great friend there was Sir Arthur Hallam Elton, who succeeded to the baronetcy in 1853, and was himself the author of two novels, and a contributor to the *Saturday Review* and other journals. His nephew Charles Elton, was a poet in his youth, but is best remembered as the author of *Origins of English History*; *Shakespeare and his Friends* and similar works, and it was he who introduced Andrew Lang to the house. In earlier times Clevedon Court had been a haunt of Coleridge, Lamb and Southey, for the Eltons have always been noted for their keen literary interests.

The famous Elton Ware was made in the grounds of the Court about the beginning of the century by Sir Edmund Elton, and was noted for its artistic shape and wonderful colourings, particularly a lapis lazuli blue. Elton Ware won many first-class awards and gold medals at international exhibitions, and is still eagerly sought after by collectors. There are specimens in the Clevedon, Bristol, Bath, Taunton and other museums, and the town clock of Clevedon is set with typical pieces of the pottery.

Clevedon Court lies about two miles from the sea-shore and is one of the most perfect examples of a fourteenth-century manor-house in the present day, and has been inhabited uninterruptedly since it was built by John de Clevedon in 1313, although altered and enlarged in Tudor and Stuart times. The beautiful old house is set close under a wooded hill in beautiful terraced gardens.

The cottage in which Coleridge spent his honeymoon, celebrated in his poem *Reflections*, has changed but little since he lived there and Hartley was born, but its surroundings are very different, with houses crowding close.

Another association of which Clevedon is justly proud is with Nurse Edith Cavell, heroine of the 1914–18 War, who was educated there, and was confirmed at the parish church in 1884.

In the neighbourhood of Clevedon is Cadbury Camp, not

to be confused with the far more important Cadbury Camp in south Somerset; Tickenham with the remains of a fifteenth-century manor-house of the Berkeleys, now a farm, and a church with the unusual dedication to SS. Quiricus and Julietta, and effigies of the Berkeleys; and Wraxhall, once a market town, but now a charming village looking away to the Mendips. The splendid church has a gaily painted tomb with the effigies of Sir Edmund Gorges, and his wife, Lady Anne, daughter of the first Duke of Norfolk and grand-aunt of Anne Boleyn and Catherine Howard, who lies on his right to show her superior rank. There is a massive church-yard cross with four tiers of deep octagonal steps, and an elm tree at the neighbouring cross road, locally known as the Cross Tree, as it grows out of the base of the old market cross. The modernized Wraxhall Court is on the site of the old home of the Gorges family, who were settled there in the time of Edward II. Sir Ferdinando Gorges, who was born at Wraxhall about 1566, was the descendant of Sir Edmund. He distinguished himself as a soldier in many engagements on the Continent, but the most notable work of his long and busy life was the founding of the New England Colonies, when colonists were permanently settled at New Plymouth in 1628, and he has been hailed as the "father of English colonization in America".

We can find many pleasant country roads in the neighbourhood of Wraxhall, and can make our way back to the coast by way of Nailsea. Nailsea church has a fine stone pulpit, a punning epitaph to Richard Cole and his family, and a quaint verse composed by a former rector. The thirteenth-century Nailsea Court, approached through an avenue of chestnut trees, has been beautifully restored. It was the birthplace of Richard Percival, who gave Elizabeth the first tidings of the Armada by translating documents taken from a captured Spanish ship.

Kenn, on the road from Clevedon to Yatton and Congres-

bury, has a small church with a quaint little pyramidal tower
and numerous monuments to the Ken family of Ken Court,
and a little portrait of Bishop Ken, who has often been
claimed as a descendant although this has since been dis-
proved.

Yatton's immensely long main street has nothing of special
interest with the exception of the fine and interesting church
with its curious truncated spire. There are some notable
monuments, including a rich altar tomb to Judge Newton,
who was Chief Justice of the Common Pleas in the fifteenth
century. Splendid as the monuments in the church are, the
epitaph which lingers in the memory longest of all those at
Yatton is in a corner of the churchyard which has long been
a burying-place of the neighbouring gypsies, one of whose
graves has the haunting epitaph:

> "Here lies Merrily Joules, a beauty bright,
> Who left Isaac Joules, her heart's delight."

The church of Kingston Seymour has a tablet commemorating the destructive inundations of 1606 and 1703, when the
sea broke down the village defences and the water rose so
high the Norman font was filled with sea water, and the
water was above the pews for ten days.

Congresbury, where many roads meet, is a large and
modern-looking village with a history so long that its name
is said to be derived from St. Congar, a prince who fled from
Byzantium to avoid a loveless marriage, and settled at
Congresbury as a hermit. Legend tells that when he wanted
shade, he stuck his yew stick into the ground, and it sprouted
into a tree, and King Ine, hearing of the miracle, gave
Congresbury to the saint, who founded a monastrey there.
Modern historians discredit the legend, and say the name is
derived from "König" or King, and "bury" a town, but the
stump of an ancient yew is still called "St. Congar's walking
stick". Even without the legend, the history of Congresbury

goes back to the earliest times, for in the reign of Alfred it had a monastery which was given to Asser. The church has a west tower with a good spire, and an unusual clerestory with curious coloured figures between the windows. The vicarage house has a fine fifteenth-century doorway and various heraldic devices. A singular method of distribution of common lands in this parish is described in Mr. Gomme's *Village Community*.

Roads radiate from Congresbury in every direction, and we can either return to Bristol from there, or make for the coast at Weston-super-Mare, through the green country-side watered by the River Yeo, with the twisting lanes and willow-bordered meadows. Puxton's small church has some good woodwork, and a tower leaning 3 feet out of the perpendicular. Among the names of local rhines are: Blind Yeo, Old Yeo, Lythy Yeo, Grumblepill, and others scarcely less quaint. Wick St. Lawrence, near the estuary of the Yeo, has a Perpendicular church formerly a chapel of Congresbury, with some interesting features. An epitaph dated 1730 tells of an old tragedy of this low-lying country:

> "Save me O God, the mighty waters role
> With near Approaches, Even to my soul:
> Far from dry ground, mistaken in my course,
> I stick in mire, brought hither by my horse.
> Thus vain I cry'd to God, who only saves
> In death's cold pit I lay ore whelm'd with waves."

The ancient font is said to have been formerly in Worspring Priory, which lies a mile to the north.

The priory was founded in 1210, by William Courtenay, a grandson of Reginald Fitzurse, one of the murderers of Thomas à Becket, and was partly dedicated to the Archbishop. It was never a very large Priory, and after the Dissolution the church was converted into a manor-house, which is still inhabited. The great barn, chantry, court-room, and church tower are carefully preserved, and the other foundations have been excavated. Once one of the loneliest places imaginable, and still secluded in a grassy hollow, its quiet retreat may yet be invaded, as the bungalows which have broken out all over Sand Bay come ever nearer.

Kewstoke church, which makes a conspicuous landmark on great Worlbury Hill, bounding the south of the bay and hiding Weston-super-Mare, is an extremely interesting building. During repairs carried out in 1852 a wooden cup was discovered in the wall of the chancel, which is believed to have contained drops of the blood of Thomas à Becket, probably brought from Worspring Priory at the Dissolution and walled up for safety. It is now in Taunton Museum. Kewstoke village, climbing the hillside around and above the church, is a favourite haunt of artists. "St. Kew Steps" or "Old Monks Steps", a long flight of two hundred steps leading up the hill from the church, was originally connected with a landing-stage serving the Prehistoric camp on Worlbury Hill, in the days when the sea spread over the low-lying ground bordering the present-day Sand Bay, and Worle, two and a half miles from Weston-super-Mare, has a Perpendicular church with traces of Norman work. The miserere seats on the south are good modern copies of the ancient originals on the north of the choir.

Chapter Three: THE FROME VALLEY

Frome—South to Witham—North to the Avon.

FROME, the nearest Somerset town to London, is set on a steep hillside among the foothills of the Mendips. It has narrow little paved lanes, and streets with such delightful names as Gentle Street, Apple Alley, and Willow Vale converging on to the spacious market-place. Most fascinating of all is Cheap Street, where no wheeled traffic can go, and a clear rill runs down the centre of the paving.

Roman remains have been found in and near Frome, but its greatest importance dates from Saxon times, when it was a hunting centre of the Saxon Kings, in the heart of Selwood Forest—now remembered only in the town's full name of Froome-Selwood. The forest covered a large portion of east Somerset, and spread south and west over the Dorset and Wiltshire borders. It was disafforested in the time of Charles I, but as late as the eighteenth century sheltered a gang of marauders who were the terror of the neighbourhood.

The cloth trade was established in Frome by the fifteenth century, and it has been said that "Europe could not produce a wool equal to that used in the production of the broadcloth of Frome". By 1801 there were nearly 9,000 inhabitants, and it was the largest town in the county, with the exception of Bath, but in September 1826, when Cobbett visited the town, he drew a pathetic picture of the lot of the Frome wool-workers, who were unemployed and had so little from parish relief that they had pawned all their possessions. He records that he found the working people there very intelligent, although the innkeepers and their people were "flashy". Cobbett would be surprised and

31

delighted to find the woollen mill, and other staple industries of the town, have brought prosperity to the workers as well as to the manufacturers.

The parish church had the honour of being founded by St. Aldhelm himself, about A.D., 680 but it was rebuilt in Norman times, and only a fragment of a Saxon cross, and a stone curiously carved with a galloping animal, survive from the early church.

The church was energetically restored in the nineteenth century, by W. J. E. Bennett, an outstanding figure in the Oxford Movement, who spared no expense to bring his church into line with prevailing ideas of ecclesiastical decoration. The changes he made, after he came to Frome as Vicar in 1852, particularly the medallions over the nave, and other decorative work, have aroused very conflicting opinions. Professor Freeman said he felt "bound to bear testimony against what seemed to him a mere itch for change", but some are found to admire the changes, and all are agreed that the church is of lasting interest as an example of ecclesiastical taste in the latter half of the nineteenth century.

Much of the Norman work still remains, for the changes were decorative rather than structural. A flight of steps, with a Calvary beside it, approaching the churchyard, is also a part of Bennett's work. Bishop Ken is buried in the churchyard, in accordance with his own request that he should be buried at sunrise, on the east of the parish church in his diocese nearest to the place where he died. His curious monument has been described by Lord Houghton:

> "A basket-work where bars are bent—
>   Iron in place of osier;
> And shapes above that represent
>   A mitre and a crozier"

Just over a mile from Frome is Vallis Vale, so full of charm with its sunlit woods, many little streams, and deep peace, that it is surprising to realize it is very important geologically, as the place where the Mendip Hills disappear below the newer rocks of the Cotswold range. Vallis Farm, on a hill-top, is neighboured by all that remains of the ancient manor-house of the Leversedges, who held the estate until the eighteenth century.

II

The River Frome is typical of Somerset's many rivers—shallow, narrow and inconspicuous, but flowing by many attractive villages. In its twenty-mile course it links the two great Carthusian priories of Somerset—Witham, southward near the source of the river, and Hinton Charterhouse, northward near its junction with the Avon.

Only the church and dovecote of Witham Friary remain above ground to mark the site of the first English Charter-house, founded by Henry II as part of his penance for the murder of St. Thomas à Becket. Monks were sent over from Grande Chartreuse, but they had many troubles to contend with until St. Hugh became the third prior.

Born about 1135, St. Hugh had the most delightful character, and was full of loving consideration for the well-being of even the humblest. He returned every year to Witham, to live the calm and meditative life he loved, as a holiday from the cares of his Bishopric of Lincoln, until his death in 1200.

Brother Eynard, one of the monks at Witham under St. Hugh, lived to be 125 years of age, having made his profession at Grande Chartreuse 104 years before—surely a record?

Little is known of the history of the monks after St. Hugh's death, but presumably they lived the ordinary life of the Carthusians, a strict order which did not allow the monks to leave the Friary, or mingle with anyone outside the order, except in special cases. The prior and brethen lived very simply and humbly, with such a plain and monotonous diet that the curious bequest of Richard Ryborg of Salisbury to the monks of Witham Charterhouse, of "A pound of ginger, and to each brother [that is, lay-brother], half a pound of ginger", must have been most welcome.

The vanished Priory, which was situated some distance east of the church, was probably not a great work of art, for the Carthusians were not allowed to elaborate their buildings. The present parish church may be a surviving portion of St. Hugh's church, although with considerable alterations, and is still very small and plain, with a bell-cote and a high-pitched roof of red tiles. On the opposite side of the road is the monks' dovecote, which has been converted into a village reading-room.

Witham was dissolved in 1539, and passed to the Hopton family. Lord Hopton, the Cavalier general, more than once fortified and garrisoned Witham for the King. Lord Hopton, who served his King with the utmost gallantry and self-sacrifice, was so respected by the Parliamentary generals that Waller wrote to him: "My affections for you are so unchangeable that hostility itself cannot violate my friendship to your person."

North of Witham, the river flows to Frome, past Marston Bigot, where the great classical mansion of Marston House, a former seat of the Earls of Cork and Orrery, stands on a wooded hillside. The estate came into the possession of the Boyle family about 1638, and the site of the old house is still known as Marston Moat.

Roger Boyle, Lord Broghill, lived there in retirement for a time in 1647, as a known Royalist, but eventually entered the service of Cromwell, whom he served faithfully in Ireland, conceiving such an admiring friendship for him that, deeming the Royalist cause hopeless, he suggested Frances Cromwell should marry Prince Charles Stuart.

Cromwell could not believe the Prince would marry the daughter of the man who beheaded his father, and the plan fell through. His grandson, Charles Boyle, fourth Earl of Orrery, was created Baron Boyle of Marston. It was he who became involved in the dispute which led to Swift's Satire *The Battle of Books*, and whose name was given by Graham, the inventor, to the orrery, an astronomical instrument devised to represent the motions of the planets about the sun by means of clockwork.

III

Two miles north of Frome is beautiful Orchardleigh Park, with the nineteenth-century mansion built by the Duckworths high on a hill, and the remains of the ancient seat of the Champneys in the hollow below. The gem of a little church is enchantingly situated on an island in the lake.

Sir Henry Newbolt, the poet and naval historian, married Margaret Duckworth, and in his *Memoirs* gives a fleeting but vivid picture of his wedding day, when the 600 years' old church was so crowded to its small capacity by the Orchardleigh tenants that one was accommodated with a seat in the old oak pulpit! He gives, too, an illuminating account of the making of his historical novel, *The Old Country*, in which he describes Orchardleigh under the name of Gardenleigh. Although born at Bilston, Sir Henry was early acquainted with the West Country, having been educated at Clifton College, and now lies buried in the island church he loved so well.

North of Orchardleigh is Lullington, a lovely little village, with a notable church built by Geoffrey, the Norman Bishop of Coutances, which has very rich carving, probably due to the Bishop's workmen, as the figures on the capitals and doorway are similar to those at Coutances and Caen. A mile eastward across the river as the crow flies, but two miles round by the bridge, is Beckington, another quiet, picturesque village, which was once a thriving town, rich on the textile trade.

It was the birthplace of the great fourteenth-century Bishop Beckington, who did so much for Wells and lies in the cathedral there. Ever conscious of the greatness of his office, yet personally humble, wise, benevolent, and learned, Beckington's will is typical of the man, with his wish that his funeral expenses shall be "rather in the recreation and relief of the poor than in the solace of the rich and powerful".

Samuel Daniel, too, may be remembered here, for although it is known he was born "in or near Taunton" in 1562, little is known of his childhood. He was tutor to William Herbert, the future third Earl of Pembroke, and patron of Shakespeare and, later, to the Lady Anne Clifford. Daniel was praised by many of the greatest poets of his day, although his verses do not bear comparison with those of many of his contemporaries. In his old age, Daniel rented a farm at Rudge, in the parish of Beckington, where he lived for the last sixteen years of his life, and was buried in the church.

Alfred William Parsons, R.A., who was President of the Royal Society of Painters in Water Colours in 1914, was born at Beckington in 1847. One of his most charming pictures of Somerset, *When Nature Painted All Things Gay*, is in the Tate Gallery.

Beckington church has a Norman west tower which is the only one of its kind in the county, and there is much fourteenth- and fifteenth-century work, with effigies of the Erleigh family, and brasses to the Seyntmans and Comptons.

There are old houses in the village, including Beckington Castle, a gabled house near the church, and red-roofed cottages. Standerwick Court, a Queen Anne mansion, high on a hill commanding views of the Wiltshire Downs, is only a mile away, and Seymour Court, four miles east, and now a farmhouse, was once the home of Sir Thomas Seymour of Sudeley, who married the widow of Henry VIII.

Northward, on the west bank of the River Frome, is Woolverton with a quaint little tower and spire to its church. Laverton, a very remote village, has seen at least one great day in its history—June 23, 1909, when King George and Queen Mary, then Prince and Princess of Wales, went there to witness the whole process of Cheddar cheese making at the seventeenth-century Manor Farm. The church is of ancient foundation, and one of its rectors was William Keate, father of John, one of the most famous of all the Eton College Headmasters, and Robert, born at Laverton in 1777, who was a member of the council of the College of Surgeons for many years, and three times President.

There is an ancient trackway from Woolverton, carried by a packhorse bridge across the river to Rode. The parish register of Rode records that Charles Stuart passed through the village after the Battle of Worcester, and a village tradition says that he reconnoitred the surrounding country from a corner of the embattled tower of the church known as "The King's Chair".

Across the village green is Rode Hill House, where Constance Kent lived, the scene of a famous murder mystery in 1860. Constance lived there with her father, stepmother, and stepbrother Francis, apparently in complete amity, but actually cherishing resentment against her stepmother for remarks which seemed to cast a slight on her own mother. When Francis was three, she killed the child, hiding his mutilated body in a cesspool in the garden. The body was discovered a few hours later, but although it was clear the crime had been committed by someone in the house, she had planned it so cunningly that it was impossible to clear up the mystery. Five years later, she confessed and was tried at Salisbury and sentenced to death, but the sentence was commuted to penal servitude for life. It is said the whole court was in tears, and the judge broke down half-way through passing the sentence, but it is difficult to understand such misplaced sympathy for the perpetrator of such an atrocious crime. After serving twenty years at Portland she was set free and paid a brief visit to her old home before retiring to oblivion.

Tellisford, a pretty, secluded village, has a three-arched bridge across the Frome into Wiltshire, and a country lane leading to Norton St. Philip which, although a mile or more from the river-bank, is too lovely to be overlooked or neglected, for here is an enchanting black and white inn reputed to be the oldest licensed inn in England, a fine old church, and much natural and man-made beauty. It has known history, too, for it was the scene of a sharp skirmish between the Duke of Monmouth's Forces and regulars under the Duke of Grafton; Monmouth spent a night there a few days before the battle of Sedgemoor, and an attempt was made to shoot him as he stood at the window of the George Inn.

The Duke was more fortunate than the present-day visitor, for the George no longer offers accommodation, although it still provides refreshment. It was licensed as an ale-house in 1397. With its long stone-built ground floor topped by two storeys of timber and plasterwork, it is one of the most picturesque buildings in Somerset. Pepys, who visited Norton in June 1668 records "I walked to the church and there saw . . . the tombstone whereon there were only two heads cut, which the story goes, and credibly, were two sisters, called the Fair Maids of Foscott, that had two bodies upward and one belly, and there lie buried . . ." The two quaintly carved heads, strangely like a Fougasse cartoon, are now on the inner wall of the tower.

The church tower is of such curious design that it has been suggested it was either constructed of odds and ends from the dismantled monastic buildings at Hinton, or that the architect invented a plan out of his own head.

We can get back to the river bank at Farleigh Hungerford, bought about 1370 by Sir Thomas Hungerford, the first Speaker of the House of Commons, whose son Sir Walter served under Henry V at Agincourt, and held many great offices under Henry VI. By judicious marrying of heiresses, the Hungerfords grew ever greater in lands and wealth, until it was their boast they could ride from Farleigh to Salisbury on their own land—but disasters accompanied their grandeur, for several of them were beheaded. The last of the line died in the eighteenth century.

The well-preserved ruins are on a steep hillside above the Frome. The arms of the Hungerfords are over the gateway, and its chapel contains some interesting medieval armour, and numerous fine monuments and effigies to the Hunger-fords. A copy of the will of Lady Joan hangs beside the tomb, giving directions for her funeral, at which she wished twelve torches to be borne by twelve poor women clothed in russet, with linen hoods, and wearing suitable shoes and stockings. She left money for prayers to be said for the health of her soul and those of her ancestors for ever, to her grand-daughter her black mantle furred with miniver, and to her grandson a green bed embroidered with a greyhound.

The parish church of the delightful village, shaded by beech-trees above a steep ravine, was built in 1443 by Sir Walter to take the place of the original parish church, which had been enclosed in the castle.

There is no direct road to Freshford from Farleigh, which gives an excuse, if one were needed, for a brief detour to Hinton Charterhouse village, high up on the main road to Bath. The Abbey lies a mile away. This is the sister house of Witham Friary, and is in such splendid preservation that here it is possible to recapture the atmosphere of Witham. Hinton Charterhouse, which stands in a pleasant park, was

4

founded in honour of St. Hugh by Ela, Countess of Salisbury, the widow of Henry Longespée, in the afternoon of the day in May 1232 when she established Lacock over the Wiltshire border.

In spite of the extreme rigour and seclusion of the Carthusian rule, the Priors of Hinton appear to have had some worldly wisdom, for in 1255 the Prior secured from the Crown a grant of a yearly fair at Norton, and another at Hinton, although the grant was opposed by the monks of Bath, who were afraid their own fair would lose thereby—and eighteen years later, they complained that they had lost 100 shillings yearly through it. In 1279, the Prior proved his right to inflict capital punishment on the manors of Hinton and Norton with which the Countess Ela had endowed the Priory, and in 1351 the fair was extended to five days.

Among the monks at Hinton were Thomas Spenser, author of a *Commentary on the Epistle to the Galatians* and other learned works, who died in 1529 and was buried there; and Dom Nicholas Hopkins, confessor to the Duke of Buckingham, whose dreams and prophecies foreseeing Buckingham as King came to the ears of Henry VIII and led to the trial and execution of the Duke. Shakespeare mentions Nicholas Hopkins' part in the disaster in *King Henry VIII*, calling him "that devil monk, Hopkins, that made this mischief", although it appears it was simplicity rather then devilishness that led to the undoing of the monk and his patron.

The priory was on the comparatively small scale to be expected of a Carthusian establishment, but the ruins are unusually complete. They include the room used as a library, in which Prior John Batmanson probably wrote his diatribes against Luther and Erasmus. The neighbouring Hinton Abbey House, constructed from part of the Prior's lodging, has all the graciousness of Tudor architecture.

North-east of Hinton is the large, but extremely attractive

village of Freshford, in a deep hollow below its fine church, in the angle formed by the junction of the Frome with the Avon. Sir William Napier, who had fought in all the principal engagements in Portugal and Spain, wrote part of his famous *History of the Peninsular War* at Freshford House.

INNUMERABLE roads converge on Frome. Those running east to Wiltshire give access to Rodden, with a quaint little church, dating from 1640, in a farmyard, and Berkley, with a mansion dating from the time of William III and a classical church, unusual in a village, which was built in 1751, with a dome said to be a copy of St. Stephen's Walbrook. The manor came into the possession of the Newboroughs by marriage, and a monumental slab in the church traces their descent from the Conquest until 1680, when the daughter of the last male heir married John Prowse of Compton Bishop.

II

The roads running westward link up some of the loveliest villages of the Mendips. The lower road, which runs along the foot of the hills, gives fine views of Cranmore Tower, soon after leaving Frome, but all thought of the tower is soon lost in admiration of Nunney, an enchanting combination of moated castle ruins, a splendid church tower, and picturesque houses, many of them thatched, clustering near the stream whose stone bridge is neighboured by the village inn.

Nunney Castle is quaint rather than impressive, and is un-usually complete in outline, with the exception of the roofs. It was built in 1373, by Sir John de la Mere, out of the spoils of the French wars. During the Civil War it only surrend-ered on terms to Fairfax, after a determined resistance. A curious little drawing, now in the Taunton Museum, shows how it appeared during the siege, with the conical caps on its towers. It was found in the pocket MS. volume of a Royalist officer, who visited the castle in July 1644, and is just such a rough sketch as a present-day soldier might make to send home to his family.

Nunney church, although largely rebuilt in 1874, has considerable thirteenth- and fourteenth-century work. There is a late fourteenth-century wall painting and some fine effigies interestingly illustrating armour at varying periods.

Nunney lies peacefully a little off the main road, which continues under the hills below Cranmore Woods and tower past East Cranmore, half hidden in trees down a side lane. One of the Pagets of Cranmore Hall erected the tower in 1862. A spiral staircase leads to a couple of balconies, which give marvellous views of the surrounding country.

After speeding past the old Cranmore Turnpike House, and the towered church of West Cranmore, which has some interesting monuments to the Strode family, we come to Doulting, a neat village with little to breathe of its wonderful memories.

It was at Doulting that St. Aldhelm, who was born in Wessex about 639, was seized with his fatal illness in 709. His funeral procession to Malmesbury, which he had ruled at one time, was very impressive, for he was venerated all over the Kingdom, having been counsellor to King Ine, and the first English scholar of distinction. His vernacular hymns were the delight of King Alfred, and a number of his works have survived to the present day. When learning was at its lowest ebb on the Continent, it flourished under his encouragement in England. He was skilled in all kinds of music, and when he found the English, who had almost fallen back into heathenism, would not listen to preaching, he stood on a busy bridge and sang songs, attracting a crowd who thought him a professional minstrel, and then gradually introduced sacred subjects.

The restored Early English church, which has a quaint seventeenth-century brass to Robert Mawes, stands on the site of the little wooden Saxon building in which the saint died, and is dedicated to him. There is a fifteenth-century cross, for Doulting was privileged to be a place of refuge for debtors and criminals. There is also a fine fifteenth-century tithe barn, which formerly belonged to the Abbots of Glastonbury, and in the vicarage grounds is St. Aldhelm's Holy Well.

The Doulting freestone quarries, from which the medieval builders took their stone for Wells and Glastonbury, are still worked, and are of considerable commercial importance.

III

The upper road from Frome to Shepton Mallet runs over the hills through Egford, a starting-point for Vallis Vale, and the pleasant little village of Whatley, whose church has Norman work, and a thirteenth-century effigy of Sir Oliver de Servington. Dean Richard Church, a recognized leader of the older High Church party, is buried there, at his own wish. He was rector of Whatley for nineteen years before he became Dean of St. Paul's Cathedral.

After Whatley, the road runs through a pretty wooded valley to Chantry, or Little Elm, which has a modern Gothic church designed by Sir Gilbert Scott. Beyond is the rather bleak little village of Leigh-on-Mendip, nearly 900 feet above sea level. It has a surprisingly fine church tower, crowned with no less than twenty elaborately decorated pinnacles, whilst the church itself is a miniature of the great Perpendicular churches, with good roofs and stone angel corbels. There are charming views northward from the road near the Stoke Lane cross roads.

IV

There is also a choice of roads from Frome to Radstock.
One crosses wooded Whatley Bottom, south of Great Elm,
whose church has walls built of stones laid in herring-bone
formation, in the Saxon style, and a quaint saddlebacked
tower added about the year 1240. Near Great Elm the Mells
stream and Fordbury Water enclose the horseshoe shaped
Tedbury Camp; where a hoard of Roman coins was found
in 1691. The impregnability of the stronghold, on the
precipitous banks of the stream, can be realized from
the road.

Mells, with its fine old houses, has supreme beauty.
When Mells Park was built by Thomas Horner, about a
century and a half ago, the sixteenth-century manor-house
was reduced in size to about a third, but is still a building of
charm and distinction, making a perfect foil for the church,
with its magnificent fifteenth-century tower. The founder
of the Horner family is said to have been the original of the
nursery rhyme "Little Jack Horner", who pulled out the
plum of Mells from the maelstrom of the dissolution of the
monasteries.

The late Canon Hannay, better known to the public as
George A. Birmingham, the novelist, was rector of Mells
for a number of years.

In the early nineteenth century Mells was famous for its
ironworks, which exported agricultural implements to all
parts of the Empire. Gold medals were awarded James and
Thomas Fussell for scythes and reap-hooks at the Exhibition
held in Vienna in 1860, but before the end of the century the
works were taken over by a Sheffield firm.

At Vobster, which is said to derive its name from some
Dutch weavers who once worked a mill there, the road turns
at right angles, and runs north to Babington, which has no
village, but a church dating from the reign of George II, so

close to the seventeenth-century Babington House that there are tombstones on the lawn!

Kilmersdon, a pleasant little village in a hollow at the foot of Ammerdown Hill, has a fifteenth-century Perpendicular church with a graceful west tower, and traces of Norman work. Parson Skinner tells us in his *Journal* that the stained-glass window of the Mount of Olives was copied from a sketch made by Thomas Joliffe, a former owner of Ammerdown House, when on a visit to Jerusalem. Among the epitaphs is one dated 1849 to Anne Abraham, who died in her 104th year, and regularly walked a distance of a mile and a half to work until the last two years of her life, at her own express desire, "for with a laudable feeling of independence she always resolutely refused parochial relief". There is a quaint stone lock-up in the village.

Ammerdown House stands in a park four miles in circumference, and is a classical building designed by James Wyatt. The 600-foot hill in the park is topped by a memorial column 150 feet high, to Thomas Joliffe.

v

The upper road from Frome crosses the Mells river at the northern end of Vallis Vale, and runs to Buckland Denham, or Dinham, set on a hillside. Although now a small and peaceful village, it was once a busy little town with a flourishing cloth trade, which received a charter from Henry III. There are curious effigies of Sir John Dinham and his wife, of the time of Edward II, in the church. Beyond Buckland Denham there are no villages on the road itself, but lanes lead to a number of interesting places, including Hardington, consisting of two farms and a church which still has its Georgian fittings, complete with box pews. The park and a range of stables are all that remain of Hardington House, the home of the Bampfyldes from the fifteenth century until 1823, when Sir Charles died, deeply in debt.

Hemington lies at the head of a wide valley with an ancient church resembling that of Buckland Denham, and the square tower of "Turner's Folly" on a hill above. Roman pottery has been dug up in the neighbourhood.

VI

Radstock, in a deep valley surrounded by coalpits, is a flourishing little place, but with a population of only 4,000, is inoffensive to those who know "real" mining towns, for the countryside creeps so close there are innumerable enchanting places within easy reach, served by the three railway stations of Radstock, Midsomer Norton, and Hallatrow, which are set so closely together that they serve practically the same area.

Radstock is near the ancient Fosse Way, and some years before the war a small section was uncovered, showing the original paving stones, still scored by the marks of the Roman chariot wheels. There are numerous tumuli and Roman remains in the neighbourhood, and several beautiful valleys converge on the town. The church, restored out of recognition, is well cared for, and has a unique list of Rectors, painted by the daughter of Canon Bax, with tiny pictures to illustrate each era from 1297 to 1914.

Midsomer Norton, another little town of the mining area, is nearly twice the size of Radstock, but is still a pleasant little place. Its undistinguished modern church replaces a Norman building, and this disregard for the past is also shown by the neglected state of the wooden figure of a mailed knight, one of the few left in England. A large stone in the churchyard commemorates a tragedy of 1839, when twelve miners were killed by the snapping of the rope as they were about to descend into the pit. The Coroner's jury returned a verdict of "Willful Murder against some person or persons unknown"; it was believed that the rope had been maliciously damaged, but no one was ever brought to book for the crime.

VII

The road from Radstock to Shepton Mallet follows the old Fosse Way, on which the only village is Stratton-on-the-Fosse, with a tiny church preserving a few remnants of Norman work, and an organ originally made for Brighton Pavilion! Stratton House, in fine grounds half a mile away, is an ancient manor-house which formerly belonged to the Long family of Wiltshire, but the chief interest of Stratton is centred in the splendid abbey of Downside.

Originally founded by Elizabethan Roman Catholic refugees at Douai in 1605, the Benedictine community of St. Gregory's, when driven from there by the French Revolution, came back to England, and eventually settled at Downside in 1814. There is also a school, which has attained considerable fame since its inception.

The abbey church was consecrated in 1935 and is the only church in England to be raised to the dignity of a Minor Basilica. There are tombs and shrines to Oliver Plunket, Archbishop of Armagh, who was martyred in 1681; Bishop Walmesley, a mathematician who acted as consultor to the British Government on the reform of the calendar and adoption of the "new style", and consecrated Dr. John Carrol, the first Catholic Bishop of the United States of America; and Cardinal Gasquet, whose great learning shed a lustre over Downside, where he was educated, and of which he was prior from 1878 to 1885. The tower of the church was completed in 1938 as a memorial to the Cardinal, having been commenced fifty years before, when he was Prior. It is 166 feet high, on a base 600 feet above sea level, and commands wonderful views across the county.

East of Stratton-on-the-Fosse is the little colliery village of Holcome, with a small modern church in the village and an unspoiled older building a mile away, with Norman work, beautiful box pews and the graves of the father, mother, brother and sister of Captain Scott of Antarctic fame. A little further east again is the village of Coleford, known to every lover of gay Somerset dialect tales under the name of "Springfield", in the *Jarge Balsh* stories of Mr. W. M. Jones, who was born there.

There is a longer road from Radstock to Shepton through Chilcompton, a charming little village in a valley, with the little Somer river cascading through the main street, and Gurney Slade, set on the cross-road to Binegar, a small village on the top of the Mendips, once celebrated for a great fair, transferred there from Wells on account of the plague in the sixteenth century, but moved back again in 1837. South of Binegar, the old Somerset and Dorset Railway reaches its highest elevation, 800 feet above the sea, and just beyond is Maesbury Camp, whose double ramparts enclose six acres commanding a splendid view of Somerset.

VIII

Shepton Mallet, in a sheltered hollow at the foot of the Mendips, although modernized almost out of recognition, cannot be dismissed lightly, for the restored church still has a splendid tower and clerestory, with a rich parapet and notable gargoyles, and there are interesting monuments and brasses. The ceiling of the nave is the finest of its kind in existence, with 350 carved panels and bosses. Shepton also has a fine market cross, with a spire rising to 51 feet, and a hexagonal shelter, with an original brass dated 1500. Dr. F. J. Allen most justly remarked that although it has since undergone several alterations "as a piece of patchwork it is only a little less picturesque than a genuine ancient building." In the market-place is also all that remains of the old Shambles—a fragment now, it is true, but still a very special part of Shepton's claim to detain the traveller, for so few medieval shambles remain in the country.

Shepton Mallet carries its history in its name, for it was originally a Saxon village on the Fosse Way, its name of Sceaptun, or Sheep-town, indicating its chief source of prosperity, whilst the second name of Mallet perpetuates the great Norman family who became lords of the manor after the Conquest. As early as the fourteenth century, it was a place of commercial importance, and in 1790 more than 4,000 hands were employed in the cloth trade, which has since been replaced by the making of Cheddar cheese and other industries.

The oldest nonconformist chapel in Shepton is the Unitarian, first built in 1692, and enlarged in 1785, which has a richly carved oak pulpit and canopy.

Shepton was the birthplace of Hugh Inge, a favourite of Wolsey, who became Archbishop of Dublin in 1521 and Lord Chancellor of Ireland six years later, which office he held until his death. Polydore Virgil said he had the character of "an honest man . . . and put the kingdom in as good condition as the untowardness of the wild Irish would suffer him".

In the following century Simon Browne was born there. The simultaneous loss of his wife and only son unhinged his mind, and although his faculties remained perfect, he became convinced that God had "annihilated in him the thinking substance" and that his words had no more sense than a parrot's, and tried by earnest reasoning to persuade his friends he was "a mere beast".

Giving up his ministry, he retired to Shepton, where he amused himself by writing books for children, translating classical authors, and composing a dictionary, declaring, "I am doing nothing that requires a reasonable soul. I am making a dictionary; but you know thanks should be returned to

God for everything, and therefore for dictionary makers."
Even a dedication to Queen Caroline asked for her prayers
in his singular case who was "once a man" but whose "very
thinking substance has for more than seven years been continually wasting away till it is wholly perished out of him".

Dr. Walter Charlton, born in 1619 whilst his father was
rector of Shepton, became President of the Royal Society,
and was praised by Dryden in "The Epistle to Dr. C.", said
to be the "noblest poem in which English science has been
celebrated by an English poet".

Shepton has one of the world's unsolved mysteries. Owen
Parfitt, a seventy-year-old crippled tailor, was helped out
of bed one afternoon in June 1768, and put into a chair outside his cottage door, and fifteen minutes later had disappeared, and no trace of him has ever been discovered.

IX

The charming road from Shepton Mallet to Wells passes
through Croscombe, in a well-wooded valley. Its church,
comparatively plain on the outside, but with a stone spire
most unusual in the county of towers, has a marvellously
rich interior, with gorgeously carved woodwork sufficient
to satisfy the most voracious appetite for this delightful form
of decoration.

There is also a fifteenth-century village inn with much
good carving, the hall of the fifteenth-century manor-house
of the Fortescues, now used as a Baptist Chapel, and other
old houses.

A mutilated village cross topped by a ball, set beside the
road, has a fascinating story. In the latter part of the nineteenth century the local way-wardens, thinking the cross an
incumbrance, endeavoured to remove it. The villagers were
up in arms at once with a fine old English spirit of conserva-
tism, and attacked the demolishers just as the shaft had been

thrown down. They drove them off and hoisted a flag bearing the legend "Be Faithful" (we are not told how they happened to have this appropriately inscribed flag handy), and at night over thirty men volunteered to bivouac round the cross and guard it, the women preparing them beds of straw and kindling a huge fire—an evidence of determination which finally put a stop to the attempt to remove the cross. Would that other villages had been so eager in the defence of their ancient treasures!

Once a place of importance, Croscombe had charters for a market and fair granted by Edward I, and in the curious two-storied vestry of the church no less than seven guilds of the village once met—The Young Men, the Maidens, the Webbers, the Fullers, the Hogglers (or labourers), the Archers, and the Wives.

Ham Wood, a beautiful rocky glen, richly wooded, and more than a mile long, runs north-east from Croscombe. Also in the neighbourhood is Dungeon Farm, set in apple orchards. The railway line between Shepton and Wells runs at the bottom of the garden, and Alfred Parsons was so captivated by the view of Glastonbury Tor from the railway carriage that he secured rooms at the farm, and painted his most famous picture *The Heart of Somerset*, which was exhibited at the Royal Academy in 1911. He also painted his picture *Stoodley Batch* whilst staying there.

Westward from Croscombe the road passes Dinder, where the smooth green turf of the park in which Dinder House is set slopes down from the road to the mansion and the attractive Perpendicular church, behind which lie the houses of the village, and the mansion of Sharcombe, but, charming though they are, we will be content to see them from the road, and hurry on to Wells, skirting the foot of Dulcote Hill and only touching the fringe of the picturesque hamlet of Dulcote, until the wonderful view of Wells bursts upon our sight.

Wells—"On Mendip"—The Old Lead Mines

AS the road from Shepton Mallet curves round Tor Hill, the ancient city of Wells is seen lying below. First the great Perpendicular tower of St. Cuthbert's rises above the rooftops, so stately and so splendid that it might be thought the cathedral itself, until that great grey pile comes into view, dominating the city, as distant Glastonbury Tor dominates the rich plain stretching away to the horizon. Well may the returning traveller exclaim with W. H. Hudson, "O joy to look again on it, to add yet one more enduring image of it to the number I had long treasured."

Wells is beautiful from any viewpoint, but incomparably at its best when approached by the roads dropping down from Shepton, Bath, or Bristol, for then its kinship with the country is seen, and the pleasant old houses have gardens where, in late spring and early summer, the pale mauve of wisteria and deliciously fragrant lilac vie in enchantment with the pearly beauty of magnolias to deck the approach to the cathedral precincts.

Once pass into the Cathedral Close, and all is tranquillity and beauty, hidden away from the secular town behind high walls, as it has been for centuries—a complete survival of ecclesiastical self-sufficiency—the cathedral, and the houses of church dignitaries, overlook spacious green lawns which allow the stupendous west front to be seen to the best advantage; the graceful Chain Gateway gives access to the picturesque fifteenth-century Vicars' Close; and beyond is the moated thirteenth-century Bishop's Palace, backed by giant elm trees which cast their long shadows on rich meadows where cows graze placidly. It is a truly pastoral setting.

53

At first sight, the contrast between the gorgeous ornamentation of the west front, with its 600 figures, and the simplicity of the interior, with its unusual inverted arches, its spaciousness, and its sense of light and air, so unusual in a medieval cathedral, comes in the nature of a surprise, until it is gradually realized that every column and niche has its exquisitely carved miniature figures and formal patterns.

The beautiful Lady Chapel, exquisite fourteenth-century stained glass, a thirteenth-century octagonal Chapter House, two chantries, and richly carved tombs, with quiet cloisters leading to the Bishop's Palace, are among the splendid possessions of the cathedral, but we have not space here to record its treasures and there is no need, for many admirable guide books describe them fully.

The Palace and its gardens occupy 7 acres of ground, which also enclose the springs which gave the city its name. At one time the bishops had sole control of the city's water supply and were not above stopping the flow to coerce the citizens, but the great and good Bishop Beckington built a conduit in the market place for their use. Well may he be remembered with gratitude, as also the later saintly Bishop Ken, for many of the earlier Bishops were unashamedly out for their own aggrandisement and some, like Cardinal Wolsey, never even visited the city, although they never neglected to draw the revenues pertaining to the See!

Since its earliest days, the city has had no real history apart from its cathedral, for although Henry VII passed through the town on his way to suppress the rebellion of Perkin Warbeck, he was entertained at the Deanery, and when Monmouth's troops stayed there just before Sedgemoor, almost the only recorded incident is the attempt of a fanatical minority to destroy the cathedral. The many headless statues on the great west front are witness to their iconoclastic zeal, which might have had still greater effect had not Lord Grey defended the high altar with his drawn sword;

Bath, from the terrace of Prior Park

Jacobean Screen, St. Mary's Church, Bridgwater

The Staircase, Dunster Castle

a scene thrillingly described by Conan Doyle in *Micah Clarke*.

The fortunes and interests of Wells have been bound up with those of the cathedral so long that it has become a habit. There is plenty of enterprise locally, and some excellent manufactures, but all is subordinated to the interests of beauty, and no casual visitor would dream that Wells was more than a tourist centre.

With a population of under 5,000, the city has never grown unwieldy, and its older buildings have been modernized without losing all trace of their medieval origin. Every little by-way can show something of interest to those who love to poke about odd corners and make their own discoveries. There are inns whose ancient timbers and open-handed hospitality have a long tradition; quaint old alms-houses, and even a fourteenth-century bakery; there is St. Cuthbert's parish church, which would be a supreme attraction in any other town, and suffers only in comparison with the great cathedral.

There is a quaint little modern innovation in the theatre of the Somerset Players, converted out of a cow byre; and the local territorials drill in a magnificent fourteenth-century tithe barn. The Museum is in the Cathedral Close, and is of exceptional interest not only for Wells "bygones" but for prehistoric relics from Mendip Caves explored by the Curator, Mr. H. E. Balch.

A song school was flourishing at least as early as 1140. Bishop Beckington took great interest in these "queristers" and framed a special code of rules for them, which throw a profound light on their manners before he took them in hand, for among other things they were specifically forbidden to clean their teeth with their knives at table! Overcrowding seems to have been as chronic as in the present day, for they slept three in a bed. The master was required to be "sober, prudent and truthful" and "moderate in chastisement"—an

5

unusual medieval provision, but possibly due to still vivid memories of an usher who had been suspended in the thirteenth century for the violence of his punishments.

Curiously enough, although Bath drew all the wit and fashion of the eighteenth century, and is overwhelmingly full of literary associations, its sister city of Wells is almost without a mention in the voluminous diaries and letters of the period. The truth doubtless was that the eighteenth century considered itself modern and progressive, and had a well-authenticated capriciousness in its liking for "the antique"—unless it was sham antique like Walpole's Strawberry Hill. Probably Fanny Burney, who so faithfully reflected the taste of her day, was only putting into words what others would have thought had they visited Wells, when she wrote in her diary: "Hence we proceeded to Wells. Here we waited, as usual, upon the cathedral which received our compliments with but small return of civility. There was little to be seen without except old monuments and old abbots removed from Glastonbury, so inferior in workmanship and design to the abbey once containing them, that I was rather displeased than gratified by the sight. They have also a famous clock, brought from the abbey at its general demolition. This exhibits a set of horses with riders, who curvet and dance round a bell by pulling a string, with an agility comic enough, and fitted to serve for a puppet-show; which, in all probability, was its design, in order to recreate the poor monks at their hours of play. . . . The old castle of Wells is now the palace for the bishop. It is moated still, and looks dreary, secluded, and in the bad old style".

Apart from the lively Fanny's lack of appreciation, she shows a lamentable ignorance of the facts, as the west front of the cathedral was completed three centuries before the Dissolution of Glastonbury, and the bishop's palace was never a castle; but she must be forgiven for thinking the clock came from Glastonbury, for a number of modern writers have also repeated the old tradition, although it was mentioned in the account roll of the Communar of the Dean and Chapter of Wells for the year 1392-3.

Only in modern times has Wells figured as the background for any novel. It makes the briefest possible appearance, under the name of Fountall, in Hardy's *A Tragedy of Two Ambitions*, and is briefly but sympathetically described in C. N. and A. M. Williamson's *Set in Silver*, when the hero and heroine go to see the swans on the moat ring for their food—a trick taught by Bishop Eden's daughter, and handed down through generations of swans to the present day.

Among the many natives of the city who achieved fame were Jocelin, born about 1180, and Bishop of Bath and Wells for thirty-seven years, during which time he practically completed the work of rebuilding the cathedral commenced by his predecessor; Thomas Chaundler, who was Chancellor of Oxford University in 1476; George Bull, born 1634, Bishop of St. David's; and a bevy of eighteenth-century celebrities, including Elizabeth Benger, poetess and novelist, and the friend of Lamb and other notable people of her time; Thomas Linley, father of the famous Elizabeth Linley of Bath; Sir James Eyre, Chief Justice of the Common Pleas; Henry Harington, D.D., a descendant of Queen Elizabeth's godson, compiled a valuable collection of literary pieces and historical notes from family papers, known as *Nugae Antiquae*; and John Keate, Headmaster of Eton.

II

High on the Mendips above Wells is Priddy, a small and incredibly ancient village grouped round Priddy Green, and famous for the great Fair held annually in August, said to owe its origin to the Black Death, which was so virulent in the towns and villages at the foot of Mendip that the itinerant chapmen sought the purer air of the heights to sell their wares.

The sturdy little church is mainly Perpendicular, and has some interesting features, including a Norman font.

Priddy, always remote, has cherished its old customs, and Priddy folk are especially noted for their folk-dancing which in their case has needed no revival, never having died out.

The loveliest of all Somerset legends centres round this quiet village, where they cherish the tradition that Christ himself once walked there as a boy, having accompanied his uncle on one of his voyages to Britain. As with every cherished tradition, there have been found learned men to dispute it, but the early life of Our Lord is so shrouded in obscurity that they can find no facts to support their contention, any more than the believers, and surely it is ungracious not to accept such a rare and beautiful tradition with becoming thankfulness?

One of the principal sources of the Axe is near Priddy, although it is very hard to find the point where it wells up from the ground, only to plunge down again through a fern-draped hole on its two miles' underground journey to Wookey Hole. The surrounding district is honeycombed with caves and swallets, all more or less explored by the enthusiastic members of the Wells Spelaeological Society.

Priddy was in the heart of the Roman leadmining district, and there are innumerable prehistoric burial mounds in the neighbourhood. Charterhouse, about two and a half miles from Priddy, has three prehistoric earthworks, and a fine Roman amphitheatre. Charterhouse Bottom, with its miniature gorges, twelve miles from the coast and 800 feet above sea level, yields innumerable marine fossils.

The little whitewashed church of Charterhouse, isolated even from the tiny hamlet, is bright against the dark green background of hills, and commands a wide view westward to Blackdown. It is very properly dedicated to St. Hugh, for a cell of Witham Priory was established at Charterhouse early in the thirteenth century. In 1250 the monks were exempted from the forest laws to which, being within the bounds of Selwood Forest, they would otherwise have been subject. Nevertheless, there was a tremendous commotion ten years later, when a woodman of the monastery was convicted of taking two bucks and a hart, and of carrying venison to the Priory, although apparently nothing much came of it.

The traditional site of the monastery is marked by an Elizabethan farmhouse, near the old Roman road from Uphill, and still known as Charterhouse Manor Farm.

Mining on Mendip began at a very early period, and massive pigs of lead bearing the names of Roman emperors have been found. Mining was chiefly, although not entirely, confined to the Mining Forest, which was not the same as the Hunting Forest, but was divided into four Mineries under the control of the four Lords Royal of Mendip—the Bishop of Bath and Wells, the Abbot of Glastonbury, Lord Bonville of Chewton, and Lord Richmond.

A dispute between the miners or groovers, as they were called and the Prior of Green Ore, a monastic cell belonging to Glastonbury, led to the framing of the famous code of mining laws, in the reign of King Edward IV. The Prior having complained to the King, no less a person than Lord Chief Justice Coke was sent to the spot to settle the quarrel. He sat at a place called Forge, commanding the Lords Royal and all the commoners to appear, to the number of 10,000 people.

A map was prepared, giving the boundaries of the Mining Forest, which quaintly pictures all the churches and has agreeable little drawings of packhorses and wagons. Copies are preserved at Taunton, Wells, and other places. The results of his mission were recorded with a long preamble. "The olde Ancient Custome of ye occupation of ye Meynderies in and upon ye Kings Ma^tles forrest upon Meyndeepe within his Ma^tles County of Som'set being one of ye foure staples of England which has been exercised and continued through the said forrest from ye time whereof man now living hath no memory is hereafter as doth particularly ensue". Then followed minute details, providing that miners should be licensed, that those who stole were to have their tools and instruments "belonging to the same occupacion . . . put into house or works and set fire and the thief banished from Myneders for ever". Anyone killed by falling earth must be brought out to Christian burial, even if he was three-score fathom under the earth.

The Mendips were enclosed by Act of Parliament about 1725, and the old mining laws became obsolete, although the industry was of great importance long after that. Vast heaps of refuse left at some of the old mining centres suggest that the amount of lead obtained must have been very large. The deposit at Priddy was originally a mile long, and is estimated to have contained half a million cubic yards, the original methods of working ore being very rough and ready. In the eighteenth century it was worked over again, but the process was still wasteful, and in the latter half of the nineteenth century a company was formed to resmelt the slag. Collinson describing the process in his day, said that the occupation was so lucrative that with proper assiduity a miner could earn a guinea a day—an enormous wage in the eighteenth century.

There are records of prospecting for iron, lead, and copper in 1856, but the glowing prospectus was not then justified. Later, in 1890, another company acquired the property and started mining operations, but the undertaking also failed. No less than thirty varieties of minerals have been discovered on Mendip, including some of great rarity, but although the deposits are not exhausted, in modern times it has been found cheaper to import from abroad.

The village of Shipham, at the western end of the main range of the Mendips, about two and a half miles from Charterhouse, was also a mining village, and the broken and uneven ground in the neighbourhood, with grass-grown hillocks and hollows, deep trenches and old mineshafts, prove its former importance. Many Shipham and Priddy men fought under Monmouth at Sedgemoor, but their intense patriotism was also shown by their readiness to volunteer for defence against the Armada, and they also volunteered for service when the French landed at Fishguard in 1797.

Shipham villagers at one time had a reputation for being turbulent and defiant of authority. Hannah More has left on record that in her day no constable dared venture into Shipham to arrest a man, for fear he should be made away with, thrown down some old mineshaft and "never heard of more; no uncommon case". When Hannah More started a Sunday School for the neglected children, the incumbent repaired the rectory, which had had no tenant for a century, and allowed her to use it for a school, but she said "as he is but 94 years old, he insists upon my taking a lease, and is as rigorous about the rent as if I were taking it for an Assembly Room".

Dr. George Smith, of Axbridge, in a paper read before the Somerset Archaeological Society, drew attention to certain marked characteristics in some of the inhabitants of the Mendip Hills which seemed to him to suggest foreign influence, particularly French. It is well known that French Huguenots did settle on the Mendips, and in Shipham such names as Thiery, Sawtell, Moger (Maugre) and Fountain (Fontaine) were common until recently, and some may still be found, whilst a number of French coins have been dug up in the parish.

A great stone in the neighbourhood, called the Wimblestone is believed to have treasure hidden under it, and an old story tells that at night the old stone is up and about, ranging the fields until dawn. The name wimble means, quick and active, but whether the name gave rise to the story, or the story to the name, is not clear.

Rowberrow, more out of the world even than Shipham, was another of the Mendip mining villages. It lies on the slopes of the wild, uncultivated Rowberrow Warren, and its picturesque little church, quite away from the village and only neighboured by the rectory and manor house, lies under Dolbury Camp. The old church records were incredibly badly kept, with astounding spelling, and entries include such Christian names as "Moreya, gob, gosyer, Sarrahawn, iams, Socelia and fillopp".

Dolbury Camp is another place with a longstanding tradition of buried treasure, and Leland quotes a local rhyme:

> "If Dolbyri dyggèd were
> Of gold shulde be the share".

Originally of Celtic construction, Dolbury Camp was used by the Romans, who built the great stone ramparts inside the earlier earthworks.

Wells to Axbridge—Winscombe—Down to the Sea—Along the Northern Face to Weston-super-Mare

THE road skirting the south-western foot of the Mendips from Wells to the sea soon gives a rich foretaste of its lovely scenery, with the high ridge, seamed with combes, on the one hand, and on the other the great plain of Sedgemoor, broken by Glastonbury Tor and other knolls and low ridges of hills, stretching away to the distance.

Wookey village has a Perpendicular church at which Alexander Barclay, author of the rhymed satire *The Ship of Fools*, was incumbent in the sixteenth century. He was a very prolific writer, and exercised an important influence on English literature helping to sound the death-knell of medieval allegory and lead the way to the drama, novel and essay of character.

Another writer associated with Wookey is Sir Cyril Arthur Pearson, a great-grandson of the Rev. H. F. Lyte. Sir Cyril was born in the village in 1866 when his father was curate of Wookey. He founded *Pearson's Weekly*, the *Daily Express* and other papers, and when he found himself going blind, conferred a lasting benefit on fellow-sufferers by founding St. Dunstan's.

A detour to the village of Wookey Hole is absolutely obligatory for those who have not lost their youthful love of caves—and for serious archaeologists, too, for there is nothing in England quite like Wookey Hole. A pleasant footpath up a green tree-shaded valley leads to the great caves, with their history, legends, underground river and ever-fascinating problems.

There are many who imagine only scientists and geologists

have the necessary equipment and knowledge to discover really important caves, but those of Mendip have more often been discovered by pure chance. The famous Hyaena Den at Wookey Hole was found by a schoolboy during the construction of a canal for the paper works, and the fascinating series of caves through which the River Axe runs were explored by the local postmaster in his spare time. It is true both these men became pre-eminent authorities, for the boy was the late Professor Boyd Dawkins, and the postmaster was Mr. H. E. Balch, who is now curator of the Wells Museum, but their fame came after their discoveries.

No caves yet discovered in England have the human interest of those found by the two young men, or have yielded such a rich store of relics, with such an appeal to the layman. The expert can revel in the story unfolded in the museums at Wookey Hole and Wells by the huge collection of bones and relics, but even the "tripper" in his joyous ignorance, loves to see the skeleton and crystal which prove beyond possibility of doubt that the Witch of Wookey really lived in the days of King Arthur, even if she did not have all the supernatural powers ascribed to her.

Wookey Hole has yielded many tangible proofs of ancient traditions. The phenomenon described as long ago as A.D. 189 by Clement of Alexandria—an extraordinary sound of clashing cymbals regarded in his day as supernatural—has been heard in modern times and ascribed to its true source: the natural suction of the river in flood times.

Bones, cooking pots, and weapons of the tribe which inhabited the caves from 250 B.C. to A.D. 400, remaining undisturbed all through the Roman occupation, have been found, and even the toys of the children, the combs and ornaments used by the women, and delicate bone needles, which can pass through the finest material without leaving any mark.

Relics and bones of men and animals found in the Hyaena

Den enable the whole story of man's fight for life against giant denizens of the forest, 40,000 years ago, to be reconstructed, Professor Boyd Dawkins, in his preface to Mr. Balch's monumental work *Wookey Hole, its Caves and Cave Dwellers*, says the exploration "has added an important chapter to the story of Britain at the obscure time when pre-history was shading off into history."

The paper mill which led to the discovery of the Hyaena Den stands beside the entrance to the valley. It is one of the only five hand-made paper mills left in England, and is believed to have been founded at Wookey in 1610.

Further along the road from the entrance to Wookey Hole is Ebbor Gorge, an unspoiled valley, where lovely woods gradually close in and climb the limestone cliffs.

Back on the main road, we pass Easton, which commands a good view of Wells cathedral and the tower of St. Cuthbert's; and Westbury, with a fine Perpendicular church, and an old yew tree shading the churchyard, and a village cross at the cross-roads. Rodney Stoke, little more than a mile further, was originally Stoke, and took the additional name of Giffard when it came into the hands of the Giffard family during the reign of King John, changing again to Rodney Stoke when the last of the Giffards married Sir Richard de Rodney in the time of Edward I. The ancient church is full of memorials of the Rodneys, one of whom is shown rising out of his coffin, draped in a shroud. There is a seventeenth-century carved screen, and some modern bench ends carved by a group of village workers. Speeding past Draycott— unless it is the strawberry season, when the fame of its beds of Cheddar strawberries will excuse us for lingering—we come to Cheddar.

Remains of paleolithic cave men and of Romans have been found in and around Cheddar, but the earliest known mention is in the will of Alfred the Great, dated 901, in which he mentions his family at "Ceodre", and three further documents of the same century are dated from the "King's palace at Ceodre", but all trace of the Saxon palace has long vanished.

King Athelstan and his brother and successor, Edmund, often came to the district to hunt, and a document preserved at Axbridge recounts the legend of King Edmund's miraculous escape from death on the cliffs of Cheddar. Having yielded to evil councillors, the king had deprived St. Dunstan of his honours, and dismissed him from the council. Shortly afterwards, when hunting in Cheddar forest, he found himself, in the excitement of the chase, on the brink of Cheddar Gorge, and unable to control his horse. He "commended his soul to the pleasure of Almighty God, saying 'I give thanks Lord Jesus Christ, that at this time I do not remember having injured anyone, but Dunstan only: and this fault I will, with ready zeal, amend by a hearty reconciliation, if Thou only grant me time. Immediately, he was able to control his horse, and after giving thanks for his escape returned home, told his assembled nobles all about it, and bestowed on Dunstan the office of Abbot of Glastonbury.

There is a note of fresh green beauty around the grand old church, and village gossips still meet around the time-worn market cross with its hexagonal shelter. The interior of the church is gay with colour and rich in woodwork, and the tomb of the de Cheddres is bright with gilding and red paint. The fifteenth-century stone pulpit is one of the finest in the county. William Chatterton Dix, who wrote the hymns *Come to me, ye weary*; *As with gladness men of old* and many others, is buried in the church. There is also a mural tablet to Hannah More, who established the first Sunday Schools there, the effect of which is strikingly illustrated in the church records, where most people made their mark on marriage until the schools were established, after which all the couples could write their names.

The Cheddar Caves were mentioned as far back as 1130

by Henry of Huntingdon, as one of the four wonders of England, but although traditions of their existence persisted, their entrance was only re-discovered in the nineteenth century—Cox's by accident in 1837, and Gough's in 1877. Cox's is the smaller cave, but its stalactites and stalagmites have the lovelier and more delicate colouring.

Many flint tools and bone implements were discovered in Gough's cave, and the famous "Cheddar Man" was found in the entrance, at a depth of 9 feet below the surface, and under 18 inches of stalagmite, surrounded by paleolithic flints which lead experts to date it at between 40,000 and 80,000 years old. When it is remembered that half an inch of stalagmite or stalactite takes a thousand years to form, it is enough to make the brain reel at the thought of the ages which went to the making of such formations as the pillar 11 feet high, and the stalactite hanging 15 feet. The Cheddar river emerges from its underground course close to Gough's cave, and falls in a series of cascades into the flower-decked lake.

The road through the gorge was constructed in 1801, and winds through the cliffs for over a mile. The Great Cave Man restaurant and the cheapjack stalls and teagardens rather detract from this part of the valley, but beyond is silence, and a dignity in which intruding man becomes so puny in contrast with the great cliffs that he cannot detract from their grandeur.

There are many higher cliffs than those at Cheddar, but few more overwhelming in their impressiveness, due to the narrowness of the gorge, and the winding of the road, with the consequent impossibility of gaining a distant view, or, more lamentably, of photographing it to advantage. Rising to 480 feet at their highest point, the Wind Rock, they are scantily clothed in the ferns, alpine flowers and dwarf trees of yew and mountain ash which cling to every nook and cranny. These cliffs are the only place in the British Isles where the Cheddar Pink (*Dianthus caesius*) grows wild, and is the chief habitat of the Self-heal (*Prunella laciniata*) and other rare flowers and ferns, and are the only inland breeding-place in southern England of the Peregrine Falcon and the Raven.

Cheddar is also, of course, famous for its Cheese, mentioned by Camden, the sixteenth century historian, who says in *Britannia*: "Cheddar, famous for the excellent prodigious cheese made there, some of which require more than one man's strength to set them on the table, and are of a delicate taste equalling, if not exceeding, the Parmesan." In the seventeenth century Cheddar cheese was in such high favour that it was difficult to procure any, as they were "bespoken by the Court before they were made", and Fuller says, in his inimitable way: "They may be called *Corporation Cheeses*, made by the *Joint Daryes* of the whole Parish, putting their Milk together, and each one, Poor and Rich, receive their share according to their proportion. So that some may think, that the Unity and Amity of those Female Neighbours, living so lovingly together, giveth the better Runnet and Relish to their handiwork."

The normal weight of a Cheddar Cheese is from 80 pounds upwards, but smaller sizes are made especially for the benefit of tourists, and the making of them is no longer confined to Cheddar.

It is nearly half a century since the first Cheddar strawberries came on the market; they are said to owe their distinctive flavour to the chemical composition of the soil.

Axbridge lies close under the shelter of the main range of the Mendips, looking away across the moors. Its name is misleading, as it has no bridge, and the River Axe is some distance away. Axbridge is the perfect expression of the smaller Somerset towns, with a pleasant consciousness of a long history, and a friendly contentment, preferring to live quietly and pleasantly as an agricultural centre, without that itch for change and bustle which has despoiled so many English country towns of their charm. Some of the most unlikely corners have rich medieval work to show. There is a butcher's shop with a magnificent doorway of carved oak, and many of the private houses have doorways, window frames, or a touch of carving to show their age.

The very complete Church Registers and town archives show that Axbridge was a place of considerable importance in Saxon times, when the Saxon kings made the town their headquarters for hunting in the Mendip Forest, and developed it as one of the five military centres for the defence of the county—the others being Watchet, Lyng, Langport, and Bath.

Among the documents preserved at Axbridge is a fourteenth-century MS. describing the privileges enjoyed by the thirty-two burgesses of Axbridge, which included exemption from serving on juries, interference from the sheriff and fines for murder—this last, surely, rather a perilous concession?

The records in Axbridge Town Hall are among the most remarkable and interesting in the county, and are extraordinarily complete, with all the town charters since the time of Henry VI, and numerous earlier MSS.; sixteenth-century Convocation Books containing minutes of the proceedings of the Corporation, and nearly a thousand deeds deposited with the Town Clerk during the Middle Ages, in accordance with a local custom by which buyers and sellers of land placed these documents with the Town Clerk or the Guild Stewards. Some of these deeds are as early as the reign of Henry III, and are a mine of information on local affairs and medieval and Elizabethan customs.

The house known as King John's Hunting Lodge, although it has been said there is no work earlier than Elizabethan times, is a fine old building. An early seventeenth-century moneychanger's table, some old stocks, and other town relics are preserved in the Town Hall, which faces the noble Parish church across the market place. A fine flight of stairs leads up to the church, with its great tower in the Cheddar Valley style. The curious plaster ceiling in the nave, with its long pendants, dates from a restoration carried out in 1636. The Axbridge Panel, a curious fourteenth-century painting on wood, has unfortunately been injudiciously restored. There are several interesting monuments, including one to the Rev. Elias Rebotier, a French Protestant refugee from Languedoc who left France to escape being forced into the Roman Catholic priesthood, and after many adventures, including an attack by pirates on the ship in which he was sailing to Barbados, found a quiet haven at Axbridge where he was rector for forty-five years.

William Naish, who was born at Axbridge in the eighteenth century, studied under Sir Joshua Reynolds, and was a well-known miniature painter. He exhibited at the Royal Academy almost continuously from 1783 until his death in 1800.

West of Axbridge the long, and hitherto unbroken ridge of the Mendips which we have followed from Shepton Mallet breaks up into a group of hills and valleys, with a road going north between Shute Shelve Hill and Winscombe Hill to Weston-super-Mare, and another continuing directly west to the sea at Uphill.

II

Winscombe lies a mile off the Weston road, and its scattered houses are bowered in trees, its roads quiet and deserted, and its grey old church, on a hillside above, presides benignly over its green byways and flowery fields. The station is away by the main road—a trim little place of conspicuous neatness, with geraniums in the waiting-room window. Not many trains call there, but the enchanting

The Packhorse Bridge, Kentsford

The River Parret

Huish Episcopi

St. Mary Magdalen, Taunton

view from its single platform certainly encourages a placid contentment in waiting for them.

Theodore Compton's delightful book *A Mendip Valley* gives a discursive account of life and natural history at Winscombe towards the end of the nineteenth century, and it is pleasant to find that in spite of his distrust of innovations, Winscombe has changed but little, although the hamlet of Woodborough on the main road has been modernized with a big garage and some excellent shops.

On the way to the church a signpost "To Max" points the way to Maxmills, with the ruins of an ancient mill, possibly the same one that is alluded to in Domesday book, neighboured by the old manor-house, and lovely with woods and wild flowers, old orchards, and many water-birds. Wild snowdrops and bog bean can be found there, where many brooks join to form the picturesquely winding Lox Yeo river.

There are carved wooden bosses of winged angel heads in the nave roof of Winscombe church, and carved stone corbels in the aisles, and a mural tablet to the Hon. Colonel Samuel Knollis "whose memory time itself cannot obliterate from the hearts of all who knew him", from whom are descended Lord Knollys and the Hon. Charlotte Knollys, of the households of Edward VII and Queen Alexandra.

Sidcot School is delightfully set in a large garden, on a hillside above the valley. There has been a Quaker School at Sidcot for nearly two and a half centuries. The advertisement of the charges in John Benwell's time makes envious reading for parents of the present day—£16 a year for board and teaching, for which "Much care will be taken to accommodate the Children in an agreeable Manner and great Attention will be paid to their Behaviour and Morals, as well as to the Literary Improvement."

The seventeenth-century meeting house is now a cottage. It was from there the Friends hurried one Sunday in 1789

6

in an endeavour to lay the ghost of George Beecham, a local "conjurer" or wizard, who had expressed a wish to be buried at the cross-roads, and threatened his wife, "If 'ee don't, I'll trouble 'ee." He was buried at Winscombe churchyard, but twelve months later, to the day, all the chairs, tables, pots and pans in his old home began dancing about the floor, and the dead man's boots clattered slowly downstairs. A number of responsible Friends from the meeting house witnessed the disturbance, but neither they, nor Hannah More, who came over from Wrington, nor the curate, Mr. Jones, afterwards Rector of Shipham, could decide whether the phenomena were genuine or not. There was no evidence of trickery, nor even any object in trickery, and it remains an unsolved mystery to this day.

III

Compton Bishop lies a little off the main road, in a valley between Wavering Down and Compton Hill. Its church contains a Norman font, a magnificent fifteenth-century stone pulpit, and some ancient glass.

The road then skirts the southern foot of Crooks Peak and crosses the Lox Yeo valley to Loxton. Although only a little over 600 feet in height, Crooks Peak has the most conspicuous and characteristic peak in the whole range of Mendip, and is used as a steering mark for ships in the channel.

Loxton, high on the south-eastern slopes of Bleadon, and Christon hidden away in the hills, have delightful Norman churches, whilst westward, near the sea, is Bleadon, with many modern houses on the hill top, but the still attractive old village apart, grouped round its fourteenth-century church.

IV

The villages which lie on the north-east of Mendip can be reached by taking the Bristol Road from Wells to Chewton Mendip, which is beautifully situated in a slight dip, below a fifteenth-century church with a noble tower. There are traces of Norman work in the church, many carved bench-ends, some pre-Reformation communion plate, and one of the only three frid-stools left in England —a stone seat let into the window-sill of the sacrarium for the use of those claiming sanctuary.

Chewton Priory, a pleasant modern building, is on the site of an ancient monastery, but thoughts of the monks pale beside memories of a far different personality associated with the mansion, for Edward Lear, author of the *Nonsense Books* not only stayed there, but wrote delightfully amusing letters to Lady Waldegrave, brimful of fun and nonsense, and expressive of his curiously child-like qualities, and his enthusiastic pleasure in the success of himself or any of his friends.

The attractive villages of East and West Harptree have interesting churches. Harptree Combe, a deep and narrow ravine, has the slight remains of Richmond Castle crowning precipitous cliffs, where once the notorious Azelin de Percheval, nicknamed "Lupus", and his equally ferocious son, "Lupellus", pillaged the countryside with their foreign mercenaries in the twelfth century, until their fortress was captured by Stephen and destroyed.

There are numerous fine caves in the neighbourhood and several interesting manor-houses, now farms. Gourney Manor and Tilly Manor date from the seventeenth century, and Harptree Court, a classical building of the Adams school, is in a charming park. Gourney Manor perpetuates the name of Sir Thomas Gourney, a former lord of the manor who was associated in the murder of Edward II.

Compton Martin, set on a slope giving wide views, and backed by wooded hills, is a pretty little place, with its church perched high above the village pond. Compton Martin took its second name from the family descended from Martin de Trèves, all of whom were great church builders, and the village probably owes its splendid Norman church to them. A unique twisted and carved Norman column, a richly carved screen of black oak brought from Bickfield nunnery, now a moated farmhouse, and the recumbent figure of a knight with his sword, make this church one of the most interesting in the county.

At the time when the church was built, a boy was born in the village who grew up to be a medieval version of the hunting parson. He was turned to more holy ways after conversing with a beggar, became a hermit at Haselbury Plucknett, in the south of Somerset, and was venerated as St. Wulfric.

The turning to Ubley is reached at the Saw Mills, where Blagdon Lake comes into view in the distance. Ubley is set beside a stream hurrying to join the lake, and the church, with a quaint pyramidal cap to its stair turret, and a low spire, stands opposite a fine restored cross on a little green.

Blagdon, with the main road high above the lake, gives charming views of the church beside the sparkling waters and the little bays and capes of this most natural-looking reservoir of the Bristol Corporation. Only the stately Perpendicular tower remains of the church where two literary clergymen have worked. The Rev. John Langhorne, who was rector there in the eighteenth century and is buried in the church, was famous for his translation of Plutarch's *Lives*, made in conjunction with his brother; and the Rev. A. M. Toplady, wrote *Rock of Ages* when he was curate in sole charge of the parish. The church was rebuilt by W. H. Wills, first and last Lord Winterstoke of Blagdon, a munificent benefactor to the village, where a branch of the famous tobacco king's family is still seated. Both Lord and Lady Winterstoke are buried at Blagdon.

Beyond Blagdon, the road winds through Rickford Combe, with its rounded, wooded hills and its ploughed fields glowing with the good red earth of Somerset, to Burrington, a picturesque village at the foot of Blackdown Hill. The Perpendicular church has a memorial tablet with an inscription composed by Hannah More, to the memory of Albinia Jackson, one of the twenty children of Vicar Wylde. Eleven of his twenty children were married in the church, including Albinia, who was drowned when the East Indiaman *Elizabeth* was wrecked off Dunkirk in 1810.

In the churchyard there is an epitaph to John Jones, baby, "Born Novr. y 15th, 1708, Dyed March ye 14th, 1708." The dates are quite correct, the apparent mistake being due to the fact that the New Style of the calendar was not adopted until 1752, and under the Old Style, the year began on March 25th.

Burrington Combe, which runs up to the shoulder of Blackdown, the highest point on Mendip, is a bleak valley, golden in summer with stone crop and ragwort, and only sparsely covered with dwarf yew trees and small storm-beaten bushes clinging precariously to the ledges of the limestone. There are many caves in the combe, where quantities of prehistoric weapons, and bones of men and animals have been found, of great importance archaeologically, but the chief interest for tourists is the cleft rock under which Toplady sheltered during a sudden storm, and which is said to have inspired him to write *Rock of Ages*.

The summit of Blackdown, bright with gorse, heather and ling, commands magnificent views across the Severn Sea to Wales and across Sedgemoor to the heights of Exmoor.

There are two roads from Burrington to Churchill, one of which keeps close under the hills, through Upper Langford, and the other by way of Lower Langford and beautiful Langford Court, long the home of the Latch family, whose tombs will be seen in the Perpendicular church of Churchill, a delightful village in a lovely valley below Dolbury Camp. One of the monuments shows a Cavalier gazing with a quizzical melancholy on the form of his wife lying beside him, swathed in a shroud. The whimsical epitaph is almost invariably ascribed to Dr. John Donne, but he died in 1631 and the monument dates from 1644.

Churchill Court, the mansion near the church, was once the home of the ancestors of Mr. Winston Churchill and, curiously enough, a sixteenth-century brass in the church to Ralph Jenyns and his wife is believed to commemorate ancestors of Sarah Jennings, wife of the great John Churchill, first Duke of Marlborough.

Westward from Churchill the road runs below Sandford Hill and Banwell Camp, with its prehistoric earthworks, to Banwell, with its long main street on a slope, and the splendid church. The great church tower, the strikingly beautiful gilded screen, the coloured wooden roof of the chancel and the gilded bosses of the nave roof, the carved wooden bench ends, Flemish glass brought from Belgium in 1855, and many other treasures, go to make up the glory of Banwell church.

There is a brass to John Martock, physician to Bishop King, dated 1503, and a mural tablet to William Beard, a native of Banwell, who was a self-taught zoologist, and explored the famous bone caverns of Banwell Hill.

Banwell has many associations with the Bishops of Bath and Wells, whose palace was built on the site of a Saxon monastery. The great hall built by Bishop Beckington survives in Court House.

Banwell fire station preserves a fire engine dating from 1610, with two thatch hooks used at that time to drag burning thatch off the houses.

V

Beyond Banwell Hill a road branches off to run along the foot of the hills to Hutton, a charming little village at the foot of Bleadon Hill with a small but attractive Perpendicular Church. Hutton Court, close by, dates from the fifteenth century.

The road reaches the sea at Uphill, near the mouth of the River Axe. Uphill was once a Roman port. Its Norman church is high on the grassy, wind-swept hill above the modern town, which has sprung up as a suburb of Weston.

The Roman road which ran along the top of the Mendips and continued to Old Sarum, had its seaward end here. There are wonderful views from the church, which is a landmark for many miles around, and well worth the steep climb to visit it.

VI

The main road continues to Weston-super-Mare past Locking church, with its beautiful carved stone pulpit and elaborate square font, and the vicarage with its miniature stone circle on the lawn, said to have been brought by a former vicar by bullock cart from a site on the Mendips.

VII

After wandering in the towns and villages of Mendip, which time has touched so lightly, it is strange to find the hills ending with Somerset's largest and youngest holiday town.

At the beginning of last century, Weston-super-Mare was a hamlet of fishermen's huts. The first hotel was built about 1808, and was for many years such a white elephant to its owner that it was usual to obtain custom by sending a bellman to announce that beer was to be had at the hotel in the evening!

In 1811, the entire population only numbered 163 people, but Weston was already becoming known for its health-giving climate, and eight years later Mrs. Piozzi, who had been sent there by her Bath physician, wrote to Sir James Fellowes: "The breezes here are most salubrious; no land nearer than North America when we look down the Channel. . . . I enquired for books. 'There are but two in the town,' was the reply: 'a Bible and a *Paradise Lost*.'"

Letters were addressed "Weston, near Worle", and delivered by the Worle postman in a red coat, blowing a long horn, and riding on a donkey, or in a dog-cart. When Beachfield Villas were put up, Archdeacon Law, then Rector of Weston, asked the owner what on earth possessed him to build two such big houses in Weston, as they could never be required, and he would never find anyone with money enough to live in them!

A curious little book, published in 1882, gives reminiscences and pictures of the Old Farm House at Weston in 1826. The illustrations show a long, low thatched house, with comical sketches of some of the furniture in use there —the table propped up with stones to make it stand straight, and chairs in various stages of dilapidation. The village then "consisted of only four streets, two inns, and a few scattered houses, some of which had been newly built by the rustic inhabitants of Weston, who, themselves resided in small cottages with mould or stone floors."

It was undoubtedly the coming of the railway which led to the sudden rapid development of Weston, as it did in so many other towns. At first the railway station was a mile and a half away. A comical account of the first railway excursion to Weston, from Taunton, shows that even war-time travelling was luxurious in comparison with the early days of railways. It is true the fare was only 1s., but the excursionists certainly got a great deal of excitement for their money, even if not quite what they expected. The train probably consisted of open trucks, and it is known that a large and excited crowd gathered to see the intrepid travellers commence their journey. The whole of the morning was taken up with false starts, and eventually the train "dashed off" at two o'clock—six hours late!—and reached Weston Junction, thirty miles away, at 6 p.m. As the train was due to return at 8 p.m., the excursionists decided it was too risky to walk the mile and a half to the sea, so they waited at the Junction, where it began to rain heavily, and were soon soaked through. They arrived back at Taunton at 2 a.m. Their comments are not on record; nor is it clear whether they had anything to eat during all that time, but being excursionists, doubtless they had provided both food and, even more important, liquid refreshment.

So rapidly did Weston grow that two local papers were firmly established there by 1845, and are still friendly rivals in the present day, and guide books, of course, followed. *The New Handbook to Weston-super-Mare*, published in August 1865, described the scene on the beach in the magniloquent language of the period " . . . attention is arrested by the bustling activity of bathers presented on Weston Beach. Verily, people begin to discover with what amazing gusto, after a marine immersion, they can demolish the luxurious comestibles of a seaside breakfast. The ladies think of becoming Nereids; the gentlemen renew their outworn classical acquaintance with Neptune and Amphitrite."

To-day, with a population of nearly 30,000 Weston-super-Mare has no links with the village from which it has sprung, apart from its parish church, and part of the old thatched cottage built by the Rev. W. Leeves, Rector of Wrington. He composed the tune to which the ballad *Auld Robin Gray* is sung, and the fragment of his house is still known as "Leeves" or "Auld Robin Gray's" Cottage.

In Grove Park, presented to the town by the Smith-Piggot family, who have been lords of the manor since 1696, there is a curious and completely irrelevant eighteenth-century survival, in four busts purchased by the Smith-Piggots from the estate of Horace Walpole, Earl of Orford, which have an inscription saying they formerly stood in the garden of Walpole's famous villa, Strawberry Hill, Twickenham.

Although perfectly content to be the Mecca of excursionists, gay, friendly Weston scarcely deserves the slighting references so often accorded to it, by people who seem to think popularity the unforgivable sin. Popular it is and always will be, so long as it continues to make its visitors healthy and happy, but even the oldest towns might well envy its two great and unique features—Worlbury Hill and Brean Down. These last outcrops of the Mendip range before they plunge into the sea to emerge finally as the islands of Steep Holme and Flat Holme, do more than ward off cold winds and lend beauty to the views from Weston's Marine Parade, for Brean Down has been recognized as a national treasure, and scheduled as a bird sanctuary, and Worlbury Hill, with its lovely woods, has another national possession in its great prehistoric camp.

Chapter Seven: THE BURNHAM LEVEL AND EAST SEDGEMOOR

Along the Burnham Level to Brent Knoll and Burnham—South to Wedmore and Meare—Glastonbury

THE country stretching from Bleadon Hill to the Quantocks, and bordering Bridgwater Bay, stretches in a series of "Levels"—Bleadon, Burnham, Huntspill, and Pawlett Levels—and well may they be so called, for the land is as flat as a billiard table—the greatest stretch of flat coast in the west of England.

There are people who extol the charms of Holland, yet never give a thought to the Somerset moors, although their willow-bordered "rhines", as the ditches are called, have a charm as great as the Dutch canals. In early summer the rich meadows are a sheet of gold with buttercups, and always there are strangely beautiful atmospheric effects, and wonderful sunsets. Here is history, too—the dawn of our race in the lake village of Meare—the dawn of Christianity in Glastonbury; and of English freedom when Alfred's wanderings ended in the peace of Wedmore. Sedgemoor saw the Civil War in many a town and village, and the ending of all England's Civil Wars in Sedgemoor's fight.

The main road from Weston-super-Mare passes Lympsham to the isolated hill of Brent Knoll, a landmark for miles around, with its two neat little villages among the orchards and trees on its lower slopes, and a prehistoric camp on the grassy crest.

East Brent has a famous Harvest Home, started in 1857 by Archdeacon Denison, who was rector for over half a century. Lunch is served in the great marquee, which has seating accommodation for about 1,400, and in peace-time the feast calls for over 500 pounds of beef, 400 pounds of ham, 400 pounds of pudding, 100 pounds of cheese, 120 quarterns of bread, 2 hogsheads of beer, half a hogshead of cider, and enormous quantities of lemonade. Ninety plum puddings are made at the vicarage, in a special boiler installed by Archdeacon Denison, and are carried by the ladies, two and two, escorted by the band, whilst the feasters cheer and clap their hands. Afterwards there is the triumphal march of the Monster Loaf and the Giant Cheese, borne on trenchers by four men to the same accompaniment.

On the west of the hill is Brent Knoll village, which stretches along the road with its church beautifully situated on the hillside. The church has a wonderful series of bench ends, some of which are very humorous, and there is a fine wooden roof, and a mural monument to John Somerset "found fit for bliss" in 1663.

The sands and dunes of Brean and Berrow, on the coast, have had the usual fatal attraction for caravans, huts and bungalows. Brean village, near the estuary of the Axe, has an isolated church in whose graveyard are many sailors drowned on Brean sands, and the small and ancient Berrow church is right in the middle of the golf-course laid out on the dunes.

Burnham is a typical family resort, with glorious sands and every concomitant of holiday joys, but it has two distinguishing features—the superb sunsets, which Turner loved and painted, and its church on the sea-front, with an unexpected feature worth going far out of the way to see, in its carved altar-piece by Grinling Gibbons.

Originally designed by Inigo Jones and executed by Gibbons for the chapel of Whitehall, it was saved when the chapel was burned down, and given by Queen Anne to Westminster Abbey, where it was entirely out of place. When it was taken down before the coronation of George IV, Bishop King, at that time Canon of Westminster, asked that it might be given to Burnham church, of which he had been vicar. It was so large that it was divided into several sections, some of which were lost and have only recently been restored to the church.

Four panels form the present altar-piece, three well-nourished cherubs cluster round an open Bible in the north aisle, and under the tower are two huge kneeling angels, each on a pedestal, whilst on the tower wall are winged cherub heads flying round the inscription I.N.R.I. set in the gilded rays of a glory.

A mile and a half inland from Burnham is Highbridge, on the River Brue, a busy market town which is the centre of some of the richest grazing land in the Kingdom. Surprisingly enough, it is completely modern, and one of the few places in Somerset without any antiquarian interest, but it is a road, rail, and river centre of considerable importance.

The village of Pawlett, on a slightly higher level than the surrounding flats, has a church dating from Norman times, with much carved woodwork on the bench-ends, box pews, and a painted and gilded fifteenth-century chancel screen. From there the road runs between the River Parret and the western end of the Polden Hills to Bridgwater.

II

A road from Highbridge runs by way of Mark Causeway to Mark, whose great Perpendicular towered church dominates the flat meadows. There is a fine panelled roof over the north aisle, and carved figures of the Evangelists, brought from Bruges Cathedral by a former rector. The many ancient carved wood corbels of kings and queens and bishops surprisingly have new and easily recognizable additions—the heads of King Edward VII, Queen Alexandra, and Bishop Kenion.

Wedmore is for ever famous as the scene of the treaty

between Alfred and the Danes, which brought much-needed peace to England, and was followed by the christening feast of Guthrum and his nobles.

Alfred's palace was probably on the site now occupied by the manor-house, and not, as once supposed, at Mudgeley, where excavations have brought to light nothing earlier than the thirteenth century.

Wedmore is on rising ground, and its Perpendicular church has a central tower and some interesting features, including a fine Jacobean pulpit, a remarkable wall-painting, and a seventeenth-century brass to George Hodges, said to be the last ancient brass portrait of an English soldier. A hoard of silver coins dating from the time of Sweyn and Hardicanute was found in the churchyard in 1851 and is now in the British Museum. One of Wedmore's two beautiful old crosses still stands in the churchyard, and the other in front of the house where Judge Jeffreys lodged. It was on this cross that Jeffreys hanged a doctor who dressed the wounds of a dying Puritan.

Up to 1913, a Court Leet was held annually at Wedmore at which portreeves, bread-weighers, ale-tasters, and a hayward were appointed, although the proceedings were latterly no more than a formality.

South of Wedmore is Meare, which derives its name from the moors or meres with which it was formerly surrounded, and which were once overflowed by the sea. Three islands are mentioned in old records, all of which were given by Kerelwach, king of the West Saxons, to the Abbots of Glastonbury, and their old manor-house, built about 1300, can still be seen, although it is now a farm. Meare Pool, once the fish-preserve of the Abbots, covered 500 acres in Elizabethan days, and was five miles round. Later a stagnant pool, it has since been drained and has become valuable land.

The Abbot's Fish House, beside the River Brue, is unique.

This fourteenth-century home of the abbot's head fisher-man has an upper floor where he lived, and storage-room below, where he kept his tackle and stacked his fish. It is to be hoped he liked the smell of fish.

The lovely group made by the church with its low tower, and the abbot's manor-house and fish-house, shaded with trees, and surrounded by flower-starred meadows, charms the average visitor rather more than the site of the Lake village which gave the place European fame, and has such a fascination for archaeologists.

The site at Meare, which was probably occupied longer than the site near Godney, is believed to have been in con-tinuous occupation from about 250 B.C. until well into the Roman period, and the antiquities discovered show that these prehistoric men and women could spin and weave, make pottery, cast metals, hunt, sow, reap and cook, and liked to decorate their implements, utensils, and pottery with elaborate curvilinear designs. The women decked them-selves with rings and beads of glass and amber, and the dice found show that the villagers shared the modern passion for a gamble. The Meare Lake Village consists of two parts (the east and west villages), and at least one-half of the whole area yet remains to be examined by skilled archaeologists. Dr. Arthur Bulleid and Mr. H. St. George Gray have done many seasons' valuable work there, and all the remains from this site are preserved in the Somerset County Museum at Taunton, where the life of the villagers can be better under-stood by unskilled observers than on the site itself.

The antiquities found in the Glastonbury Lake Village, near Godney, between 1892 and 1907, are beautifully dis-played in the little museum at Glastonbury. An astonishing number and variety of relics were brought to light, all of which are illustrated and minutely described by Dr. Bulleid and Mr. St. George Gray in their authoritative monograph *The Glastonbury Lake Village*.

III

Michael Drayton says in his *Polyolbion:*

"O three times famous Isle, where is that place that
      might
   Be with thyself compar'd for glory and delight,
   Whilst Glastonbury stood? exalted to that pride,
   Whose Monastery seem'd all other to derive?
   O who thy ruin sees, whom wonder doth not fill
   With our great father's pomp, devotion, and their
      skill? . . . "

Site of the first Christian Church in England, setting for the legends of St. Joseph of Arimathea and King Arthur, birthplace of St. Dunstan—Glastonbury has a thousand wonderful associations for those who seek it in a reverent spirit. What matter if some ungrateful souls seek to disprove the legend of St. Joseph and the Holy Thorn? We will be content to accept the age-old tradition which in 1434 gave the English bishops precedence over those of France and Spain at the Council of Basle, on the ground of "Britain's conversion by Joseph of Arimathea". Certain it is that Christianity was established at Glastonbury at a very early date, and was maintained there when the rest of England had reverted to paganism. Ancient Welsh triads mention Glastonbury as one of the three perpetual choirs in Britain, and no less a person than St. Augustine bore testimony that Christians still lived peaceably at Glastonbury when he landed in Kent to convert the heathen Angles.

It is a happy circumstance that the earliest Christian site in England is associated with memories of King Arthur and his Knights of the Round Table, those doughty champions of the Christian faith during some of the darkest days of England's early history. It is, unfortunately, all too true that

Geoffrey of Monmouth is more given to pleasant romancing than an historian should be, and it is equally true it has never been proved that Arthur lived at all, but there are so many age-old traditions in Somerset linking the hero king with Cadbury Camp and the Isle of Avalon that we may be forgiven if we dwell on those proud tales of chivalry, which are enshrined in some of the greatest literature of England.

In Arthur's day Glastonbury was indeed an island, as it is still, in times of flood, and Mallory gives a vivid description of Arthur's last voyage, when Sir Bedivere carried him to the waterside and placed him in the barge with the three queens in mourning, and afterwards followed him to the chapel and hermitage "between two hills" at Glastonbury.

But whether we believe in the lovely legends of Glastonbury or not, there are abundant records of its early foundation. A charter is known to have been granted to the Abbey in A.D. 601, which gave evidence that it had been in existence for many centuries, whilst charters granted in A.D. 708 and 1032 are still in existence, and from the time of St. Dunstan onwards detailed facts emerge.

St. Dunstan, who was probably born at Glastonbury about 924, had a passion for acquiring knowledge, and became celebrated for his great learning and many accomplishments. He excelled as a musician, sculptor, worker in metal and at illuminating MSS., and was particularly fond of old folk songs. Tradition says he always carried a harp with him on his journeys. In his youth at court his good looks and charming manners made him such a favourite with the ladies that the courtiers became exceedingly jealous of him, but when he was made Abbot of Glastonbury by King Edmund, he became an ascetic. He gradually replaced the secular occupants of Glastonbury by Benedictine monks, and made it a great centre of learning and religious observance.

As adviser to King Edred, and his successor, King Edgar,

7

St. Dunstan also initiated a far-seeing policy of national unification and moral reform, and was successively Bishop of Worcester and London, and Archbishop of Canterbury, and the sixteen years of King Edgar's reign were notable for the reforms instituted by the Primate. The year A.D. 973 saw his plans for unification brought to fruition with the crowning of Edgar at Bath as King of All England. He was appointed papal legate in 961, but on the death of Edgar in 979 he retired and devoted himself to pastoral work, until his death in 988.

All through the centuries from then, until the Dissolution, the Abbey grew in size, beauty, wealth, and power, until the fateful day when the gentle, saintly, and fearless Richard Whyting refused to be false to his trust and surrender the abbey to Henry VIII, and paid for his refusal with his life, for the wealth of the abbey was too great to be lost by mere scruples of justice. The abbey lands alone were valued at about half a million of modern money, and there were the rentals and many treasures to add to the spoil.

Although Abbot Whyting was the last abbot to rule Glastonbury Abbey, it is not generally realized the title has survived through every vicissitude in an unbroken connexion with the Benedictine community, and since 1893 has been vested in the Benedictines of Downside Abbey.

A disastrous fire in 1184 destroyed practically the whole abbey, which was rebuilt on a magnificent scale. The surviving ruins of the Abbey date from periods varying from 1184 to the fifteenth century, and patient excavations have uncovered the foundations of the little church built by King Ine in the seventh century, and the additions of St. Dunstan in the tenth century, and late work, but many detailed accounts of the gracious ruins make it unnecessary to describe them in full; richly decorated, nobly proportioned, and lovingly tended, they are worthy of the fame of the once-great abbey.

A few yards away, in the High Street, is the George Inn, with its splendid carved stone front dating from 1475, and still one of the finest, as it is the earliest example of its kind. It was originally built for the accommodation of pilgrims to the Abbey. Further up the street is the Tribunal House which was built in the reign of Henry VII and was originally the Abbot's Court House, and near by is the magnificent fourteenth-century Abbey Barn, and some almshouses founded by Abbot Bere in 1512. The two churches of Glastonbury are also noble and interesting buildings, one dating from the fifteenth and the other from the sixteenth century.

Glastonbury Museum, opened in 1885, contains many early British remains, and relics found during the excavations on the site of the prehistoric lake village at Godney.

There is a winding pathway to the summit of Tor Hill, which no one should fail to climb, for although it is only 520 feet in height, it commands a marvellous panorama of the greater part of Somerset. The Perpendicular tower which makes the hill such a distinctive landmark marks the site of the chapel of St. Michael which was destroyed by a landslide in 1271. At the foot of the Tor is Chalice Well, a chalybeate spring where Collinson tells us in 1750 Matthew Chandler was cured of a serious disease by drinking the water, with the result that crowds were attracted there to take the waters. The *Gentleman's Magazine* for the 5th May, 1751, said that 10,000 people came from all parts. Bathing houses were built and a Pump Room erected and the waters were also sent out in sealed bottles and sold in London. Curiously enough, although there is a chain of Holy Wells along the Polden Hills, neither the Chalice Well nor the spring in the crypt of the Abbey appear to have been regarded as Holy Wells. The water of the Chalice Well stains the stones over which it flows a deep red. It has been said that it was here Joseph of Arimathea hid the Holy Graal, but as no mention has been traced in early writers of any such legend, it has been discredited as a modern invention, although Tennyson embodied it in his *Idylls of the King*.

It was on Weary-all Hill that St. Joseph traditionally landed and stuck his staff into the ground, whereupon it took root and grew into a miraculous thorn tree which ever afterwards blossomed on Christmas Day. The original thorn was hacked down by a fanatical Puritan soldier. It is decidedly satisfactory to know that he accidentally cut off his own leg in the process! The fallen tree remained connected to the root by its bark, and survived for thirty years after, during which time grafts were taken and trees propagated, and many gardens in the neighbourhood now have a Glastonbury Thorn (*Crataegus Oxycantha praecox*), which blossoms at Christmas, and again in May. It is said that the original tree was held in such veneration that sailors carried pieces of it for luck, and men died happy if a piece could be buried with them. It is shown on the pastoral staff of Bishop Savaric, now preserved at Wells, and in olden days a spray was always presented to the King at Christmas. In 1929 the custom was revived at the express wish of King George V.

Chapter Eight: ALONG THE POLDEN HILLS

The Polden Hills—Bridgwater

THERE is nothing more delightful than to explore the little ridge of the Polden Hills which divides the great plain of Sedgemoor roughly into half. Only twelve miles long, and never more than 300 feet in height, the Poldens not only command wide views, but have the most enchanting villages down byways which have escaped the notice of the multitude.

The road leaves Glastonbury by way of Street, with its mile-long main street very neat and modern-looking. It owes its prosperity largely to the well-known West-Country Quaker family of Clark, who established a shoe factory there, and have been munificent in their donations to the town. John Aubrey Clark, who was a land surveyor of Street, discovered several new fungi, and two books of his drawings of fungi are in the library at Kew.

Joseph Glanvill, who became rector of Street and Walton in 1672, was a voluminous writer, and his works included *The Vanity of Dogmatizing* containing the story of the Scholar Gypsy which is the subject of Matthew Arnold's poem. John Xavier Merriman, son of a rector of Street, who was born there, in 1841, was Premier of Cape Colony from 1908–1910. It was largely through his firm stand that the Union of South Africa was established in 1910.

Walter Raymond, the Somerset novelist, spent the latter years of his life at Street, and gave the desk at which he wrote his books, which had once belonged to the poet Cowper, to Street Library.

In the neighbourhood of Street is the twelfth century Ivythorne Manor, and southward, at Marshall's Elm, are

the Ivythorn and Walton Hills, which have been presented
to the National Trust. The first blood of the Civil War was
shed at Marshall's Elm, on 2nd August, 1642, twenty days
before the King set up his standard at Nottingham.

Walton is almost joined up with Street. It has an unusually attractive modern church, a fifteenth-century farmhouse which was formerly the rectory, but its greatest
attraction lies down a byway to the north, where a farm
represents all that remains of Sharpham House, once a manor
of the abbots of Glastonbury. It was here that Abbot
Richard Whyting was arrested at the Dissolution, and here
that Sir Edward Dyer, poet and courtier, and Henry Fielding
were born.

Gabriel Harvey, in a letter to Spenser, bracketed Dyer
with Sir Philip Sydney as "the two very diamondes of her
maiesties courte for many speciall and rare qualities". Dyer
was frequently abroad on diplomatic missions, and fell into
and out of favour with Elizabeth from time to time because
he would never "fawn and cringe" at Court. His best-
known poem is on Contentment.

Henry Fielding, the "Father of the English Novel", was
born in the Harlequin's chamber, a small room over the
chapel, on Shakespeare's Day, a hundred years after the
death of Dyer. He was highly connected, and was descended
from William Feilding, the first Earl of Denbigh. It is said
he accounted for the difference between his name and that
of the Feildings by saying his branch of the family had been
the first to learn to spell!

Soon after leaving Walton the road climbs the hills to run
along the top of the ridge to Bridgwater. There are no
villages on the crest of the hills, and the road is chiefly
notable for its wonderful views on either hand, but at
Loxley Wood a little wicket gate leads to the famous
Swayne's Leaps, which commemorate a sequel to the Battle
of Sedgemoor, when one of the prisoners was bidden by the

Royalist soldiers to leap for his life. His legs were bound together, and there is little doubt it was intended he should die, however great his prowess, but the young man gave three great leaps—now marked by small stones—and bounding into a coppice, managed to effect his escape.

On the south-western slopes of the hills are several peaceful little villages looking away across King's Sedgemoor to the Quantocks—Greinton, whose Perpendicular church has an embattled tower with a pyramidal top and seventeenth-century bench ends; Moorlinch with its Early English church, pillar piscina, carved bench ends, Norman font, old oak seats and the fourteenth-century effigy of a lady, and its fine views of the battlefield; Sutton Mallet and Stawell, with modern Chilton Priory on the hillside above; and Bawdrip which, although it has a station on the Somerset and Dorset Railway, and is within four miles of Bridgwater, is so retired and unsought that it has not even an inn, lodging, or village shop. Well hidden behind a hill, its pretty, rose-bowered cottages cluster round an interesting little church, in which are the effigy of a knight in fourteenth-century plate-armour; a panel of oak carved with Tudor roses; and an inscription to Eleanor Lovell the "daughter and heiress of the family honour and estates who died June 14th, 1681, taken away by a sudden and untimely fate at the very time of the marriage celebrations"—a rather vague inscription which has given rise to a local version of the famous legend of the Mistletoe Bough Chest—that tragic tale of the young bride who hid in a chest carved with mistletoe boughs on her wedding day, in a spirit of playfulness, and was imprisoned by a spring lock and suffocated.

II

On the north-eastern slopes are Ashcott, which commands a fine view of Glastonbury Tor and the long line of the

Mendips. It is said to have been the birthplace of Thomas Pride, the Parliamentarian General, who was one of the signatories to the death-warrant of Charles I.

Shapwick's Early English church has mural tablets to the Bull and Strangways families, dating from 1657. Shapwick House was built by Judge Rolles when Cromwell deprived him of office, on the site of the old court-house of Abbot John de Taunton; and Down House has been the seat of the Strangways since the seventeenth century. One of them is praised on his memorial for the "sweetness of his manners", and another was Premier of South Australia from 1868 to 1870.

According to an accepted legend, St. Indractus and his sister Dominica and their companions were martyred at Shapwick by pagan Saxons in 710, and the Holy Well near the church may have been dedicated to him. In the eighteenth century a small bath-house and pump-room were erected for the accommodation of patients resorting to the well, but in modern times the spring has been diverted.

Catcott has a quaint old church with oak seats and an odd arrangement for lengthening them.

Edington, not unnaturally, claims to be the site of the great battle of Ethandune, in opposition to the Wiltshire town of the same name, and has many learned supporters for its claim. The protracted arguments and wordy battles which have been waged are too long to recapitulate here, but the fact that Guthrum's forces are admitted by all to have been concentrated in the Poldens, and that Alfred's army was probably gathered in the Quantocks under Earl Odda, and that the battle was followed by the treaty of Wedmore, and Guthrum's baptism at Aller, makes the claim of the Somerset village plausible, to say the least, and the records of the time are too confused to settle the dispute finally.

Chilton-upon-Polden, another pretty little village, has a sham priory on the hillside above, said to incorporate

material from a Benedictine priory established there as a cell
of Glastonbury, and certainly incorporating bits and pieces
collected from churches and manor-houses all over the
county.

The National Trust own a little viewpoint on Cock Hill,
on the crest of the Poldens above Chilton.

Cossington is so delightful that it needs nothing else to
recommend it, but it has a manor-house neighboured by a
thirteenth-century church with a sixteenth-century brass to
a lord of the manor and his wife. In the centre of the village
is the great yew tree called the Preaching Tree, because there
is a tradition Wesley stood in its shade to preach.

The neighbouring village of Woolavington is also enchanting, not only picturesque in itself, but commanding an
amazingly fine view across the fertile Burnham level to the
Mendips, ranging over Brent Knoll and Glastonbury Tor,
Uphill Church, high on Bleadon hill above the Severn Sea;
and the coast of Wales—a breathtaking expanse.

There is a duck-pond beside the fine old church with its
Norman nave, Early English chapel, and a stone carved with
the initials of Sir John Hody, who was Lord Chief Justice
in the reign of Henry VI. He died in 1441 and was buried
there. He had an estate at Stowell, near Templecombe, and
his second son Sir William, who became chief Baron of the
Exchequer, had many connexions with Somerset.

General John Jacob and William Stephen Jacob were the
sons of Stephen Jacob, vicar of Woolavington-cum-Puriton,
and were born in the village. General Jacob sailed for India
in 1828 and spent thirty years there without ever returning
home on leave. He proved himself a soldier of a rare type
—a brilliant cavalry leader and swordsman, a courageous
and beloved leader, and a gifted administrator. He invented
an improved rifle, planned the reorganization of the Indian
Army, made good roads all over Upper Sind, and multiplied
its irrigation system fourfold. In 1851 the village of Kan-

ghurto, which had become a flourishing town under his rule, was re-named Jacobabad in his honour.

His younger brother William also earned fame in India and at home, as an astronomer, and was appointed Director of the Madras Observatory in 1848.

On the hill-top above Woolavington is a sham ruined tower in the grounds of the Georgian manor-house of Knowle, said to have been built about 150 years ago, by a former owner, who had married a French lady and built it to please her when she pined for her home. Benjamin Greenhill, who built the tower, and his French wife, are buried in the Early English church of Puriton. Modern Puriton manor is said to be on the site of a manor-house which belonged to Admiral Blake.

III

There is little that is really old in Bridgwater now, but its streets have a pleasantly old-world air, and there are fine seventeenth-century houses in quiet King's Square and Castle Street; the tall church spire peeps over the top of the impressive Corn Market, and down a little byway is the house in which Blake was born, now a most interesting little museum.

Bridgwater is logically and inevitably the centre from which to reach the site of the last real battle on English soil, for did not Monmouth himself watch the defeat of his un-trained troops from the top of the church tower, and did not those deluded unfortunates set out from Bridgwater on their fatal campaign? But memories of the rebel Duke with his handsome face and winning ways, but hopelessly unstable character, pale into insignificance before the memory of one of the most gallant and successful leaders in our history—Robert Blake, Bridgwater's greatest son, who combined in his own person a brilliant soldier and a victorious admiral.

Bridgwater is justifiably proud of Blake; the striking statue to his memory in front of the Corn Market is the first thing the visitor notices on entering the town, and there are reminders of him everywhere.

Born in 1599, of a family which had formerly belonged to Bishop's Lydeard, he was the eldest of twelve sons of a Bridgwater merchant of some standing, and was educated at Bridgwater Grammar School before proceeding to Oxford. On the death of his father he took to business with his brother Humphrey, was elected Member of Parliament for Bridgwater in 1640, and joined the Parliamentarian forces two years later.

Shortly afterwards his brilliant series of successes began with his defence of Lyme Regis, followed by his prolonged and brilliant defence of Taunton, and his siege of Dunster, which proved he was as successful at attack as in defence. In 1648, when the fleet mutinied, and went over to Prince Rupert, he was given his first naval command, defeated the Prince's fleet, "whipped" the Dutch from the seas, and in spite of illness, set out on his last great expedition, when he destroyed the great Spanish Plate Fleet at Teneriffe in an action of almost unbelievable daring. Even Nelson, two centuries later, with all the improvements of naval armament, failed in the same enterprise at Teneriffe.

The news of this great victory, which compares with the most brilliant naval achievements in history, excited the greatest enthusiasm in England. A public thanksgiving was ordered, and the Protector sent Blake a portrait set in gold and diamonds ". . . as a testimony of our own and the parliament's good acceptance of your carriage in this action".

The great Admiral, who longed to see his native land again, died just as he entered Plymouth Sound in August 1657, which inspired Sir Henry Newbolt to write his touching ballad on *The Death of Admiral Blake*. Blake's body was embalmed, and taken by sea to Greenwich, where he lay in state until taken in solemn procession up the Thames to be buried in Westminster Abbey.

Blake had made England's name respected all over the world. His chivalrous soul was filled only with an unselfish patriotism, and his only object was to uphold the interest and honour of England, without regard to politics, and it is one of the greatest blots on Charles II's reign that the body of this great Englishman was dug up and thrown ignominiously into an unknown pit.

Among other natives of Bridgwater is John Oldmixon, the historian who was a member of a family which settled at Axbridge as early as the fourteenth century, and afterwards held the manor of Oldmixon, near Bridgwater. Two years after the accession of George I he became collector of customs at Bridgwater, and also acted as a political agent. He incautiously attacked Pope and other writers of the day, which Pope revenged by a scathing satire in his *Dunciad* and in *The Art of Sinking in Poetry*.

Oldmixon died at Bath and was buried at Ealing with his son and daughter, and the tomb at Bridgwater sometimes asserted to be his is probably the burial-place of his wife.

Andrew Plimer, a painter who exhibited at the Royal Academy from 1786 to 1819, and whose beautiful miniatures are much sought after by collectors; and Henry Phillpotts, Bishop of Exeter, a great controversialist, were born at Bridgwater in the eighteenth century, and Canon George Trevor, who was instrumental in reviving the Convocation of York; Frederick Horniman, founder of the Horniman Museum; and George Deacon, a civil engineer who took part in laying the second Atlantic cable, invented the waste water meter which bears his name, and projected the scheme for the utilization of the River Vyrnwy as the Liverpool Reservoir, were born at Bridgwater in the nineteenth century.

Bridgwater is set on Somerset's chief river, and however

much its enterprising merchants may regret that vessels of over 800 tons cannot reach the town, the visitor rejoices in the result that Bridgwater is prosperous without being completely divorced from the pleasant things of life. There are gardens along the river, from which the daily tidal "bore" can be seen, and the countryside is very close.

The peculiar sediment of mud and sand brought up by the tide and deposited on the banks of the Parret provides the material for the bath-brick manufactures, which can be found nowhere else in the world. The value of the deposits were first discovered about the thirteenth century, but it was a Mr. Bath who first took out a patent for the manufacture of "Bath's patent scouring bricks" which, contrary to widespread belief, have no connexion with the city of Bath.

The town's chief links with the Monmouth Rebellion are the Parish Church, and the old house known as Judge Jeffreys' House, in which the Judge stayed a night on his way to Taunton to hold the Assizes which resulted in the wholesale hangings and deportations meted out to the unhappy followers of Monmouth.

The parish church, which dates from the fourteenth century with various later rebuildings and additions, has a slender spire rising 120 feet above the tower, and has a wonderful abundance of magnificent wood carving in black oak, and a famous picture *The Descent from the Cross*, about whose origin there are many conflicting opinions. Some accounts say it was taken from a Spanish privateer, others from a French vessel during the Napoleonic wars. Sir Joshua Reynolds thought it was painted by Seuer, others have attributed it to Murillo, Tiepolo, and Guido, or other Masters, and the whole question remains unsettled.

At the time of the Civil War, the castle was considered impregnable, and its surrender without any attempt at defence was a serious blow to the Royalist cause. Forty years later, Monmouth was proclaimed King on June 21st, 1685, at the High Cross. On the 6th of the following month he was utterly defeated, and nine days later he was beheaded on Tower Hill, whilst by September no less than 331 of his followers had been hung, 850 sold as slaves, and 408 fined, whipped, or continued in prison, although the other leaders had escaped and some even rose to honoured positions which they seem to have deserved but little.

Bridgwater has been famous for centuries for its Guy Fawkes celebrations, held on the Thursday nearest November 5th, and people come from all parts to see the torchlight procession of masqueraders, the huge bonfires, and giant squibs.

Chapter Nine: KING'S SEDGEMOOR AND THE CURRY COUNTRY

The Battlefield of Sedgemoor—The Isle of Athelney—the Curry Country—Langport—High Ham Hill.

SOUTH of Bridgwater lies King's Sedgemoor, with the battlefield at Westonzoyland, but in picturing that piteous rout it is necessary to explore the whole area between the King's Sedgemoor Drain and the River Parret, from Chedzoy in the north, to Middlezoy in the south. On the night before the battle Feversham, with the Royal cavalry, lay at Westonzoyland, Pembroke and the Militia at Middlezoy, and a detachment of cavalry under Sir Francis Compton at Chedzoy, the great church towers of these villages indicating their positions to the Duke of Monmouth.

Each of the villages is on slightly rising ground, and the termination "oy" is probably a corruption of "ey" or isle. Chedzoy church has sixteenth-century bench-ends, a lectern, pulpit and other seventeenth-century work; a fifteenth-century brass, and an altar cloth made from an embroidered cope. Dr. Ralegh, a nephew of Sir Walter Ralegh, was presented to the living of Chedzoy in 1620, and became Dean of Wells in 1641. He was a staunch Royalist, and was persecuted by the Parliamentarians at the instigation of a man who wanted to secure the rectory for himself, and was finally murdered in his own Deanery at Wells.

A curious custom has been observed at Chedzoy since the fifteenth century, when a piece of land was left to be sold every 21 years to provide for repairs to the church. The auction lasts during the burning of half an inch of candle, and the last bidder before the candle is consumed becomes the purchaser. A similar auction is held at Tatworth, near Chard.

The battlefield lies between Chedzoy and Westonzoyland. Those who do not wish to study the many detailed accounts of the battle cannot do better than read Conan Doyle's brilliant novel *Micah Clarke*, which gives an accurate picture of the whole rebellion and its aftermath, with a vivid description of the battle.

The quickest way from Westonzoyland to the battlefield is by way of Langmoor Drove, Zog Drove and Penzoy Drove, but the site has changed considerably. At the time of the Monmouth Rebellion it was a large common cut with the rhines which proved so fatal to the rebels, but the moor was enclosed by Act of Parliament in 1795, and as part of the scheme the River Carey was diverted and carried across the level to the Parret at Dunball, under the name of King's Sedgemoor Drain, and the moor is now fertile pastureland. In tracing out the battlefield, all the present hedges and ditches must be disregarded, and it must be remembered the old rhines have disappeared, or only left faint, dry tracks. Marsh Lane, however, is still only a track for cattle, as it was when Wade led the foot along it, and Bradney lane still has Peasey farm on its little hill, and the ancient drove leading to the moor, where Godfrey guided the rebels.

Two trees were planted in 1927 to mark the battlefield, and a year later a "Stone of Memory" was set up. The roughly hewn block of Cornish granite bears an inscription commemorating those who fell in the battle, and those who suffered death, punishment, or transportation.

No church in England has a more direct or tragic connexion with national history than Westonzoyland, where 500 miserable prisoners, wounded and dying, were locked into the church after the battle, some dying whilst the bells rang out for the Royalist victory—and these, as it proved, the more fortunate.

Westonzoyland's Perpendicular church tower is one of the finest in Somerset, and there are splendid roofs and a

Whitestaunton

Babcary

Wookey Hole Cave

remarkable series of bench-ends. The church records contain an account of the battle, probably written by the Rector Richard Alford. Five of the King's soldiers were buried in the churchyard after the battle, and twenty-two of the rebels were hanged. According to these registers, King James visited the battlefield on the 27th August, and 8*s.* 10*d.* was "expended in beere on the next day when the King came through Weston". A tablet with an inscription written by Professor Boyd Dawkins, was unveiled in the church on July 6th, 1930, the anniversary of the battle.

Middlezoy has a church with a massive tower, an oak rood-screen and pulpit dating from 1606, and a brass commemorating a French chevalier, Louis de Misières, who, after serving eighteen years in the British army "with great courage and gallantry" fell in the "Battle of Weston" having "behaved himself with all ye courage imaginable against ye King's enemies commanded by ye rebel Duke of Monmouth".

Fairfax and Cromwell, with their forces, were at Middlezoy in July 1645, after the Battle of Langport, and before storming Bridgwater.

Othery, at the southern end of the "Island" of Zoyland, although with no known associations with the battle, is in some ways the most interesting of the marsh villages. Its thirteenth-century church has a gable cross—a great architectural rarity; an octagonal tower; and a curious low side window, constructed with great difficulty for no known purpose; a fourteenth-century chair and a fifteenth-century cope made into an altar frontal.

The great plain is broken up into smaller moors, each with its different name. Immediately south of Othery is Aller Moor and the village of Aller, where King Alfred stood sponsor to Guthrum when the Danish leader and thirty of the principal men of his army were baptized after their defeat at Ethandune.

8

Aller church at the foot of High Ham Hill, is small but interesting, and has two remarkable turrets, an effigy of Sir William Botreaux, dated 1420, and an ancient font which has been claimed to be the identical font in which Guthrum was baptized, although this has been disputed.

Aller was the birthplace of Dr. Ralph Cudworth, whose father was rector there, and whose mother had been nurse to Henry, Prince of Wales. As Regius Professor of Hebrew, he advised in the preparation of the Polygot Bible, and as Master of Clare College, Cambridge, he became a leader of the Cambridge Platonists. He preached and published a remarkably enlightened sermon protecting against the exaggerated importance attributed by the Puritans to dogmatic differences, but his greatest work was on the *True Intellectual System of the Universe* published in 1678, which proves him to have been the most learned able and sensible of his school of thought. His daughter Damaris, second wife of Sir Francis Masham, was a friend of John Locke.

It was at Aller that Fairfax consolidated his victory over the Royalists at Langport in 1645 by capturing the remnants of their forces.

The Isle of Athelney, where the events were planned which led to Guthrum's defeat and baptism, lies directly west, on a slight rise in the angle made by the junction of the Parret and the Tone, and its immediate neighbourhood abounds in osier- and reed-beds producing the withes for the basket-work industry.

Asser, who visited Athelney in Alfred's lifetime, described it as "surrounded on all sides by water and by vast and impassable peat bogs". Access to the Isle was gained by "causeways, or by a single bridge built and lengthened out with great labour between two elevated posts, towards the western part of which a fort of very great strength and most beautiful construction" had been erected by Alfred. Two centuries later, William of Malmsbury described it as "an island surrounded not by the sea, but by fens and overflowing marshes, so as to be altogether inaccessible except by boats. On this island is a forest of alders of vast extent, giving shelter to stags and roebucks, and many other kinds of game. Of dry there is barely two acres. There is a small monastery, with offices for the monks."

It was an ideal hiding-place for the hunted King to make his plans for the overthrow of the Danes. He commemorated his victory by building the monastery of Athelney, of which nothing now remains. The story of his burning of the cakes, known to every schoolboy is highly probable—every housewife knows that it is essential not to get absorbed in thought when baking cakes!

The site of the abbey is marked by a small stone pillar erected in 1801, with an inscription commemorating King Alfred's stay on the island, but giving the date of 879, a year later than the date given in the *Anglo-Saxon Chronicle*. The so-called "Mump", a mile away near Borough Bridge, marks the extremity of the island, and was probably the site of Alfred's fort. It is now crowned by a church which was garrisoned by Goring with 120 men during the Civil War, and destroyed during the conflict. An attempt was made to rebuild it in 1724, but it was finally left as it now stands, above a bridge across the Parret which only recently ceased to be a toll bridge—the last in Somerset.

Lyng, to the west of Athelney, on the River Tone, has a little, aisleless church which was once a chapelry of Alfred's monastery at Athelney. It has a small but beautiful Perpendicular tower, some fine carved sixteenth-century bench-ends, an oak pulpit, and a chest hollowed from a single trunk.

II

South of the main road and railway line lies the Curry country, which gives its name to an interesting little group of villages and hamlets.

The flat waterlands, or moors, as they are called in Somerset, lying north and south of the railway, supply large quantities of the willow of commerce, which is grown and cultivated very carefully. In the winter it is a wild, desolate country, haunted by the cry of marsh birds, but as the year advances the green and silvery grey moors grow brighter as the willow buds unfold their pale yellow catkins, buttercups spread the fields with sheets of pure gold, and the orchards are gay with apple blossom. Fluffy little yellow ducklings congregate on the silver waterways, and shoals of tiny, thread-like eels known as elvers come up from the sea, only to be caught and cooked and eaten.

The willow rods are cut in spring, and left to dry, or boiled in special tanks, and are stripped by the women.

The varieties of willow grown in Somerset include Red Bud; Black Mould; Champion; Black Spaniard Osier; Dicky Meadows and Canadian, and the colours vary from white and golden yellow to vivid emerald green and bright gold, red, or deep purple.

Among the articles made from the withes are lobster pots, eel-hives, fish kiddles, wickerwork garden and indoor furniture and, of course, every kind of basket. Withes are also used to bind such vegetables as celery and spring onions.

The Curry villages are chiefly set on the low hills above West Sedgemoor. North Curry, originally a royal manor, was a place of importance in Norman times, and held several charters which were confirmed by King John, who also granted them a weekly market. Several odd customs were observed in North Curry, and one, directing the tenant to superintend the haymaking in the kings-meade in white gloves, with a white rod in his hand, may date from the time of King John, who visited the manor on several occasions, and is usually credited with the founding of the famous Reeves Feast, although some authorities maintain it dates back to Saxon or Early British times, and was only confirmed by him.

The provisions and ceremonies for the Reeves Feast, which was held annually on Boxing Day, were most minutely specified, and involved the provision of three fat heifers, a pig, a large quantity of "good marketable wheat" and certain sums of money from the Lord of the Manor and holders of stated estates. There was a generous distribution of food to the poorer tenants, and the Feast itself was provided for the Lords of the Manor of Knapp and Slough, who were called the "Jacks", and their attendants. Among many specified dishes at the feast were a collar of brawn, served up with a sprig of Rosemary, and a large mince pie, with an effigy of King John in pastry, properly painted, stuck up in the middle of it. When they sat down to dinner, two candles, weighing a pound each, were lighted, and until they were burnt out the Jacks and their attendants had a right to sit drinking ale. After dinner, the regular toasts were "To the immortal memory of King John"; "To the Real Jack of Knapp" and "The Real Jack of Slough". Similar feasts, on a smaller scale, were held at Stoke St. Gregory and West Hatch. The Reeve of West Hatch, a neighbouring village in the Vale of Taunton Deane, received a special amount of half a bullock, and the hind quarter of half a pig for the use of the tenants of that manor, on his paying five shillings to the Reeve of North Curry, but before he was allowed to enter the Reeve's house he had to sing the song:

> "King John he was a noble Knight
> I'm come to demand my right
> Open the door and let me in
> Else I'll carry away my money again."

The last feast was observed in 1865, after which the money was converted into a charity. A large marble tablet on the north wall of the vestry in North Curry church has a full account of the feast, with an old painting hung above representing a king playing a harp, with a crown lying on the ground and angels in flight. It has been said to represent King John, but much as they appear to have liked him at North Curry, it is difficult to imagine him among the angels, and it is more likely to represent King David, or King Alfred, both of whom were harpists. The two candlesticks used at the feast are also preserved in the vestry.

There are fine views of the Vale of Taunton Deane and the Quantocks from the churchyard, which is on the verge of an abrupt descent to the moor. A seventeenth-century epitaph in the churchyard reads: "My good lads, do not sit on this stone, on account you do disfigure it with your heels. Lean on it if you please. Yours etc. R. Pocock".

Lillesdon Court Farm still has its old mullioned windows. It was first mentioned in the time of Edward I, and there was a chapel there in the fourteenth century. Slough farm has part of its old moat, and arrow slits in the walls.

Stoke St. Gregory, originally East Curry, has a twelfth-century tower to its church, and beautiful woodwork. The Stoke Club Pudding, which was especially associated with Stoke St. Gregory Club-day, was a plum pudding baked in an oven.

Curry Mallet takes its second name from the great Norman family of Malet, who had a castle there of which all trace has disappeared. The church contains a large altar tomb and some curious mural tablets. Valentine Pyne, master gunner of England, was born at Curry Mallet in 1603. His brother Richard was appointed master-gunner of Gravesend in 1673.

Between Curry Mallet and Fivehead is Cathanger Farm, with a Court Room and an ancient gatehouse built by John Walsh, father of Jane Seymour, who married the eldest son of Protector Somerset. Both father and daughter are buried in Fivehead church. Langford Manor, a mansion of the

Spekes, was altered in Stuart times. Swell Church is chiefly Perpendicular, with a Norman doorway, and has fragments of ancient glass, a seventeenth-century pulpit and reading desk, and a brass to John Toose and his wife, with their twenty sons and daughters. There is a heronry in Swell woods.

Curry Rivel took its second name from its twelfth-century lord, Sir Richard Rivel. The Perpendicular church has a lovely thirteenth-century chapel and some fine monuments, but Curry Rivel's chief interest is its associations with William Pitt, Earl of Chatham, and that strange and vivid character, Lady Hester Stanhope, his brilliant, witty, and imperious grandchild.

Burton Pynsent steeple, which stands on the ridge of a hill overlooking Sedgemoor, was erected by the Earl to the memory of Sir William Pynsent, the last of an old Somerset family, who left him the estate "in his veneration of a great character of exemplary virtue and unrivalled ability". They had never met, and on the occasions when Sir William called at the Earl's town house to acquaint him with his intentions, the servants turned him away on account of his eccentric clothes.

In the spring of 1800 Lady Hester accepted the offer of her grandmother to make a home at Burton Pynsent. She rode about the countryside on horseback, and made friends with the country-folk, but three years later she left to keep house for her uncle, William Pitt the Younger. When she finally settled down on the slopes of Mount Lebanon, she never forgot her old Somerset friends, and used to send them flagons of attar of roses, and strings of amber, and it was his Mother's stories of the strange and wayward girl that fired Kinglake with his ambition to travel in the Near East. He described in *Eothen* how he visited the old autocrat at Lebanon.

Langport, on a low hill above the meeting of the Yeo and

the Parret, is a tranquil little town of which it may still be said, with Collinson, that it "was anciently more celebrious than now". It has been identified by some authorities with the Llongford of Welsh poetry, where the great battle was fought between the Britons and Saxons at which Prince Geraint was killed. Always of the greatest strategic importance in ancient times, it was a "key" position during the Civil War, and it was the defeat of Charles I's forces under Lord Goring in 1645 that gave the Puritans their hold over the West Country.

The east window of the church has some ancient glass, and the west window has modern glass to the memory of Walter Bagehot and Vincent Stuckey, both natives of Langport, and to Thomas Gillett, who founded the Grammar School. There is a mural tablet to William Quekett who was master at the school.

There is a wonderful view southward across the moors to Muchelney and the Blackdown Hills, and an equally fine view westward across the Curry country, when descending the hill to the High Street. Langport's most curious possession, the little Perpendicular chapel on a gateway, has known various vicissitudes, having been a Grammar School, a museum and a Masonic Hall, and more recently had to be repaired when an American tank carried away part of the arch.

Walter Bagehot, who was born in Langport in 1826, received his earlier education at the Grammar School there. He became one of the chief authorities on finance, and was consulted by both Liberal and Conservative Chancellors of the Exchequer, and devised the "simple, practicable and intelligible" Treasury Bills in use to-day. He was a prolific writer on a wide range of subjects, and his *Literary Studies*, still widely read, have a charm all their own. When he died at Langport in 1877, Augustine Birrell said he "carried away into the next world more originality of thought than is now to be found in the three Estates of the Realm". President Woodrow Wilson confessed to a great enthusiasm for his writings, and wrote two brilliant and appreciative articles on the man and his work, and Forest Morgan undertook the editorship of all Bagehot's published works because his writings had been for many years "one of the choicest of intellectual luxuries, and a valued store of sound thought and mental stimulation ".

Walter Bagehot's mother was one of the Stuckeys of Langport, who founded the famous Stuckey's Bank in 1770. It was one of the earliest County banks in England, with branches all over Somerset, Dorset and Devon, and remained a very prosperous concern until absorbed by Parr's Bank in 1905. "Safe as Stuckey's" is still a Somerset saying.

Edwin and John Quekett were born at Langport when their father was master of the Grammar School. When only sixteen years of age John gave lectures in microscopic subjects, illustrated by original diagrams, and by a microscope which he had made himself out of a roasting-jack, a parasol and a few pieces of brass. He became Professor of Histology in 1852, and President of the Microscopic Society, and his work is commemorated by the Quekett Microscopical Club. His third brother, Edwin, was the founder of the Royal Microscopical Society. He was a lecturer on botany at the London Hospital, and a Fellow of the Linnean Society; and his name is commemorated in the Brazilian genus of orchids, *Quekettia*. William Quekett, the eldest of the brothers was appointed to a curacy in London, where his philanthropic energy attracted the notice of Charles Dickens, and inspired his articles on "What a London Curate can do if he tries" and "Emigration". In co-operation with Sidney Herbert, Quekett founded the Female Emigration Society in 1849.

III

Almost immediately after passing under the Hanging
Chapel, on the Somerton Road, is Huish Episcopi Church
with its grand Perpendicular tower, spacious south porch,
and Burne-Jones window.

North of Langport is High Ham Hill, and its villages.
High Ham church was built in 1467 by Abbot Selwood of
Glastonbury, and has a superb rood-screen, a richly carved
roof, some good bench-ends, a curious lectern, and some
very expressive gargoyles, including a medieval Darby and
Joan over the porch. Adrian Schael, who was rector in the
reign of Elizabeth, wrote a description of the parish in Latin,
and left a donation for the schools when he found his
churchwardens could not sign their name.

Low, or Nether Ham has exceptionally interesting
Roman remains, and a curious church in the middle of a
field, which was built by Sir Edward Hext in 1650 in
imitation Gothic, and contains the effigies of him and his
wife, and a monument to Lord Stawell, his great-grandson,
who declared that "as he had the most beautiful wife and
most beautiful horse in the world, he would also have the
most beautiful house". Only the gateway was completed
before he died, and that was carried away in twenty wagons,
and now stands as an entrance to Hazelgrove House, near
Sparkford. An extraordinary maze-like series of embank-
ments near Low Ham church remain to tell of his ambition.

Pitney's Perpendicular church has several interesting
features. A Roman pavement was found in the parish,
and some specimens of the tiles are now in the Taunton
Museum.

Chapter Ten: AROUND WINCANTON

Wincanton—Vale of Blackmoor—The Wiltshire Border—The Dorset border—North to Bruton and Castle Cary

SET in south-east Somerset, very near the meeting of Somerset, Dorset, and Wiltshire, Wincanton is a typical little Somerset market town, with a long main street climbing a hillside above the little River Cale, which winds south through Blackmoor Vale.

Although known to Romans and Saxons, and a possession of fierce Norman Lords, Wincanton's first known taste of warfare was in 1645, when its active little Parliamentary garrison made it a base for skirmishes against Sherborne Castle. Twenty-three years later, it saw the first bloodshed in the Revolution of 1688, when the troops of William of Orange were unsuccessfully attacked by a party of James II's dragoons, and in the early nineteenth century it was a depot for French prisoners-of-war, nearly 300 of whom lived there at one time.

Wincanton was devastated by a fire which destroyed over forty houses in 1707, but the old manor-house, with a dog's head over the door, in which William of Orange stayed for a night or two after his landing, survives, and there are attractive nooks, particularly the yard of the Greyhound Hotel, and a little thatched inn. Every little byway from the High Street quickly reaches fields and lanes giving fresh viewpoints over the lovely, rich lands of Blackmoor Vale, stretching away over the Dorset border with all the charm which made it so dear to Hardy and William Barnes. Still higher up the hill there are views north-east to the wooded hills crowned by Alfred's Tower.

The church, at the foot of the main street, was entirely

rebuilt in the nineteenth century, with the exception of the fine Decorated tower. A quaint old relief in yellow oolite stone, portraying the legend of St. Eligious, the patron saint of metal workers, is preserved in the north porch. In the churchyard is an effigy erected by Nathaniel Ireson to himself. Ireson settled at Wincanton early in the eighteenth century, and left many examples of his work as builder, sculptor and potter in the neighbourhood. He had a pottery at Ireson House for many years, and many of his named and dated pieces are sought after by collectors or can be seen in the British Museum.

In the Council Offices of Wincanton are two very fine paintings by Samuel Woodforde, R.A., of Castle Cary, one of which is said to be a portrait group of the Baker family of Wincanton. The paintings were presented to the town by a descendant of the Woodforde family.

Dr. John Ring, who was born in the town in 1752, did spendid work for vaccination under Dr. Jenner; and Maurice Newport, a Jesuit who escaped to Belgium after the Oates Plot in 1678, has been claimed as a native of Wincanton, but the most famous son of Wincanton, was Sir James Dyer, Lord Chief Justice, and Speaker of the House of Commons, who was born at Roundhill Grange in 1512. His integrity of character and profound legal knowledge made him trusted by Edward, Mary and Elizabeth—no uncommon feat for a man of honour, and George Whetstone, in his obituary poem, wrote:

"Alive, a refuge of those whom wrong did payne,
A Dyer such as dyde without a stayne".

II

At Physickwell House, on Horwood Common, south-east of Wincanton, there is a well mentioned by Collinson "for purifying the blood of scarbutick taints". It lies beside the road to Cucklington, a pleasant little village, so superbly placed on a hill above the Blackmoor Vale that every cottage has a far-reaching view across Somerset and Dorset.

Cucklington church has been restored, but has exceptionally spirited oak carvings of Flemish work. The pulpit, given in memory of a former Rector, depicts him as the Sower. The bench-ends in the choir were carved by a local lady, who also carved the triptych in the north chapel when she was over eighty years of age. The great weights of the old clock hang down in the south porch, and there is a fragment of ancient glass in one of the windows, showing St. Barbara to whom a well in the village, known as Bab well, was probably dedicated. It is believed St. Aldhelm may have baptized converts in the well, for he frequently preached in the neighbourhood. A road zigzags steeply through the village to the top of the hill, said to be on a level with the spire of Salisbury cathedral, and giving enchanting views across the Vale.

Delightful roads lead through Stoke Trister, where grass-grown mounds in the fields below Clapton Farm mark the site of the old cock-pit, to Penselwood on high ground close to the Dorset border, which in early times was strongly defended by the British earthwork known as Cenwealh's Castle. The moated mound of Orchard Castle marks the site of the Norman fortress.

Penselwood has been claimed to be Caer Pensauelcoit, one of the British cities mentioned by Nennius, and Dr. Guest identified it as Peonne by Gillingham, where in 658 Cenwealh of Wessex defeated the Welsh and annexed Somerset to his Kingdom. Pen Pits, the curious circular cavities in the ground, extending over two hundred acres and long a puzzle to archaeologists, are now believed to have been excavated for the purpose of obtaining grindstones.

The high ground of Pen Ridge, at the junction of the three counties of Somerset, Dorset, and Wiltshire, merges into the wooded heights of the Stourhead estate, with the famous landmark of Alfred's Tower, in the Somerset parish of Brewham, which was built in 1772 to mark the site where King Alfred raised his standard in A.D. 879 against the Danish invaders. Standing 854 feet above sea level, the 160 feet triangular tower has a flight of 222 steps leading to the summit, and commands wonderful views over the counties of Somerset, Dorset, and Wiltshire.

In the foothills below is Stavordale Priory, founded by the Lovells in the thirteenth century for a small brotherhood of Black Canons. It was so scantily endowed that it was always in a bad way, and constantly sought special dispensations on the plea of poverty. The chapel was rebuilt in 1440, and later annexed to the Priory of Taunton. It was granted at the Dissolution to John Vere, Earl of Oxford. Only the shell of the church remains, and the choir has been converted into a house, and the nave into a barn, although a beautiful chapel remains on the north of the choir.

III

A considerable part of the lovely Blackmoor Vale lies in Somerset, and the main road south from Wincanton to Sturminster Newton, in Dorset, runs along the west of the valley, by way of North Cheriton with its restored church, and a manor-house where the French prisoners of war from Wincanton used to play fives; and Horsington, with its remarkable preaching cross. The church has been rebuilt with the exception of the tower, but has a fifteenth-century octagonal font, with roughly carved figures of angels, and a Perpendicular window in the sanctuary which has had some unusual adventures, for it was originally in the manor-house, and later in the rectory dove-cote. The manor-house of the Gawens is neighboured by the church house, dated 1611 and some picturesque old cottages. The rectory, which dates from 1686, was built by the first of the Wickhams, who were rectors at Horsington for over 200 years.

South of Horsington is Templecombe, with a church at the foot of the village, which sustained considerable damage by bombs. The rather drab little village climbs a hill to the manor farm, which incorporates the remains of the preceptory of the Knights Templars founded in the twelfth century by Serlo Fitz-Odo. The long barn has a fireplace at one end, and may have been the refectory, and there are the ruins of a small chapel in an orchard.

Still further south are the cross roads at Henstridge Ash and the Virginia Inn, where an ash-tree by the roadside is the successor of an earlier tree—one of the many traditional settings for the tale of Sir Walter Ralegh and his pipe. Last of all, there is Henstridge, close to the Dorset border. Here again, the church was rebuilt in the nineteenth century, with the exception of the tower, but it contains two unique monuments: the splendid altar tomb of William Carent of Toomer and Margaret Stourton, his wife, constructed in 1463 with an aumbry and well-preserved effigies, and a miniature altar tomb with a canopy of Purbeck marble, probably commemorating a William Carent who died about 1516. The earlier William Carent's brother, Nicholas, was Dean of Wells, and in 1463 Bishop Beckington published an indulgence of forty days to all true penitents who said a paternoster and ave at the tomb for the souls of "that worthy man" William Carent, his brother the Dean, and their relatives.

IV

The most direct way south from Wincanton to Milborne Port is by the Stalbridge road as far as Templecombe, but it is possible to make a slightly longer trip by taking the main road westward to the verge of the Camel country, and then turning south at Blackford, or, by a judicious use of a map, tracing out the byways to glimpse the villages which lie just off the highway. There is Holton, with cottages bowered in climbing plants, and a small Early English church containing a Norman font, a fine oak roof, and a stone pulpit discovered at the restoration; and Maperton, set among hills and woods beautified with masses of rhododendrons.

Blackford, not to be confused with Blackford near Wedmore, is a low-lying village with a small, plain church which formerly belonged to Glastonbury Abbey, and has a Norman doorway and font, and an Elizabethan chalice among the church plate. Compton Pauncefoot, whose Perpendicular church has a low spire, unusual in this district, a fine south door, and some modern Brussels glass, of which a nineteenth century guide said discreetly "on the merits of which opinions may be allowed to differ". Compton Castle is a modern castellated building in beautiful grounds.

A tangle of country lanes leads south to remote Corton Denham, in the shelter of Corton Hill, a grassy height crowned by a little group of trees, from which it is said the firm of Cadbury took their well-known trade-mark, under the impression it was Cadbury Camp. There is a more direct way south through Charlton Horethorne, which formerly belonged to Kenilworth Priory. A portion of the church dates from 1441. Three round barrows in the parish yielded a quantity of pottery, a bark coffin and human bones, and in the neighbourhood are such fascinatingly named places as Silver Knap, Dark Harbour, Golden Valley, and Wilkin Throop. The restored fifteenth-century church has a Norman font and part of the church plate dates from 1573. The ever-present passion of some people for cutting their initials is illustrated on the chancel seats, on which C.T.T. cut a peacock and his initials in 1760, and R.A.C. cut a cock with his initials in 1913.

Milborne Port, in a valley between two little hill ranges

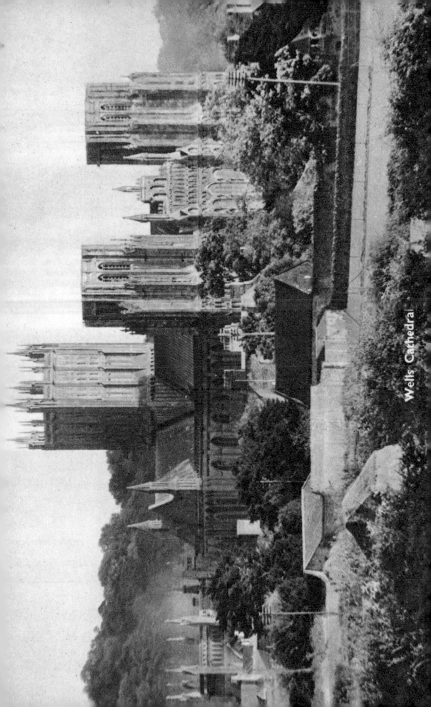

Wells Cathedral

Dunkery Beacon from Selworthy Green

Danesborough

running down to the Dorset border, was anciently a place of importance, with six mills at the time of Domesday Book and two Members of Parliament in the fourteenth century. In spite of ups and downs, it remained a borough until the Reform Bill, and has an old guildhall, and a church of outstanding architectural importance, with arches probably dating from the end of the Saxon period, a Norman doorway and a fifteenth-century screen of exceptional beauty and delicacy. There are also monuments and effigies to the Medlicott family.

Within the last century an old custom was still observed at Milborne Port on the evening of Shrove Tuesday, which was known as Pan Shard Night, when the youngsters paraded the town in search of pots and pans, with which they bombarded the doors, shouting:

"Flitter me, Flatter me Floor;
If you don't give me some pancakes,
I'll beat down your door!"

East of Milborne Port, on the Salisbury Road, is Ven House, the seat of the Medlicotts, begun 1678 and completed in 1701 by James Medlicott. It is one of the most perfect examples of a country house and garden, brought to perfection in the reign of William and Mary. It was probably designed by Richard Grange, who signed the drafts, and although alterations were made in 1836 under the direction of Decimus Burton, the architect of Hyde Park Corner, the work was in keeping with the original conception, and is one of the loveliest memories of the Dorset borderlands.

v

The Bruton road runs north from Wincanton, past the lane which leads to Charlton Musgrove with its early Perpendicular church, and past Roundhill Grange, formerly

9

attached to Stavordale Priory. It came to the Dyers after the Dissolution, and was the birthplace of Lord Chief Justice Dyer, mentioned under Wincanton. It was rebuilt about 1557 and again in 1701, by the Churchey family, who succeeded the Dyers.

Northward lies Redlynch Park, a seat of the Earls of Ilchester, and formerly of the ancient family of Draycot, the heiress of which married James Fitzjames early in the fifteenth century. Richard Fitzjames, who became Bishop of London, did much to beautify St. Paul's, and built the palace at Fulham.

The original house was built in 1673 by Sir Stephen Fox, father of the first Earl of Ilchester and the first Lord Holland, and grandfather of Charles James Fox, the statesman. It was Sir Stephen, who was born at Redlynch, who inspired Charles II with the idea of founding Chelsea Hospital for disabled soldiers, the credit of which is generally ascribed to Nell Gwyn. He planned the building and gave largely towards the foundation, and Evelyn, who describes their talks in his *Diary* says that although Fox was worth a huge fortune it was "honestly got and unenvied, which is next to a miracle." Pepys also has much praise for him and his family.

VI

There are two roads from Wincanton to Castle Cary, of which the upper is one of the prettiest in south Somerset, winding over the hills and giving charming views, and the lower road is scarcely less delightful. Byways lead to Shepton Montague and Pitcombe, each with a restored church; Godminster Farm, which dates mainly from the fifteenth century; Bratton Seymour, high on a hill backed by trees near a tumulus where the remains of a Roman watch-tower have been discovered; and Hadspen House, the attractive mansion of the Hobhouse family.

At the first cross-roads on the lower road is the site of Jack White's Gibbet. Although the gibbet has long vanished, the gruesome story has given rise to innumerable tales, poems, articles, and even plays. At least two companies of players are known to have acted the story at Castle Cary and it was acted at Taunton as recently as 1912.

Chapter Eleven: ALONG THE BRUE AND ALHAM

*Bruton—Along the Brue to Glastonbury—The River Alham—
The Pennard Ridge*

THE first villages to take their name from the River Brue
are North and South Brewham which face each other across
the very diminutive stream, not far from its source in Selwood Forest.

North Brewham is only a small hamlet, but South Brewham, half a mile away in a dell, beside the Brue, has a Perpendicular church with a curious doorway, and a brass to
Edward Bennett, "who by a suddain surprise fell asleep in
Christ the 8th day of November Anno Dom 1673".

After leaving the Brewhams, the river runs along the edge
of Cogley wood, parallel with road and railway, to Bruton
which, even from the railway, is an enchanting little place,
and on closer acquaintance is even more delightful. Not so
very much larger than a big village, it has preserved an old-
world atmosphere, and has kept its little packhorse bridge
across the Brue, building the modern one further along,
instead of destroying the older one.

Bruton is surrounded by grassy hills more like artificial
mounds, one of which is crowned by the ruins of a sixteenth-
century dove-cote. Truth compels the admission it looks
more like a dismantled house, but to the loving eye of
knowledge it is very fair to see, as one of the few square
dove-cotes remaining, and the National Trust consider it one
of the two finest in their care.

Bruton was formerly the seat of a brotherhood of Black-
Canons, whose priory was built by William de Mohun of
Dunster in 1142, on the site of a Benedictine monastery. The
Abbey is said to have possessed a girdle of the Blessed Virgin

Mary, and the Bodleian Library at Oxford preserves the account of the Commissioner Richard Hayton, to Cromwell, "By this bringer, my servant, I send you reliques . . . alsoe Our Lady's girdell of Bruton, sed silke, which is a solemn relique sent to women travelling, which shall not miscarry in partu".

The abbey was granted to Sir Maurice Berkeley, the Standard Bearer, in 1546. The Berkeleys later became Lords of Stratton, and gave their name to Berkeley Square, Stratton Street, and Bruton Street in London. The great Hall of the Abbey House was burnt in 1763, and the remainder was pulled down in 1786, a few years after the Berkeley family died out. Charles I stayed there in 1641, and heard a sermon preached by Bishop Lake, and visited it again with Prince Charles in July 1644, when he spent two nights at the Abbey House "A faire and noble habitation of his loyal servant Sir C. Berkeley". General Goring made it his headquarters in 1645, but evacuated it on Cromwell's approach.

The parish church is one of the finest in east Somerset. The nave roof is an example of the enriched king-posts of mid-Somerset type, each king post having an angel on each side. There is a fourteenth-century crypt, a beautiful screen dated 1620, four strips of embroidered vestments, two chained books, a huge thirteenth-century oak chest, and gorgeous monuments to Sir Maurice Berkeley, Viscount Fitzhardinge, William Godolphin, and eighteenth-century Berkeleys.

In the registers there is a verse of thanksgiving for deliverance from a local raid in 1642:

> "All praise and thanks to God still give
> For our deliverance Matthias eve;
> By His great power we put to flight
> Our foes, the raging Batcombites,
> Who came to plunder, burn, and slay,
> And quite consume our town this day."

The hospital founded by Hugh Sexey's trustees in 1638 is a picturesque building forming a small quadrangle, and includes a hall and chapel. Hugh Sexey's bust is above the door, looking singularly Shakespearean. Little is known of his life beyond the fact that he was the son of poor parents residing in or near Bruton, and was baptized there in 1556. He began life as a stable boy at one of the Bruton inns, but was afterwards "advanced by the help of a little learning"— probably acquired at the Bruton Grammar school—and by a "regularity of meritorious conduct", but nothing more is known until 1599, when he became one of the seven auditors of the Exchequer, an important post he held for twenty years. The objects of the foundations were to maintain a number of old men and women from Bruton and neighbouring parishes, excluding all "drunkards, swearers, unquiet or disorderly persons", and the funds he left were so generous that they also support three schools at Bruton and another at Blackford near Wedmore.

The free Grammar School founded in 1520 by Richard Fitzjames, Bishop of London, and his nephew Sir John Fitzjames, Lord Chief Justice, was suppressed by Henry VIII, but was refounded by Edward VI, and is now a flourishing modern school known as King's.

Stephen Batman, who was born at Bruton in the sixteenth century, and educated there, became domestic chaplain to Archbishop Parker, and collected for him the library now in Corpus Christi, Cambridge. He was himself an author and translator of some repute, and certainly gave the most entrancing titles to his works: "*Travayled Pilgreme, bringing Newes from all Parts of the World, such-like scarce harde before*"; "*The Golden Booke of the leaden goddes, wherein is described the vayne imaginations of heathen Pagans and counterfaict Christians*", which Shakespeare is believed to have consulted; and "*Preface . . . Displaying of an horrible Secte of grosse and wicked Heretiques naming themselves the Family of Love*". He seems to have had a good conceit of his work, or a very modern publicity sense, for he describes one of his books as ". . . Taken foorth of the most approved Authors, the like heretofore not translated in English. Profitable for all Estates, as well for the benefite of the Mind as the Bodie".

Wyke Champflower, a mile from Bruton, is a little hamlet with a small church, interesting as an example of Jacobean Gothic. Built in 1623 on the site of a chapel dating from 1482, it has a ceiling ornamented with escutcheons, a fine stone pulpit, box pews, each with its own hat pegs, and a seventeenth century black letter bible. The manor-house is in the same garden, and both are shadowed with fine elms.

After leaving Wyke there is hardly a house to be seen from the river banks until the ford and bridge at Castle Cary station is reached. Originally called Almsford—a very suggestive name—it has been corrupted to Ansford, with a village of that name half-way between Castle Cary station and Castle Cary itself. It was at Ansford that James Woodforde, the diarist, was born, but we shall meet him and his friends when we come to Castle Cary. Now we will hurry on to Alford, where the River Alham joins the Brue and flows past the church and the grounds of Alford House in which it stands, and where we meet with the Thrings, three of whom achieved fame in the nineteenth century—Henry, afterwards created Lord Thring, as a legislator; Godfrey who was Rector of Alford-cum-Hornblotton from 1858 to 1892, as an hymnologist whose best known works were *Fierce raged the Tempest*; *The Radiant Morn hath Passed Away*; *Saviour, Blessed Saviour* and *Thou, for whom the sick and dying*; and Edward, as Headmaster of Uppingham.

East Lydford, or Lydford-on-the-Fosse, is, as its name implies, on the Fosse Way, and West Lydford is on the Brue. East Lydford church was rebuilt in the nineteenth century but retains the font and carved wooden pulpit from the old church, and has an attractive little alabaster St. George on horseback, charging a dragon with the king and queen praying on the top of a castle and the princess kneeling close by. At West Lydford there are arched openings on the old bridge wall to let out floods, as a reminder that the Brue can get out of control in the winter floods.

The River Brue turns north after leaving the Lydfords and flows to Baltonsborough, skirting a group of hills with some interesting villages. Keinton Mandeville's church is in a field at the extreme south of the village, but interest centres on a grey stone house, one of a row, now marked by a brass, where John Henry Brodribb was born in 1838. He became Sir Henry Irving, the greatest actor of his time, and fulfilled one of his dearest wishes by raising the theatre from a despised profession to one of the highest art and honour.

It is said that when he was only three, having seen a stone-cutter rolling homewards singing at the top of his voice, he re-enacted the scene on the kitchen table, to the horror of his mother, a deeply religious Methodist. Only four of his sixty-seven years were spent at Keinton Mandeville, but the family records show a long association with the county. Their name was derived from the village of Bawdrip in the Poldens, in the twelfth century, and there are numerous family tombs in Clutton churchyard, near Bristol.

Kingweston's church, which stands in the park of King-weston House, has been rebuilt, but has a Norman doorway and font from an earlier church on the site; Barton St. David was the birthplace of Henry Adams, a founder of New England. Its churchyard cross has the figure of a bishop on the shaft, probably intended to represent the Welsh patron saint, from whom the village takes its name, and to whom the church is dedicated.

The road from Barton St. David crosses the Brue at quaintly named Tootle's Bridge, where a hatch is lifted over the week-ends to give water to land near Barton. The original supply was cut off by an engineering feat of St. Dunstan, who is said to have diverted the river so that the mill at Baltonsborough could have more water-power. The river still divides into two branches at Catsham, and a stretch of the Brue is known as St. Dunstan's Dyke. The fifteenth-century church at Baltonsborough is dedicated to St. Dunstan, and has a number of old benches, one of which has a hinged seat at the end. There is an interesting old door and lock, and fantastic metal work on the tower which was made and fixed by a local smith. The church has a seventeenth-century epitaph to the memory of William Martin and his wife:

> "Would you know whom this tombe covers,
> 'Tis the nonparell of lovers?
> It's a sweet william, sweeter far,
> Than the flowers that so stil'd are.
> And Elizabeth his dear wife
> Both expecting a beautifying life."

Butleigh, on the wooded hill above Baltonsborough has a church which was enlarged and restored in modern times, but preserves effigies from an old tomb. Its chief interest, however, centres on the many memorials to the Hood family. One epitaph was written by Southey, to the three brothers Arthur Hood, who was lost in the *Pomona* in the Caribbean Sea; Sir Samuel, who died of fever on the Coromandel coast; and Alexander, who sailed round the world with Cook, and was killed in the *Mars*. Southey's nephew Thomas, then a midshipman, was severely wounded in the same action.

There is also a memorial to Samuel Hood, who was vicar of Butleigh for thirty-eight years and, whose two sons, born in the vicarage there, became Viscount Hood and Viscount Bridport respectively. So many of the Hoods of Somerset and Dorset achieved fame in the navy in the eighteenth century that it is difficult to disentangle their separate achievements, particularly as they were closely related, but Samuel, afterwards Viscount Hood, has a life which reads like a Marryat romance, and won the praise of Nelson, who described him as "the best officer, take him altogether, that England has to boast of; great in all situations which an admiral can be placed in". His younger brother Alexander, who was created Viscount Bridport, became rear-admiral of the White on the same day in 1780 that his brother became rear-admiral of the Blue, and their careers were somewhat similar in other ways, although their characters were unlike, for it was said of Lord Hood that he was never rich, but exceedingly generous, whilst Lord Bridport was rich but penurious.

There is a monument on the hilltop above Butleigh Wootton, a hamlet a mile and a half from Butleigh, to the memory of Vice-Admiral Sir Samuel Hood, commander of the fleet in the East Indies, who was commemorated in Southey's memorial.

The naval tradition has continued in the family in modern times, and it was Horace Hood, a son of the fourth Viscount Hood, who sank with his flagship *Invincible* at the battle of Jutland in 1916, of whom Admiral Lord Beatty said he had distinguished himself "in a manner worthy of his great ancestors".

After leaving Baltonsborough, the Brue takes a wide curve round Glastonbury Tor and Wearyall Hill, and flows by way of Meare across East Sedgemoor and the Burnham level, to Bridgwater Bay.

II

The River Alham has its source in the hills above the tiny hamlets of Higher and Lower Alham, and flows south to Batcombe, whose church is a good example of the earlier and plainer Somerset church towers. The south porch, a curious blending to Gothic and Classical styles, was built in 1629 by James Bisse, one of the family to whom the manor passed at the Dissolution of Glastonbury Abbey. There are several quaint monuments to the Bisse family, including Philip Bisse, Archdeacon of Taunton, who was rector in the sixteenth century. He gave 2,000 books to Wadham College, Oxford, which so greatly pleased the foundress that she caused his portrait "drawn in his formalities" to be hung in the library and named him a co-founder. He was succeeded by Richard Bernard, the great Puritan divine.

Although Bernard was not above invective in some of his works, his greatest books show he was far ahead of his generation in many ways. In the dedicatory epistle to his remarkable book *The Isle of Man, or Legal Proceedings in a Man's Hert (of Manshire) against Sin*, his plea for "an unbegun work" of caring for prisoners anticipated the work of John Howard. The second part of *Seven Golden Candlesticks* entitled "The Great Mysterie of God's Mercie yet to Come" is a plea on behalf of the Jews; and he anticipates the charitable organizations of the present-day church in his *Ready Way to Good Works*. Bernard's successor was Richard Alleine, another great Puritan Divine who was born in the neighbouring Ditcheat.

III

Below Batcombe the river flows under a bridge and past a mill at Spargrove which was once a parish, but is now only a hamlet in Batcombe parish. The old moated manor-house dating from the reign of Charles I is now a farm. It was built by a Thomas More, which may account for the fact that it is said Sir Thomas More had a house there.

Milton Clevedon, on the northern slopes of Evercreech Hill, has a small Perpendicular church containing an effigy of an ecclesiastic, some ancient glass, and a curious inscription on the external east wall, dated 1615. Lamyatt, on the western slopes of the hill, also has an interesting church.

The road which crosses the river at Milton Clevedon runs north to Evercreech, with a typical mid-Somerset church, of no great size, but a beautifully-proportioned tower. Some grotesque gargoyles are the work of a local mason who possessed exceptional skill, and were added when the church was restored in 1843. The grotesque at the south-east corner is said to be a skit on a former vicar and is in the best medieval tradition. There is fourteenth-century tracery in the east window, a fine wooden roof, a quaint sixteenth-century inscription behind the organ, and a modern pulpit has some cheerful-looking angels. The fifteenth-century churchyard cross is now in the village square.

The only monument of interest is one to a former vicar, James Dugdale, who held the living from 1619 to 1641. He was an ardent royalist and endured much for the cause, and was so beloved by his parishioners that when a troop of horse came to arrest him the women of Evercreech beat them off with stones.

Richard Jenkyns, Master of Balliol College, was born at Evercreech in 1782.

IV

Ditcheat, on the south-east of the Pennard Ridge, has a church which alone is sufficient to tempt the tourist out of his way, and there is much else to see and hear in the village. The exquisitely carved wooden reading desk in the church was made from the pew of the Leir family, who provided rectors for the parish from 1699 to 1891. An earlier rector was Richard Alleine, who was rector of Ditcheat for over half a century and had two famous sons born there. Both Richard and William received their early education from their father. Richard became rector of Batcombe in 1641, where he remained for twenty years, idolized by his parishioners. He was willing to acquiesce in the Restoration, being a believer in monarchy, but when the Act of Uniformity came, he felt it necessary to cast in his lot with the ejected. Owing to the Five Mile Act, he could no longer preach at Batcombe, and removed to Frome, preaching there and in the neighbourhood, and was so beloved that the Vicar of Frome preached his funeral sermon and paid testimony to his piety, meckness and moderation. His writings have a searching spiritual force which made them popular, and even the royal printer, who seized his *Vindiciae Pietatis* to be burned, because it was not licensed, was so struck by what he accidentally read that he not only bought back the sheets, but sold them in his own shop!

His brother William was living at Ilchester at the beginning of the Civil War, and was robbed and illtreated for his opinions. He was rector of Blandford when the Act of Uniformity was passed, and preferred ejection to going against his conscience, although his parishioners held him in the utmost veneration, and he "dearly loved them". He died in Yeovil in 1677, revered and respected for his learning, piety, modesty and meekness, which appears in his writings.

The Priory, which stands in a fine park, was built in 1473 by John Gunthorpe, Dean of Wells and private chaplain to Edward IV. It was moated and had a large tithe barn, and although much restored, the old features have been carefully preserved.

The churchyard cross has been so thoroughly restored as to be modern. The lovely sculptured head was rediscovered in the nineteenth century. It dates from about 1332, when Edward III granted Abbot Adam de Sodbury a charter of free warren, together with a market and fair.

A remarkable native of Ditcheat was William Kingston, who was born there in 1765, and was known as "The Armless Wonder". He was born without arms, or even shoulders, but his unusually flexible feet enabled him to feed and shave himself, write, plough and follow all the pursuits of his age, outshining all his neighbours in mental and physical pursuits. Collinson gives a full account of his remarkable abilities, and John Wesley gives an account of him in his *Journal*, under the date August 31st, 1790: ". . . at breakfast he shook off his shoes, which are made on purpose took the tea-cup between his toes, and the toast with his other foot. He likewise writes a fair hand, and does most things with his feet which we do with our hands". Kingston was twice married, and had numerous children, all perfectly normal. He died at Ditcheat in 1831, at the age of sixty-six.

Various authentic accounts of his life, and extracts from contemporary newspapers have been collected by Mr. Douglas Macmillan in one of the Folk Press booklets, which also contains a facsimile of the title page of a contemporary tract of "A true and most Dreadfull difcourfe of a woman poffeffed with the Deuill: who in the likeneffe of a headleffe Beare fetened her out of her Bedd, and in the prefence of feuen perfons, moft straungely roulled her thorow three Chambers, and doune a high paire of Ftaiers, on the fower and twentie of may laft. 1584. at Ditchet in Somerfetfhire. A matter as miraculous as euer was feen in our time"—as well they might say! It is probable that the woman was an epileptic, but her neighbours were firmly convinced that the devil was responsible for these strange happenings.

There is a road back to the river running directly south to the hamlet of Alhampton. Lower down the river, just before it flows into the Brue, is a ford and bridge carrying a narrow path across the river to Hornblotton, anciently Hornblawerton, which was given to the monastery of Glastonbury in the time of King Ethelwolf. The church is hidden behind the manor-house, near the Fosse Way. The architect, Sir Thomas Jackson, in collaboration with the

Rector, Godfrey Thring, produced a very attractive type of small village church.

The Fosse Way is only a short distance west of the village, and runs in an undeviating line to climb the Pennard ridge on its way north. There are no villages on the Fosse Way itself, as it crosses the hills, but there are several delightful villages within easy reach.

East Pennard has a Perpendicular church with a low, plain tower and a Tudor rose on the north face, and has the original fifteenth-century nave roof, supported on large corbels, Jacobean stalls, and a richly carved Norman font. There is a fine view from the neighbouring Wraxall Hill, particularly in spring when the orchards are in bloom.

On the northern slope of the ridge is Pylle, a mile from its station on the Fosse Way. Delightful roads lead north to the enchanting village of Pilton, deep in a hollow of the hills, with a handsome church in a mixture of styles, one of whose chapels is said to be on the site of a church built by Joseph of Arimathea, who is believed to have used Pilton Harbour as well as Glastonbury. There is a noble cruciform barn on a hill overlooking the valley, near the church. The modern Working Men's Club, built in 1892, is on the site of an ancient hostelry belonging to the abbots of Glastonbury, of which, externally it is an exact reproduction. North Wootton, sheltered by curiously shaped hills, has a church with a low west tower and pre-Reformation bell; and Worminster has a fine Prebendal House turned into cottages.

Turning south again, we come to West Pennard, on the Shepton Mallet road, at the end of the Pennard ridge. The church, which is some distance from the village, was built in the reign of Edward IV, and is a strikingly handsome building with a good screen. The Court Barn, although perhaps one of the smallest tithe barns of its kind completed in the early fifteenth century, is a simple but beautifully designed building, eminently suited to its purpose. A mile west of the village, on the road to Glastonbury, is Ponter's Ball, which, next to the Wansdyke, is probably the most important earthwork in the county.

It was at West Pennard that the largest Cheddar cheese ever known was made for Queen Victoria in 1839. It weighed eleven hundred-weight, and was made from the milk of over 700 cows, in a vat specially constructed for the occasion. Whilst it was maturing, it was exhibited at the Egyptian Hall, Piccadilly, after which it was exhibited in various towns, and eventually brought back to its original home, but unfortunately quarrels and arguments broke out, and when it was finally tried, it was found so lamentably wanting that it was eventually given to the pigs! Various contemporary accounts of the great cheese appeared, and a humorous version appeared in Dickens' *All the Year Round* in 1860.

SET in lovely country, typical of the fair beauty of south-east Somerset, the little town of Castle Cary has that settled and contented look which no modern town ever achieves, although it has few really ancient buildings. The main street runs up a hollow between two hills, with batches, or raised pavements which are sometimes five or six feet above the level of the road, and are said to denote a sandy trackway dating back to Saxon, or even British times.

Only a grassy mound at the foot of Lodge Hill remains to indicate the site of the castle which in Norman times was the seat of the fierce Lovells, descendants of Robert, lord of Breherval, one of the companions of the Conqueror. The Lovells threw in their lot with the Empress Maud, ravaging all the countryside from Castle Cary, until Stephen forced them to surrender in 1138, after which the fortress fell into ruins.

The church was practically rebuilt in the nineteenth century, but is effectively placed on a hillock above green fields. It has a font dating from the time of Henry VI, and a richly carved pulpit with elegant figures of the apostles. In the churchyard is a small headstone known as the Swallow stone, to the memory of Edward Swallow, with two birds forming a rebus on the name.

The house in which Charles II stayed after the Battle of Worcester, posing as the groom of Jane Lane, is not known for certain, but the ancient George Inn is conspicuous in the main street, and there are two cottages dated 1623, but Cary's most cherished possession is the quaint little round house, formerly used as a lock-up. It contains a single cell 7 feet in diameter and 10 feet high, and is almost unique.

In the sixteenth century David Luellyn "Chirugion" of Castle Cary "gave unto the poore of this parishe tenn poundes to remayne in stock to their use for ever, and to be ordered yearly by the Churchwardens and Overseers of the poore for the tyme beinge". A similar sum of ten pounds was also left for the poor by a John Francis, and these amounts were administered until 1779, when there was a solemn parish discussion on the provision of a "long-felt want" for a lock-up, and it was decided the cost of £23 should be defrayed out of these benefactions. Six years later it was enacted that any children above the age of seven found breaking the Sabbath or dodging Sunday school should be locked up in the Round House during school hours. The views of the poor, who lost their annual Easter gifts, and of the children, who lost their freedom, were not, of course, canvassed, but can be imagined!

Collinson says that after the visit of Cromwell and Fairfax in 1645 the church retained "the marks of Cromwell's fury, which entirely demolished the organ, and defaced many of its ornaments". The church accounts show that the bells had to be re-cast and the roof re-leaded.

The church of Ansford, a mile to the north, near the River Brue, has been robbed of much of its interest by restoration, but the tower has some notable gargoyles, and there is a modern stained-glass window to the memory of the Wood-fordes, who provided rectors, doctors, and lawyers in the locality for many generations, and some of whom also settled in America and Australia. The only member of the family to achieve a wider fame in his own day was Samuel Wood-forde, who was born in Castle Cary in 1763, and sent no less than 133 pictures to the Royal Academy.

It was with the publication of the Woodforde Diaries,

soon after the 1914–18 War, that the Woodfordes and their friends became more familiar figures than many an historical personage, for the Rev. James Woodforde, whose diaries extend over the years 1758 to 1781, had a happy knack of hitting off relations and friends in a revealing phrase—Mrs, Melliar "fashionably frightened into a fit by a cat"; William Woodforde and his wife, who "shot away in their second-hand flashy one Horse-Chaise with plated furniture"; Miss Woodforde and Miss Pounsett exhibiting "two new purple veils at church this morning, it being fine weather"; Brother Jack, who is "inclined to be wild", and is "very indifferent by his being too busy with girls".

The diarist was born at Ansford in 1740, when his father, the Rev. Samuel Woodforde, was rector of Ansford and Vicar of Castle Cary. James held curacies in Somerset from 1763 to 1773 before he finally settled in Norfolk as rector of Weston, and even then paid many visits to Somerset, lasting three months or more at a time. His delightful, gossipy diaries are full of innocent fun, with accounts of theatricals, masquerade balls, visits to Wincanton and Yarlington races, prodigious walks and gargantuan meals, the latter frequently followed by doses of rhubarb to counteract the effects of overeating!

Parson Woodforde and his times come very close as we wander through the streets of Castle Cary, or walk across the fields to Ansford—perhaps by the very path he trod, and certainly seeing the same entrancing view, away across the moors to Glastonbury Tor, high on the horizon.

Cary gave its name to a special kind of coarse material known in the Middle Ages as cary or caurimaury, which is referred to in Langland's *The Vision of Piers the Plowman*. Cary cloth is forgotten, but in the present day the town has the only firm now in existence which deals with the manufacture of horsehair in all its branches. The manufacture of hair seating originated in Somerset. It was at first handwoven, but a member of the Cary firm invented the power loom now in use.

II

The diminutive Cary river rises in the town, and flows away across Cary Moor, past Lovington's ancient stone church, with poppy heads to its seats, and the remains of the village stocks in the churchyard; and Wheathill, where cows graze around the forlorn church, which has sittings for only 60 people, although restored and enlarged twice in the nineteenth century. The manor formerly belonged to Glastonbury, but a farm now occupies the site of the ancient buildings connected with the abbey.

South of the river are North and South Barrow, the latter on the edge of a hill rising from Cary Moor to Camelot, with a restored fifteenth-century church said to mark the site of the passing of Arthur to his last embarkation. There is an acrostic epitaph to Richard Moriss on the wall. South Barrow, after centuries of obscurity, has found itself in the limelight since the recent publication of *The Chronicles of Church Farm* by Monica Hutchings, which gives a pleasant picture of farm life in the village.

As no road follows the many windings of the supremely unimportant little river, we shall do well to cut across country from either North or South Barrow to the first of the Cary villages—Babcary, with an over-restored church which, however, still retains a fifteenth-century font and pulpit dated 1632, and monuments to the Newman and Strode families. In January 1764, James Woodforde, the diarist, came to Babcary as curate, and made the village live for us in the present day, by recording its simple happenings in his now famous diary. South of the village the river flows past Wimble Toot, an early burial mound or look-out station, which may have guarded the neighbouring Fosse

Way, beyond which the river winds in a series of curves around the hamlet of Cary Fitzpane, under the Fosse Way at Popple Bridge, and between Lytes Cary and Kingsdon.

Lytes Cary, a very interesting example of domestic architecture, has a chapel dating from 1340. The house itself dates from the fifteenth century, and the parapetted south front bears the arms of Lyte, and the initials of John Lyte and Edith Horsey. The hall has a minstrels' gallery, and an open timber-roof with angel corbels, and there are no less than 58 coats-of-arms, illustrating inter-marriages of the Lytes, painted in the chapel.

The Lytes appear to have settled at Lytes Cary in the middle of the thirteenth century. Henry Lyte, born there about 1529, was the eldest son of John Lyte by his first wife, Edith Horsey. Wood tells us "after he had spent some years in logic and philosophy, and in other good learning, he travelled into foreign countries, and at length retired to his patrimony, where, by the advantage of a good foundation of literature made in the university and abroad, he became a most excellent scholar in several sorts of learning". Unfortunately, the "several sorts of learning" did not include an ability to recommend himself to his stepmother, or overcome her tendency to make discord between him and his father. In 1578 he produced one of the earliest works on scientific botany published in England, *A Niewe Herball or Historie of Plantes*, which he translated from a French edition of the *Crudeboeck* of Rembert Dodoens, which is now in the British Museum, whimsically endorsed in his neat handwriting "Henry Lyte taught me to speake English". He established a botanical garden at Lytes Cary, which his distant connexion, Aubrey, said was "a pretty good collection of plants for that age". He also wrote *The Light of Britayne; a Recorde of the honorable Orignall and Antiquitie of Britaine*, dedicated to Queen Elizabeth, and presented to her by the proud author in November 1588, when she went in state to return thanks for the defeat of the Armada.

He was succeeded by his second son, Thomas Lyte, who devoted himself to the study of history and antiquities, and was highly praised by Camden in his *Britannia*. Thomas Lyte drew up the "most royally ennobled Genealogy" of James I, "extracted from Brute, the most noble Founder of the Britains", beautifully written and illuminated on vellum. Camden wrote underneath, in his own hand, six Latin verses in commendation of it, and in 1610, when Lyte presented it to King James, after a "long and serious perusal" the King gave him his portrait in gold, set with diamonds.

His brother, another Henry, was one of the earliest users of decimal fractions, and published in 1619 *The Art of Tens and Decimall Arithmetike* which naturally does not endear his memory to any normal child.

The Rev. Henry Francis Lyte, the famous hymn writer, was a lineal descendant of Thomas Lyte, and it was he who married a Miss Maxwell and brought the name into the family. His grandson, Sir H. C. Maxwell-Lyte, Deputy Keeper of the Records, was the author of numerous authoritative histories.

On the opposite bank of the river from Lytes Cary is Kingsdon, whose Perpendicular church contains the thirteenth-century effigy of a knight thought to be Guy de Briene, to whom Edward III gave the manor of Kingsdon.

At Lytes Cary we take leave of Caryland, which has been called by that name since the thirteenth century, but we follow the little river to Charlton Mackrell, with the church in which so many of the Lytes were buried. The church has been much restored, and their tombs have disappeared, but the chancel roof is very fine, and there are carved seat ends, and a fifteenth-century churchyard cross carved with the emblems of the four apostles on the socket.

Last of all comes Somerton, set in a charming countryside

of hills and apple-orchards, and once the capital of Somerset. The grey stone houses, with their dark red roofs, make a very attractive group on their hill top, and closer acquaintance confirms the impression, for the wide main street has an avenue of trees, and opens into a spacious square, where the Parish church with its octagonal tower, the seventeenth-century market cross, surrounded by an open arcade with fearsome gargoyles, the Town Hall, and two old houses, make a characteristic group. The earliest part of the church dates from the thirteenth century. There is a gorgeous nave roof, a pulpit, and a finely carved and painted communion table dating from 1615. Some prisoners locked into the church after the Battle of Sedgemoor amused themselves by playing at ball, and when the church was repaired a large number of the balls were found, and are now in the Taunton Museum. There is a row of almshouses founded by Sir Edward Hext in 1604.

Somerton became the capital of the county about the end of the seventh century, with a fortress which probably occupied the ground between the modern White Hart Hotel and the Mill Lands. Under the year A.D. 733 the *Anglo-Saxon Chronicle* says briefly: "This year Ethelbald took Somerton." It was completely destroyed by the Danes in 877, and although it had recovered sufficiently in the following century for a Witenagemote to be held there in 949, and the Normans made it a walled town, it never fully regained its importance.

Somerton was the birthplace of Joseph Sams, the orientalist, in 1784. He made many visits to the East, and formed a valuable collection of Egyptian mummies, sarcophagi, and jewellery, including a ring believed to have been presented by Pharaoh to Joseph. The bulk of his collections were purchased by Joseph Mayer, who presented them to the city of Liverpool.

There is a charming walk from Somerton to Hurcot Hill,

where there are alabaster quarries, and wide views of the
countryside are obtained from the top of Somerton Hill.

After leaving Somerton, the Cary river flows through
Somerton Moor, which is bounded on the north by Dundon
Hill, and on the south by High Ham Hill. Compton Dundon
is made up of the three hamlets of Compton, Dundon, and
Littleton. There are the slight remains of a wayside cross at
Compton. The church is half a mile away in the hamlet of
Dundon, at the foot of Dundon Beacon, and has been care-
fully restored.

After rounding High Ham Hill, the little Cary river is
usefully, if rather ignominiously, turned into the King's
Sedgemoor Drain, until it joins the Parret near Bridgwater,
skirting the Poldens in a straight line very different
from its earlier amblings across the countryside.

III

The Camel country, which takes its name from the incon-
spicuous river Cam, is a land of legend, for this is King
Arthur's country, and the highroad from North Cadbury to
Yeovil runs through the heart of it.

The Cam rises near Yarlington, in an enchanting district
of small green hills and flowery valleys. The attractive little
village has a rebuilt church with an ancient carved font. A
stone coffin found during the restoration is curiously set up
on its side against the churchyard wall.

North Cadbury church was built by Elizabeth, wife of the
last Lord Botreaux, early in the fifteenth century, with the
intention of also founding a college of priests. The great
nave roof of the enriched king-post type is one of the
earliest of its kind. There is a remarkable series of carved
bench ends added in 1538. The living has been in the gift of
Emmanuel College, Cambridge, since the days of the third
Earl of Huntingdon. Among the rectors was Benjamin

Whichcote, who was presented to the rectory of North Cadbury in 1643, but resigned when he was installed as Provost of Kings in 1644, and was succeeded by the equally celebrated Dr. Ralph Cudworth of Aller.

The earliest parts of Cadbury Court date from 1417, with Elizabethan and Georgian alterations.

North Cadbury is a model village, with a club-room housed in an early fifteenth century building.

The church is reached by the same splendid avenue of beeches as the mansion, and contains the tomb of Lady Elizabeth Botreaux and her husband, under a vaulted canopy. The brass to Lady Magdalen Vernon has disappeared, but the inscription remains to tell how she was forced to marry an elderly husband, but on his death married her old sweetheart, Sir Francis Hastings, son of the second Earl of Huntingdon.

South Cadbury village lies in the valley under Cadbury Camp, with its church standing picturesquely under the rampart. Although rebuilt, it has some interesting features, including a fresco of a bishop, possibly intended to represent St. Thomas à Becket, to whom the church is dedicated, but it pales into insignificance beside Cadbury Camp, which overshadows it both in fact and in fancy, for this is claimed to be the veritable Camelot of Arthurian legend.

This great hill, with its grassy slopes and its crown of trees and bushes, gives a wide-spreading view over the entrancing countryside the half-legendary Arthur and his Knights knew and loved, and where they hoped and fought and prayed. Over there at Langport, Geraint fell, and there at Glastonbury, Arthur and his queen sleep. Here Arthur first saw Excalibur, the sword "whose light was as the light of thirty candles", and his knights set out on many of their high adventures. Camelot, invested with all the magic of great writers and poets in every age, is more real and dear than all the finds of archaeologists, even though at Westwoods, close by Arthur's lane, were found trenches filled with the skeletons of men and boys who fought despairingly against the invading Saxons.

Nevertheless, even without the spell of chivalric romance, Cadbury is full of interest, ranking with the prehistoric camps of first-class importance, and dating back to the Pre-historic Iron Age. Set 500 feet above sea level, it has four successive ramparts of enormous proportions, with interven-ing ditches, the highest vallum 190 feet above the lowest, measuring vertically, and consequently of immense strength. The base of the hill is over a mile round, and the upper vallum enclosed an area of about 18 acres, with a fine series of cultivation terraces on the Southern slopes of the fortress. There are two wells, King Arthur's and Queen Anne's.

Cadbury Castle was essentially an Iron Age fortress, but Roman occupation of the camp was also proved by excava-tions, and in the centre, in addition to the remains of numer-ous pit dwellings is the great mound traditionally known through all the centuries as King Arthur's Palace. Arthur and his knights are said to gallop round the fortifications on steeds shod with silver shoes, on moonlight nights, and other legends tell how they ride by on these same silver-shod horses on Christmas Eve, along the causeway to a wishing well near Sutton Montis church. The causeway, still just traceable, originally ran the whole way to Glastonbury and has been known to country people time out of mind as Arthur's Causeway.

Sutton Montis church, on the south of Cadbury Camp, has an interesting Norman church with a low tower and an incongruous classical porch. Westward, where several streams swell the little Cam to slightly larger proportions, is Weston Bampfylde, which takes its name from the twelfth-century lords of the manor, and has an ancient little church. North of the stream is Sparkford, which has so vigorously restored its church that there is little left of interest, but the

Cam flows by the churchyard, and Cadbury Castle is in sight.

Now we come to the Camels, south of the river in the shelter of Camel Hill. Queen Camel church, bowered in trees, and looking attractive from the Sparkford road, is a fine building with a great tower and a splendid interior. It was given by Hubert de Burgh, Earl of Kent, to Cleeve Abbey in 1202, but is chiefly Perpendicular, with another of those incongruous classical porches. In 1778 the curate was Thomas Charles, a Welshman, who could not manage to win the friendship of the villagers, and found the rector too mean to pay his small wages of £45 a year. Although befriended by the Vicar of Milborne Port, he abandoned his curacy in 1783, and married and settled at Bala, where he started his life work as a Methodist preacher and writer, becoming the John Wesley of Wales.

There is a mineral spring on the banks of the Camel, just outside the village, of curious colour and with an unpleasant smell, which was formerly reputed to cure the King's Evil. Recent analysis showed its waters to be similar to those at Harrogate, and it is extensively used for scrofulous diseases. It is also reputed to be a wishing well.

The manor of Queen Camel was transferred by the Crown to Sir Walter Mildmay, M.P., in 1555, in exchange for an estate in Norfolk, and there are mural monuments to the family, including Sir Humphrey, who was wounded at the battle of Newbury, in the church. The Mildmay pew is also of interest. Hazelgrove House, the old home of the Mildmays, is in a beautiful park north of the river, and is still partly Elizabethan, although the remainder was transformed into an exact copy of a Genoese palace in 1720, by Carew Hervey Mildmay. The entrance arch beside the Sparkford Road is the gateway which was brought from the unfinished house of Lord Stawell at Low Ham.

Pretty little West Camel has an interesting cruciform

church with a Norman font, and an elaborately carved fragment of a Saxon cross discovered during the nineteenth-century restoration. The Cam flows through the village, under a packhorse bridge. There is a great barn and a large round pigeon house at the rectory, and a mile away on the slopes of Steart Hill is Parson's Steeple, which looks like a derelict chimney, and around which many old tales cling. The most general version of its origin is that it was built by Henry Parsons, a retired pirate, who was buried there in 1794, and has since haunted the neighbourhood.

After West Camel, the shallow little river soon flows into the Yeo, east of Yeovilton.

Chapter Thirteen: AROUND YEOVIL

Yeovil—East to the Dorset Border—Along the River Yeo—Around the Cokers—Ham Hill

YEOVIL, by far the largest town in the south of Somerset, can scarcely be blamed if it does not, at first sight, seem an ancient town. It has had such disastrous fires that it is fortunate anything at all escaped, and its modern prosperity has not helped matters, for in the change and growth inseparable from commercial prosperity it has lost much of its Somerset character. Nevertheless, it has many attractive corners, and in the woods of Nine Springs and Summer House Hill it has beauty of which any town might be proud. It is also a superb centre for some of the loveliest and least spoiled villages of Somerset.

At the end of the fourteenth century, Henry V granted the manor and lordship of Yeovil to the Abbot of Sion House, which he had founded in Middlesex in 1414.

Little more than thirty years later 117 houses were destroyed by fire. Forty days of Indulgence were granted to charitable contributors on this occasion.

The noble parish church dates chiefly from the fourteenth century. Its great windows make the church wonderfully light, and there is a sense of harmony, due to the whole building being in one style of architecture. Its greatest treasure is the great brass lectern, on a pedestal supported by four amiable-looking lions, and dated 1450, It is one of five examples of a fifteenth-century desk-lectern remaining in England, and was shown in the Exhibition of English Medieval Art at the Victoria and Albert Museum, London, in 1930.

The beautiful carved head of Yeovil's old cross was found

147

accidentally in the nineteenth century, and has been incorporated in a modern cross outside the Roman Catholic church.

Among the records of Newton Surmaville house is the commonplace book of Martin Strong, details of which were collated by Mr. John Goodchild for the Somersetshire Archaeological Society's Journal in 1932. Martin Strong was vicar of Yeovil for many years. He found the parish completely disorganized, and gives interesting details of his up-hill fight to set things right. He established a lending library, and revived the old charity school in 1707. He also planted in the vicarage garden "all the codlin-hedges, archichoaks, asparagas, gooseberries, cherries and hedges" and concludes "I did all this willingly and cheerfully. I find a great deal of satisfaction now 'tis done. I did it all as an act of charity to the Church. I blesse God who gave me both a will and ability to do it. I conjure my successors by all that is sacred to keep up and maintain what is by me left well repaired for them, and I humbly hope for my reward in Heaven."

Yeovil's most fascinating industry is that of glove making, which dates back three and a half centuries. There are about forty firms, employing over 4,000 people, in normal times, and much of the work is done by country folk in their own homes. Yeovil's great aircraft works provided the first aeroplane to fly over Everest.

Yeovil has been in the centre of events since the earliest times, and many prehistoric and Roman finds have been made in the neighbourhood. One of the tesselated floors is on exhibition in the Yeovil Museum, which also has the most important exhibition of firearms in the south-west of England.

The half-timbered George Inn still stands in the High Street, but the other old coaching inns, and the Woborne's Almshouses have been modernized.

The most lovable son of Yeovil was the kindly Walter

Raymond, who typified in himself and in his books the highest type of Somerset countryman. He was born and educated at Yeovil, and joined his father as a glove manufacturer, but his heart was never fully in the work, and in his fortieth year he retired to devote all his time to writing, and recording the country life that was passing. He died at Southampton whilst on a visit to one of his married daughters, but happily he was brought back to lie in the Somerset he loved so dearly, and was buried with his wife at Yeovil in 1931.

Raymond's books have a fragrant charm and simplicity all too rare in these days of hustle, and perfectly suited to his picture of the hard-working, independent countryman, before the advent of machinery, bus services, pictures, and broadcasting changed the tenor of the English countryside so greatly. No one has more perfectly captured the spirit of Somerset than Walter Raymond. His work is rather uneven, but the best of his tales and essays win a debt of gratitude from all who enjoy trying to re-create the everyday life of the past.

The woods and dells of Nine Springs are reached from the Hendford Road, and Summer House Hill rises immediately above the town station, but looks away to the hills of Dorset over the beautiful Elizabethan mansion of Newton Surmaville, still the seat of the Harbins, and the winding River Yeo which flows through the Park.

II

Immediately east of Yeovil there is only Dorset, with which we are not now concerned. North-east, the road runs to the Camel country and Caryland through Mudford, on the Yeo or Ivel, to Marston Magna, which has a small, plain church with a low square tower, and several interesting features, and is neighboured by a house with the date 1613 on the back, and a moated site known as Court Garden, said to mark the site of a grange of Polshoe Nunnery.

The road from Marston Magna to Corton Denham has to pass through a little peninsula of Dorset, near Rimpton with its small, well-restored church, original carved bench-ends and Jacobean pulpit.

III

If we follow up the River Yeo or Ivel from Yeovil, the first Somerset village is Mudford, passing the Hundred Stone at the highest point, from which an old joke says it is possible to see seven "hundred" churches. A two-arched bridge across the Yeo carries the road on to Castle Cary, and Chilton Cantelo, which is said to take its name from the Cantilupe family. The church has been entirely rebuilt, but has a memorial stone to Theophilus Broome, who died in 1670, whose head is traditionally preserved at Higher Farm, Chilton Cantelo, and is credited with making heartrending noises at any attempt to bury it. Charles Goodford, Headmaster of Eton in 1853, and Provost in 1862, was born at Chilton Cantelo, and held the family living there from 1848 until his death.

As, however, Chilton Cantelo is on the east bank of the river, where the roads are not so convenient to our purpose, we will follow the west bank through Ashington, to Limington, the first living held by Cardinal Wolsey.

The river divides into two for a short distance at Limington, making a little island, and a road from the village crosses two bridges, which give a glimpse of a waterfall and yellow waterlilies, to Yeovilton. There is a direct road from Limington to Ilchester, and another from Yeovilton through Northover which is very little further. A paved Roman ford once crossed the river from Northover to Ilchester, where there is now a new bridge replacing an ancient one.

Ilchester is a very attractive little place, with pleasant stone houses round a tree-shaded green, a tall market cross topped by a sundial, and a church with an octagonal tower, and is particularly delightful in spring, when the chestnut trees spread their blooms above the winding river—yet it is a fashion to roundly abuse the little place for its lack of the antiquities its ancient importance would warrant.

Standing on the Fosse Way, just where a branch runs south-east to Yeovil and Dorchester, it was a Roman Station and a notable town in the Middle Ages. It was besieged in the time of William Rufus and fortified in the Civil War. Only one of the four churches mentioned by Leland remain, and the walls and gates, the Dominican Priory, the Hospital of the Blessed Trinity, another of St. Margaret, the fifteenth-century almshouses, and even the old Guildhall and gaol, have vanished completely.

Ilchester lives on its proud memories, not the least of which are its "worthies". It was for many ages the county town of Somerset, with a Corporation whose thirteenth-century mace is preserved. Until the Reform Bill, it was the only polling place in the county, and its gaol the only prison. It sent Richard Brinsley Sheridan to represent it in the House of Commons in the eighteenth century, when it was as rotten a pocket borough as any in England. Elections lasted for fifteen days, or until one or more of the candidates withdrew, and at one time the party spirit there ran so high that electors are said to have desired on their death beds that they should be buried in *true blue* coffins. The wishes of the opposing party have not been recorded. Some houses at the south end of the town are said to have been built by Lord Huntingtower to increase his votes—only to have them declared outside the boundary.

Ilchester or its neighbourhood was the birthplace of Roger Bacon in 1214. Countless legends and inaccuracies have gathered round his name in the course of centuries, which

11

modern investigation has cleared away to show him in his true light as a scientist and philosopher unique in the medieval history of Europe.

It was during his stay in Paris, when his deep knowledge attracted many students, that he earned for himself the name of "Doctor Admirabilis". All through his life he sought for knowledge, and once said, "During the twenty years that I have specially laboured in the attainment of wisdom, abandoning the path of common men, I have spent on these pursuits more than two thousand pounds, on account of the cost of books, experiments, instruments, tables, the acquisition of languages, and the like."

Strongly opposed by the leaders of the church, he was often forcibly prevented from pursuing his studies, and it is the most incomprehensible act of his life that he joined the Franciscans, of all orders the most opposed to study.

In his own day and long afterwards, Roger Bacon was regarded with horror as a sorcerer, a dabbler in the black arts, and in league with the devil, a tradition encouraged by *The History of Friar Bacon* published in the sixteenth century. Only in the present day is his greatness appreciated, and the tragedy of those twenty-five years of his life spent in close confinement, without the means to record his brilliant thoughts—the tragedy of the man born too soon.

His invention of gunpowder is widely known, but he also invented the camera obscura and optical lenses, and contended that machines to drive ships through the seas were possible, that cars might be made to move without draught animals and machines might fly.

A more fortunate native of Ilchester was Mrs. Elizabeth Rowe, the poetess, who was born there in 1674. Elizabeth commenced writing verses at the age of twelve, and she completed her famous paraphrase of the twenty-eighth chapter of Job at the request of Bishop Ken before she was twenty. She had many suitors, including Mathew Prior, the poet, and is said to have been the nameless lady to whom he dedicated one of his books of poems. Dr. Isaac Watts wrote some lines "on her divine poems" and she was also highly praised by Dr. Johnson who described her as "the earliest English writer to employ with success the ornaments of romance in the decoration of religion". She met her charming and gifted husband at Bath, but he died only seven years after their marriage, and she never fully recovered from her bereavement. She died in 1737 and was buried at Frome.

Richard of Ilchester, twelfth-century Bishop of Winchester, was probably born at Sock Dennis, a mile south of Ilchester. He was the trusted friend and adviser of Henry II, who employed him on many important foreign embassies and other state business.

After leaving Ilchester, the River Yeo crosses the flat meadowlands by way of Long Load to Langport, where it flows into the River Parret.

IV

Some of the most remote and lovely of the villages round Yeovil lie southward, where the Dorset border takes another of its sudden bends and leaves Somerset in possession of an enchanting district of wooded hills and quiet valleys.

Barwick is reached through a deep lane with yellow rock walls crowned with high hedges—a little village with an eighteenth-century mansion and a charming church which has several interesting features, including an oddly placed tower, and fine sixteenth-century bench-ends.

Still farther south, and well hidden away close to the Dorset border, is Closworth. In the churchyard is the tomb of Thomas Purdue, a bellfounder of repute, complete with a carved bell. The rectory orchard marks the site of his foundry which cast bells still to be found in all parts of

England and even in Scotland. He died in 1711 at the age of ninety.

The lanes in this hilly country are few and far between, and although Sutton Bingham is near enough as the crow flies, it is necessary to take quite a roundabout way to get there. Sutton Bingham has a station and little else but its fascinating old church and manor-house, so hidden away among the trees that they are easily missed. The quaint little church is Norman, with traces of later work, and has a curious series of fourteenth-century frescoes with one figure "crossed out" with lines of red paint. There is a very ancient sepulchral cross over an unknown grave in the churchyard, which overlooks the charming garden of the manor-house.

Pendomer is beautifully situated on a hill overlooking Pen Moor. The church has a remarkable monument, believed to represent Sir John de Dummer, who died about 1321. It shows him in a full coat of chain mail, with a cornice above the monument supported by curious little figures, and bearing small prickets of iron, probably intended for a row of wax candles. The arms of Jenkyn Stourton of Preston Plucknett, a later owner of the manor, are in one of the church windows. The ancient manor-house, now a farm, is close to the church, and commands the same delightful view of hills and woods.

At quaintly named Wickets Beer there is a lane up to Coker Wood, and beside the rectory the road branches east to Coker and west to Hardington Mandeville, and although the latter's church has some ancient features, we will turn to East Coker, one of the loveliest and least-spoiled villages in England.

East Coker with its perfect blending of Perpendicular church, seventeenth-century almshouses, fifteenth-century manor-house, and grey old thatched cottages, is exquisite in early summer with lilac trees in every shade of purple and mauve, and masses of wisteria, which later give place to equally fragrant and lovely masses of roses. East Coker's beauty is lighted by a rare memory of a strange and vivid character—William Dampier, that queer blend of buccaneer and brilliant cartographer, ruffian and gentleman whose life is so much more romantic than any story, and whose books remain to this day among the most vivid, careful and fascinating travel books of all time.

Born in the old manor-house, now Hymerford House farm, about 1651, Dampier whose life has no counterpart in the history of exploration, circumnavigated the globe three times, and was obviously only stating a fact when he says he joined the buccaneers "more to indulge my curiosity than to get wealth".

The publication of his *New Voyage* secured him his rightful position as a scientist and navigator, and brought him Government employment and contact with such men as Pepys, Dean Swift, and Sir Hans Sloan. Evelyn in his *Diary* records that in 1699 he "dined with Mr. Pepys, where was Captain Dampier who had been a famous buccaneer . . . He seemed a more modest man than one would imagine by relation of the crew he had assorted with . . ." How unlucky it was that Pepys was no longer able to write in his diary and record his impressions of Dampier!

Dampier's account of Alexander Selkirk's rescue gave Defoe his idea for the immortal *Robinson Crusoe*, and his books are also believed to have provided the geographical framework of Swift's *Gulliver's Travels*.

It is pleasant to know that East Coker does not forget its greatest son, and in 1938 the children of the County Council School at East Coker exchanged letters and pictures with the schoolchildren of Broome, Australia, when a monolith was unveiled there to commemorate the two hundred and fiftieth anniversary of Dampier's landing on the site now occupied by that flourishing town.

A mile from the village down twisting lanes is Naish

Priory, a picturesque house which dates back to the fourteenth or fifteenth century and has a chapel with a fine east
window, a refectory, hall and dormitory dating from its
early conventual days, and a beautiful oriel window above
the pointed doorway. West Coker can be reached from here
by another of the deep lanes between yellow rocks topped
with high hedges—so narrow that there is only just room
for a car or cart to pass.

West Coker has a spacious church which still has small
horn windows in the turret, reminiscent of the days before
glass. There are some seats dated 1633, a collection of old
books, and a monument to two daughters of Sir John
Portman. Their home, the attractive little manor-house of
West Coker, is in the village. It belonged to the Earls of
Devon until bought about 1600 by John Portman, and a
document survives which gives an account of the burning
and pillaging of the house in 1457, as a result of a dispute
between the villagers and the Earl of Devon's agent. The
ringleader of the villagers, most regrettably, was the
rector!

Both East and West Coker were once a great centre of
sailcloth weaving. Flax and hemp were grown locally
from very early days. There is a record that in 1358 a pound
of yarn made from West Coker hemp was sent to Bridport
for the navy, and by the middle of the seventeenth century
sailcloth weaving was a cottage industry. By 1810 "Coker"
canvas was being supplied to the Royal Naval dockyards
at Chatham, Sheerness, and Portsmouth. The industry
was transferred to Crewkerne in the nineteenth century,
but "Coker" sailcloth is still famous in all parts of the
world.

The greater part of West Coker lies on the main road, and
we can either go directly back to Yeovil from there, or make
a wholly delightful round of the Chinnocks, up north to
Martock, and back by way of Montacute to Yeovil.

v

East Chinnock, set on a hillside giving charming views of hill and dale away to Crewkerne, Middle Chinnock, the prettiest of the three, and West Chinnock all cling to the diminutive Chinnock Brook.

Chiselborough, in a valley to the north, once had a fair at which the menfolk lingered so late they had to be fetched home by their wives, an event still celebrated annually by the children of Lopen and Hinton St. George.

North of Chiselborough the road runs under the great Hamdon Hill with its prehistoric camp and many ancient villages. The fine tower of Norton-sub-Hamdon church was repaired in 1894 after it had been damaged by lightning, and parts of the church are still bright pink from the effects of the fire on the Ham Hill stone of which it is built.

Stoke-sub-Hamdon, on the north of the hill, has a wonderful view northward across the moors, and a beautiful and interesting church, with fine tombs and effigies. The village has an unusual possession in the old fives court behind the Fleur-de-Lis Inn. When fives playing against church towers was discouraged, many country inns built them in their grounds. The courts were copies of the lower stage of a church tower and were always known as "towers". John Palmer and Frederic Fane, the champions of Stoke, after beating the representatives of Bath in 1855, claimed to be the champion fives players of England.

Matthew de Gourney, fourth son of Thomas de Gourney, one of the murderers of Edward II, was born at Stoke about 1310, distinguished himself as a soldier of fortune whom Froissart termed a "*moult vaillans chevalier*". It has been suggested he was the prototype of Chaucer's knight in *The Canterbury Tales*, and Fuller says, "The veneration attached to this distinguished warrior was so great that his armour was beheld by martial men with much veneration and his faithful buckler was a relic of esteem." He died at the age of ninety-five and an effigy in the church under a foliated canopy is said to be to his memory.

Now we will make our way eastward along the main road to beautiful Montacute, one of the most magnificent Elizabethan houses in England, with its ornamental gardens and two garden pavilions, built by the Phelips family, who were high in the royal favour.

Montacute Priory, which was founded by Robert, Earl of Mortain, half-brother of the Conqueror, was associated with the great abbey at Cluny in France, but was allowed to continue as an independent Priory under Benedictine rule, at the time of the suppression of alien priories in the fourteenth century. Only the magnificent fifteenth-century gatehouse now remains.

Montacute parish church, although appropriated to the monastery, was a separate entity. It has been extensively restored and rebuilt, but has a chancel arch dating from about 1130, and a wonderful series of tombs to the Phelips family from the fifteenth century onwards.

Montacute village shelters under St. Michael's Hill, or Mons Acutus. In the days of Canute, the village smith dreamed of a stone cross hidden on St. Michael's Hill and when the cross was uncovered, Torfig, the lord of the manor, had it placed on a wagon drawn by twelve white cows, and twelve red oxen, and recited the names of various English shrines. When he came to the name of Waltham, the oxen, hitherto motionless, started off of their own accord, and the cross was accordingly conveyed there and a great abbey was founded there to enshrine such a miraculous relic, whilst a chapel was built on Mons Acutus to mark the site where the cross had been found. In Norman times a great fortress was built there which became the pivot of the feudal system of Somerset. Only a ring of earthworks now marks the site.

The loveliest way up the hill from Montacute passes the

priory gateway and leads up a beautiful lane with hanging woods to St. Michael's Hill, whilst another road from the village leads to the great camp on Ham Hill, 426 feet above sea level. The camp, which covers 200 acres, was originally British, and was subsequently occupied by the Romans to command the ford where the Fosse Way crosses the Parret. The rampart is nearly three miles in circumference. Many relics have been discovered there, including a specimen of Roman armour consisting of over 300 scales of bronze. There is also a noble view, covering practically the whole of Somerset and parts of Dorset and Wiltshire.

Ham hill is honeycombed with quarries, which have been used for centuries and furnished the beautiful Ham Hill stone of which most of the great houses, churches, and villages in the neighbourhood have been built.

Odcombe with its church high on a breezy hilltop can be reached by the main road from Montacute, or by a lane over the hills. The neat little village is notable only for its association with Tom Coryat and Humphrey Hody, both sons of Odcombe rectors.

Tom Coryat was born about 1577, and was the godson of Sir Thomas Phelips, who "imposed on him" the name of Thomas. Tom dubbed himself "The Odcombe Legge-Stretcher", after walks across Europe that might well stagger even the most enthusiastic present-day hiker. He started on his travels in May 1608 and went through France and Italy to Venice, returning through Switzerland and down the Rhine, partly by getting lifts in coaches, but mostly on foot, and calculated he had travelled 1,975 miles before he returned home to his beloved Odcombe to write his famous book *Crudities hastily gobbled up in five months' travel, newly digested in the hungry air of Odcombe*—an enthralling book, in which he proves himself as detailed and accurate in his observations and as clear and conscientious a recorder of impressions as Dampier himself. Nothing is too trivial to escape his notice, and his book was not only the first, but for many years the only handbook for continental travel.

In 1612 he started out again, after hanging up in Odcombe church the boots (now lost) in which he had made the whole of his first journey, and announcing from the market cross that he would be absent for ten years. He went to Greece, Constantinople and the Middle East, Egypt, Mesopotamia, Persia, and India, and died at Surat, where he was buried in 1617.

Although one of the oddest of the many odd characters Somerset has produced, and in early life the butt of the court, he proved a student and thinker, and won the regard of Prince Henry, who granted him a pension. He introduced forks into England, having seen them in use in Italy, and his ready wit is displayed time and again in anecdotes of his travels. On one occasion he met armed footpads near Baden, snatched off his hat, and begged from the robbers, who were so taken aback they gave him enough for his supper and lodging that night!

Humphrey Hody, who was born at Odcombe rectory in 1659, was Regius Professor of Greek at Oxford, and by his will ten exhibitions were founded at Wadham College for the study of Greek and Hebrew. He wrote several learned and whimsical treatises on religious matters.

The road back to Yeovil from Odcombe is by way of Brympton D'Evercy, where the exquisite manor-house neighbours the church in a great park. Brympton has been held by four families only since the Conquest—D'Evercy, Stourton, Sydenham, and Fane. Part of the present house was built about 1650 by Sir John Posthumous Sydenham. Family traditions assert that the south front was designed by Inigo Jones, who was a protégé of the Earl of Pembroke, father of Sir John's second wife.

The smaller house, between the perfect Renaissance house and the church with its quaint square bell-cote, dates from the fifteenth century, and was probably the original manor-house. The church, which completes the perfect group of buildings, is very interesting, and has numerous splendid effigies, including a strikingly life-like and reposeful face of a priest, and an effigy of Sir John Sydenham, who died in 1626, with a curious epitaph ending "Report it, Sir, he died an honest man".

Preston Plucknett, which lies on the main road, with Yeovil reaching to its very doors, has succeeded in maintaining its picturesque village atmosphere, with its magnificent tithe barn, its fifteenth-century house, and restored Early English church. Jenkyn Stourton, who lived there in the time of Richard II, is said to have had three daughters, among whom he divided his manors of Preston Plucknett, Brympton D'Evercy, and Pendomer—each a passing fair inheritance. He himself was buried in Stavordale Priory which he had rebuilt and endowed, and was conveyed there "In his best waggon, drawn by his best team of Oxen".

Chapter Fourteen: THE NEIGHBOURHOOD OF CREWKERNE

Crewkerne—South and East—Between the River Parret and the Isle—Westward to Chard

CREWKERNE, beautifully set among the hills above the valley of the Parret, is an attractive example of a south Somerset town. Its church vies with that of Ilminster for first place among the cruciform churches of the county, and is a beautiful specimen of fifteenth-century work of remarkable richness. There are several interesting brasses, one of which, to Adam Martine of Seaborough, who died in 1678, bears his arms and crest, of a monkey looking into a mirror, with a ludicrously close resemblance to the advertisement of Monkey Brand soap. The brass dated 1525 to Thomas Gold, who is shown in armour, had a request for prayers for his soul which was scratched out after the Reformation.

There are splendid gargoyles on the exterior of the church, and a unique and puzzling feature in the double buttress of the south transept, where there is a recess with a seat. The idea that it was once a cell of a recluse or anchorite has more recently given way to a suggestion that it was the ledge where people left their offerings for the anchoress who is known to have had a cell at the west end of the church, or the hermit who had a cottage in the churchyard.

The old grammar school on the north side of the churchyard was founded in 1499, on the site of the house of the priest who ministered to the chantry founded at Crewkerne in 1310. The present building dates from 1636 and is now used as the Church Hall. Among those educated there were William Draper Best, the first Baron Wynford, and Nelson's Hardy.

General Sir Lloyd William Mathews, famous as the Prime Minister of Zanzibar, was the son of Captain William Mathews, of Crewkerne, one of the pioneers of the volunteer movement. When he became Prime Minister, slavery was abolished, farms were established, and modern methods of agriculture were introduced, the value of his work being officially recognized by the British Government as well as by the successive Sultans he served so well. His prestige grew until his name became a household word throughout East Africa for the justice and honesty of his administration. He died at Zanzibar in 1901 and was buried there. There is an intimate little sidelight on his youth in *Odds and Ends of my Life* by his sister, Countess Cave, which tells of the very modern ideas he had of exercising and training his sisters, of whom he became guardian at twenty-one, on the death of his father.

Crewkerne is also proud to remember that the father of Tom Paine, author of the *Rights of Man*, was a native of Crewkerne, although he moved to Norfolk before the birth of his son.

Crewkerne is famous for the manufacture of sailcloth, particularly for racing yachts, and such famous racers as H.M.Y. *Britannia*, the three *Valkyries*, the five *Shamrocks*, the *Endeavour* and even a number of the American yachts defending the America Cup, have carried sailcloth made in this quiet little Somerset town.

II

South of the town, and close to the Dorset border, are Henley Manor, the greater part of which was built in the sixteenth century; and Misterton. In the charming old court-house, with its mullioned windows and wisteria-covered walls Helen Beckenham Mathers, the daughter of Thomas Matthews of Crewkerne, was born in 1853. She wrote many novels and poems, but her most famous book *Coming through the Rye* was published when she was twenty-two. Her home is still much as she knew it, with mullioned windows, walls covered with wisteria, and the long stone-flagged passages she mentions in her book. Only the beautiful garden has been created since her day, and that looks across the hilly green fields, silvered with daisies, to the footpath which still leads to the stile by the ryefield where the lovers met. The book ran through sixty editions in England, and was published in many languages, and has also been filmed four or five times over.

The same road which takes us to Misterton from Crew-kerne will also take us on to hilly North Perrot, with the infant Parret flowing through the grounds of the modern manor-house, and linking it with South Perrot over the Dorset border. Haselbury Plucknett has a Perpendicular church with numerous memorials to the Hoskins family.

Leland tells us "at this place lyvid the Holy Hermite and Prophete Wulfrik yn King Henry I Dayes". Born at Compton Martin, he was changed from a medieval sporting parson to a recluse by the arguments of a beggar, and lived in a small cell at Haselbury clad in chain mail. He became known far and wide in England as a miracle worker and prophet. He was visited by Henry I and prophesied to Stephen that he would be king. When he died at the age of ninety, in 1154, he was buried in his cell, but his remains were later removed to a chapel in the parish church, which was for ages visited by pilgrims. In spite of many alterations to the main fabric, it is still known as Wulfric's aisle.

There is a pleasant two-mile cross-country walk from Haselbury Plucknett to Merriott, crossing the River Parret by a medieval bridge. Merriott, also largely occupied in the manufacture of sailcloth, has a restored church with a massive plain tower, intricate carving over the south porch, and some quaint figures over the vestry door called "The fighting cocks". A tithe barn has been fitted up as a church room.

A mile west of Merriott stands Hinton St. George, with the fine mansion in its great park, and the church with its notable series of Poulett tombs. Originally seated in the Bridgwater district, the Pouletts came to Hinton in the fifteenth century when William Poulett married the heiress of the Denebaud family, who had been at Hinton since the time of Henry III. It was their eldest son, Sir Amyas, who put Wolsey in the stocks. Sir Hugh Poulett, a strong supporter of the Protestant cause, was supervisor of the rents of the surrendered abbey of Glastonbury. Another Sir Amyas was very bitter against Mary Queen of Scots, and guarded her closely when she was made prisoner, but incurred the wrath of Elizabeth by refusing to murder her and for his pains was called a "dainty and precise fellow, who would promise much, but perform nothing".

All these and many others lie in their gorgeous tombs in Hinton church. One of the charities, dating from 1792, is for £9 for shoes and stockings for the poor each St. Thomas's Day for three thousand years—no provision, however, is made for the bestowal of the money after that time!

The great house of the Pouletts was called by Fuller "a charitable curiosity", as it was built by the owner in a dear year on purpose to employ more people. The earliest part of the existing house was probably built by John, first Baron Poulett, in 1627, the year in which he was made a peer, and is usually said to have been to the design of Inigo Jones. Charles I was entertained there. In 1669 there was another distinguished visitor, Cosmo III, Grand Duke of Tuscany, who admired its terraces and gardens. The Duke of Monmouth stayed there during the Rebellion, and when Elizabeth Parcett, a woman suffering from the King's evil, managed to touch his hand and was cured, a certificate of the cure was sent to London to prove the Duke's right to the monarchy.

North of Hinton is Lopen, where it is said Wolsey sat in the stocks after Lopen feast. The children of Hinton St. George and Lopen maintain the old custom of "Punkie Night" on the last Thursday in October, when they go round with lighted candles set in scooped-out mangolds, singing a traditional song.

III

The marvellously thatched Poulett Arms, at Lopen Head, marks the meeting of the Crewkerne road with the great main road from Ilminster to Yeovil, and is the gateway to a group of interesting villages on the hills overlooking the flat lands of West Moor between the Isle and the Parret.

South Petherton, charming with flowering shrubs, lies just off the main road, with its octagonal church tower on a little knoll beside the main street. It is a long way from North Petherton, near Bridgwater, but they are linked by the winding River Parret.

The church dates in part from the thirteenth century, and was once glowing with paintings. Richard Symonds, who visited South Petherton when he was in Somerset with the King's forces in 1644 records in his *Diary*, which is now in the British Museum, all the shields of arms he saw in the windows or on monuments in the church, and in windows of houses in the town. In the lady chapel is the effigy of a knight in chain mail, probably Sir Philip de Albini, who died in 1292. It was dug out of the roadside when a pit was being made for a petrol tank on the main road. Another of the tombs is to Sir Giles Daubeney, who died in 1445. He was the grandfather of Giles, first Baron Daubeney, the soldier and statesman, who was born at South Petherton, and served Henry VII faithfully for twenty-six years. His son was created the first Earl of Bridgwater.

Montacute House

St. Catherine's Court and Church

A Ceiling at Poundisford Park
A Mantelpiece at East Quantoxhead Court House

South Petherton's ancient oak seats have been replaced by "a desert expanse of modern pitch-pine" in the words of Mr. Bligh-Bond, but the choir stalls, added later are more attractive, and have a special interest, for they were dedicated in 1935 by a Methodist Pilgrimage in memory of Dr. Thomas Coke, the Methodist Bishop who was John Wesley's chief of staff, and created the network of Methodist foreign missions. Dr. Coke was a curate at South Petherton when he was converted to Methodism.

The so-called King Ine's palace has no work earlier than the fifteenth century. It was probably built by Sir Giles Daubeney in the latter part of the reign of Henry VI. The tradition that it marks the site of King Ine's palace cannot be traced farther back than the eighteenth century. There is also an unfounded tradition that the effigies carved on the bridge over the River Parret commemorate two children who were drowned when the previous bridge was washed away by floods, but actually the carvings came from a neighbouring castle, long since destroyed.

There is a direct road from South Petherton to Martock, one of the most delightful little market towns imaginable, which was formerly a manor of the Fiennes, and is remarkable for its noble church. The timber nave roof with its winged angels is especially fine, and there are brasses and effigies of considerable interest. Cromwell and Fairfax with their troops gave thanks in the church in 1645 for the taking of Bridgwater.

The picturesque market cross, ancient base and modern shaft, marks the site of the ancient oak tree under which the market was formerly held, from which the town is traditionally said to derive its name of "Market Oak".

Opposite the church is an old manor-house, the earliest portion of which dates from 1240. The church house was formerly the grammar school founded by William Strode of Barrington in 1661, and over the door is inscribed "Schola

Trilinguis"—the school for three languages: Hebrew, Greek, and Latin—and the motto "Neglect not thy opportunities". One of the masters was Thomas Farnaby, whose adventurous turn of mind must have thrilled the boys, for before he came to the school "being minded to take a ramble" he had sailed with Sir Francis Drake and Sir John Hawkins on their last voyage "being in some esteem with the former", and had also fought in the Low Countries. Returning to England about 1596, his poverty "made him stoop so low as to be an abcedarian, and several were taught their hornbooks by him", but his great abilities soon resulted in his opening a school in London, and by 1629 his fame as a schoolmaster and classical scholar was known all over Europe.

A ruined fifteenth-century gate-house in a waterfilled moat at Martock is said to be the remains of a manor-house given to Lord Monteagle for bringing about the discovery of the Gunpowder Plot.

IV

Two roads run from Martock to Yeovil—one by way of Montacute, which we have already visited, and the other, through Tintinhull and Chilthorne Domer. Tintinhull has some charming old houses and a church with a massive tower, bench-ends with old seats hinged on to them, and some good brasses, including one to John Heth, who died in 1464, whose inscription says, "Be thou witness, O Christ, that this stone does not lie here that the body may be adorned, but that the spirit may be remembered."

Chilthorne Domer has an interesting little church with the effigy of a knight in chain armour, believed to be Sir William Domer or Dummer, who lived in the reign of Edward I, and whose son's effigy we saw at Pendomer.

The road directly north from Martock runs through Long Load, which straggles for nearly a mile to the bridge across the Yeo which carries the road to Long Sutton, where Goring and the Royalist forces were quartered before the Battle of Langport, and Fairfax with his victorious army after their defeat.

V

Also north of Crewkerne, by many devious byways which can be linked up to make a fascinating round, are the villages which lie between the Parret and the Isle rivers.

We will make our way to Dowlish Wake, or East Dowlish, which lies at the bottom of a hill, and owes its second name of Wake to the family which died out in 1348. The church was rebuilt in the seventeenth century by the Speke family, and there is a crude early Norman font brought from West Dowlish as the only remains of a church which was pulled down in 1700. There are several brasses and monuments to the Wakes and the Spekes, including the tomb and bust of Captain Speke, the African explorer, who was born at Jordans, on the road to Taunton. The service at Speke's funeral in Dowlish Wake church was attended by David Livingstone, Sir Samuel Baker, Sir Roderick Murchison, and Captain Grant.

We can go to Ilminster direct from Dowlish Wake, or by way of Kingstone with its Perpendicular church to the pretty villages of Seavington St. Mary, set in buttercup fields, and Seavington with its duck-pond, to White Lackington, where George Speke entertained Monmouth, and the local gentry under a splendid chestnut tree, afterwards known as Monmouth's tree, until it was blown down in a gale in 1897.

North of White Lackington is the pretty village of Barrington, with its old inn, and its beautiful church, dating from 1200, with tombs to former owners of lovely Barrington Court, so happily rescued from the ruinous state to which it had sunk.

Built between 1514 and 1520, by Lord Daubeney, it is one of the most charming of the earlier manor-houses.

It was here that Colonel Strode entertained the Duke of Monmouth in 1680. The house is set in delightful gardens with flower borders and water gardens, and has its sixteenth-century stables intact.

Shepton Beauchamp, in the lovely lanes on the way to Kingsbury Episcopi, has a fifteenth-century church neighboured by a contemporary house now used as an institute, but it cannot compare in beauty with Kingsbury Episcopi, whose grand church tower rises, lovely as a dream, from the willow-bordered buttercup meadows beside the River Parret.

VI

The way to Chard is along the top of the hills, with wonderful views over Somerset, away to the Severn Sea, and south over Dorset to the English Channel. There is a steep ascent to St. Rayn Hill, where there was once a chapel dedicated to St. Reyn, or Regina, and Windwhistle Inn, the highest point, 733 feet above sea-level and a very favourite viewpoint.

There are roads leading south down to the Dorset border. Wayford with its interesting little church high on a hill is divided from Dorset by the River Axe. It has a walled pond, and a beautiful manor-house in a terraced garden, built in 1602 by one of the Daubeneys. Daubeney Turberville, who was born there in 1612, was a famous eye specialist who is said to have cured Queene Anne, when she was a child, of a dangerous inflammation in her eyes, after the court physicians had failed. He was also consulted by Pepys, who says in his *Diary* that "he did discourse, I thought, learnedly about them (his eyes)". When the Doctor died, his sister Mary, inheriting his prescriptions, and knowing how to use them, practised as an oculist in London with great success.

Winsham, also on the Axe, has a restored church with a good tower, and a much-defaced painting on wood said to date from the fourteenth century, which is the sole remaining Rood in Somerset. It depicts the Crucifixion, which is extremely rare, the last Judgment being a more usual subject for tympana.

A parchment, dated 1641, was signed by the vicar, squire, churchwardens, and parishioners to the number of over 200, declaring they would defend the Reformed Protestant Religion against Popery with their "life and power". The church registers are bound with pages from an illuminated MS. of the "Golden Legend" which may have come from Forde Abbey, just over the Border. They date from 1559, and contain an entry of an oath taken by a John Lombard that a marble stone now in the church was brought by his father at "ye Abbey of Foorde's dissolution".

The village is set on a sunny slope sheltered by high hills, and was formerly a market town, complete with shambles, and still has an ancient market cross opposite the George Inn. It was at one time celebrated for its cloths.

Two miles north of Winsham is Cricket House, formerly the seat of Lord Bridport, set in a beautiful dell far below the road, and opening on to the wooded valley of the Axe. The house dates from the early nineteenth century, and is neighboured by the little church of Cricket St. Thomas, in which Alexander Hood, first Lord Bridport, was buried.

Cricket was the ancient seat of the Prestons, one of whom was Sir Amyas Preston, who seized the Admiral of the Galeasses of the Spanish Armada, and in 1595 made a successful foray in the West Indies, "entering Jamaica with little loss, some profit, and more honour", according to Fuller.

Among other memorials in the church is one to the Rev. William Earl Nelson, brother of the famous Admiral, whose niece married into the Hood family. The first Viscount of the second creation of the Bridport Viscounty is buried in the churchyard, and a flag in the church was flown by H.M.S. *Nelson* on her first journey through the Panama Canal.

The road passes over Windwhistle Hill, high above the park in which Cricket House is set, and north of the hills lie the secluded villages of Chaffcombe, Cudworth, and Chillington, all with interesting churches, and Cricket Malherbie's handsome modern church, with many memorials to the Pitt family, who are now seated at Cricket Court.

Chapter Fifteen: CHARD, WELLINGTON AND THE BLACKDOWNS

Chard—Along the River Isle—Roads to Taunton—Along the Blackdowns—Wellington

CHARD, with a wide main street climbing the hills from east to west, has little runnels of water flowing down each side of the street, one of which flows north from the foot of the hill, right across Somerset to the Bristol Channel, and the other south across Dorset to the English Channel.

The original borough of Chard was incorporated by Bishop Jocelyn of Wells, in a charter dated 1234, and sent Members to Parliament in the fourteenth century. Charles I stayed in the town on his march west on July 24th, 1644, when he was in high hopes, and on his return, on September 23rd, with all hope of help in the West Country gone. After the fall of Exeter in 1646 Sir Thomas Fairfax encamped with his army round Chard. The Royalist insurgents, under Col. Penruddock, received a severe defeat in the neighbourhood in 1655, Col. Penruddock being hanged at Exeter, and two men and a woman at Chard. One of those sentenced to be executed after the rising was a Major Hunt, but he escaped with the connivance of his sisters. They visited him in prison, and one of them changed clothes with him and remained in his bed. He got away to France, but his sisters were treated very harshly until the Restoration enabled their brother to return.

In 1685 Monmouth marched through Chard on his way to Sedgemoor, and shortly afterwards, Judge Jeffreys swept down on the town to exact vengeance, and executed twelve of the inhabitants.

Two events arising out of its status as an assize town, apart from the aftermath of the rebellions, must have roused Chard. One is recounted by the seventeenth-century anti-quarian writer, Sir Simonds D'Ewes, who lived at Wam-brook, just over the Dorset border, and tells of the hanging of Master Babb, which he witnessed. Master Babb, having courted a rich widow at Kingston, near Taunton, was so incensed at being rejected, especially as she hit him with a candlestick to emphasize the refusal, that he stabbed her in fifteen places, and arranged the body to look like suicide. She was buried as a suicide at the cross-roads, but a Taunton justice caused her to be exhumed, and summoned all the neighbours to trial by ordeal. When it came to Master Babb's turn, he could not bring himself to touch his victim, and disappeared, but at last gave himself up and was duly hanged.

During the Commonwealth there was a trial for witch-craft, when Jane Brooke was convicted and executed on the most frivolous testimony of superstitious neighbours, after a trial by Sir John Glyn, who must have been the most credulous and superstitious of the lot!

Although Chard is set higher than any other town in Somerset, with its town hall, half-way up the main street, over 360 feet above sea-level, the streets are not unduly steep. The parish church stands in the "old town", which now shows little sign of age apart from the intricacy of its winding streets. It is a spacious building, dating from about 1400, with faint traces of mural paintings, a fine series of gargoyles, and a quaint mural tablet to the Brewers, with their children, and an inscription "William Brewer of Chard, phisitian, and Deanes, his wife, who living forty years in happy wedlock, in full age departed this life; shee dying 8th November 1614, and hee 24th July 1618, having issue only six sons and five daughter, all men and women growne and all comforts to them". Poor William Hitchcock, who died in 1793 does not appear to have been so happy, for his inscription reads:

"If life were merchandise that men could buy,
The rich would always live, none but the poor would die".

At the foot of the main street is the beautiful seventeenth-century grammar school, which numbered among its pupils Thomas Wakley, a friend of Cobbett. He is best remembered as the founder of the *Lancet*, but his humanity as a coroner won the enthusiastic praise of Dickens.

Opposite the town hall, is the beautiful sixteenth-century court-house which was used as an Assize Hall by Judge Jeffreys. It has an elaborate plaster ceiling and freizes.

Still higher up the hill is the picturesque gabled Choughs Inn, and a pleasant little house near the top of the main street is marked with a plaque to the memory of John Stringfellow, inventor of the first engine-driven aeroplane. One of his machines flew the length of the Crystal Palace, at the Aeronautical Exhibition in 1868, and the monoplane he made in 1848 is engraved on the British Silver Medal for air feats. His models are in the Science Museum now, and his grave in Chard cemetery is inscribed to his memory as inventor, but the poor old man ended his days making brass bobbins for Chard's lace industry, laughed at and ridiculed for his dreams, and died without an inkling that he would be recognized as one of the earliest pioneers of aviation.

Down by the railway station is the house in which Margaret Bondfield, the first woman Cabinet Minister, was born. She taught the boys in Chard Board School when only thirteen years of age.

Robert Adkins, who was born at Chard in 1626, and was at one time chaplain to Cromwell, was one of the most notable of the 2,000 ministers ejected under the Act of Uniformity in 1662. He was so honoured and beloved that magistrates and ministers who were active against other dissenting ministers were lenient with him, and the Bishop of Exeter quashed all procedure against him, praising his learning and moderation.

II

Apart from the lovely ridge of the Blackdowns, there are hills all round Chard, hiding some very delightful manors and villages. South of Chard, the Fosse Way climbs Two Ash Hill to Tatworth, where there is the same curious custom of holding a sale by candlelight as at Chedzoy. The property at Tatworth consists of six acres including a watercress bed, and the local property owners have held a court annually "since time immemorial" at which an inch of tallow candle is lighted, and the last bidder before the light burns out obtains the land for a year at the price he offers. There is a fine if the candle is put out by a sneeze or cough, or is doused in any way, but when it goes out in the natural order of events, a meal is served to the bidders in the local inn, at which every guest has watercress from the stream.

Still farther south is the hamlet of South Chard, which has a flint Baptist Chapel with a thatched roof, said to have been built in the reign of Elizabeth, and known by the name of St. Margarets. It was probably an ancient chapel, and still has a niche over the doorway in which an image once stood.

III

There are many roads running north from Chard, and a delightful way of reaching Langport would be to follow the course of the River Isle, or Ile, from Knowle St. Giles, on a slight rise above the infant river. Donyatt has quarries which have provided the beautiful stone from which the village with its splendid church and manor-house have been built. The manor-house was originally built by the second Earl of

Salisbury in 1345, and later came into the possession of Sir Edward Coke, Lord Chief Justice, who made considerable alterations.

Ilminster is a delightful country town dating back to Saxon times, and its church vies with that of Crewkerne as one of the two finest cruciform churches in the county.

Part of the church was built by Sir William Wadham, who died in 1440, and whose tomb is in the church, together with Nicholas and Dorothy Wadham, who founded Wadham College, Oxford, in 1610. The grammar school, a picturesque building on the further side of the churchyard, was founded in 1586 out of one of the chantry-houses, by Humphrey Walrond, who also lies in the church.

The living of Ilminster was formerly a Royal Peculiar, and until shortly before the 1914–18 War the vicar held his own visitations, and was not under the jurisdiction of the bishop.

There is a colonnaded market-house, and several old houses in the town, and the George Hotel proudly displays a notice that Queen Victoria spent her first night in an hotel there, in 1819, when she stayed for a night at the age of seven months, on her way to Sidmouth!

John Edward Taylor, who was born in Ilminster in 1791, founded the *Manchester Guardian* in 1821, remaining its editor for the rest of his life.

Ilton, north of Ilminster, and on the other side of the river, which here takes a big bend eastward, has a church containing brasses to the Wadhams, including one with an effigy in a shroud to Nicholas Wadham, who died in 1508. The Wadhams seem to have had a great liking for the name of Nicholas, which makes it a little confusing to sort out all the different members.

The Nicholas and Dorothy Wadham who founded Wadham College showed very enlightened views, and anticipated some modern reforms. It was said by Fuller that their "hospitable house was an inn at all times, a court at Christmas", but Merrifield is now only a heap of stones inside a moat.

This same Nicholas also founded a pretty row of almshouses at Ilton, and another group of seventeenth-century almshouses there have an inscription to "John Whetstone, Gentleman". He is said to have derived his name from the fact that he was found in a manger with a bundle of whetstones. He grew up to achieve success and riches, and founded the almshouses as a thank-offering.

A bridge across the river, east of Ilton, takes us to the villages of Puckington, Stocklinch and Barrington, but we will keep on the west bank to Isle Abbots, once connected with the abbey of Muchelney. It has an interesting church with a fine tower, numerous niches with statuary, carved bench-ends, a splendid south porch, and several unusual features.

Isle Brewers, which gets its misleadingly suggestive name from its former connexion with the De Bruyère family, lies in the marshes on the east bank of the river, and was formerly the incumbency of the eccentric Dr. Joseph Wolff, who rebuilt the church in 1861 and died there the following year. Few people have had more exciting and adventurous lives then Joseph Wolff, who was the son of a Jewish Rabbi. Born in Bavaria in 1795, he left home on account of his Christian sympathies, and studied languages and theology. He travelled as a nomadic missionary in Egypt, Sinai, and Palestine, and was the first modern missionary to preach to the Jews in Jerusalem. Two years later, in 1828, he went abroad again in search of the ten lost tribes, and was shipwrecked, but after his rescue continued his travels until he reached Khorassan, where he was made a slave. He was again rescued, and resumed his travels, emerging at Kabul after being robbed in Central Asia and compelled to walk 600 miles without clothing or money. He had cholera near

Madras, but survived and went to Abyssinia, and from there to the United States.

Five years later he was sent out to Bokhara from London, to ascertain the fate of Lieut-Col. Stoddard and Captain Conolley, found they had been executed, and nearly shared their fate, but escaped almost miraculously, and brought the first authentic news of their death to England, in 1845, and published an account of the mission. By this time, he apparently felt he had had his fill of adventures, and accepted the living of Isle Brewers, where he remained for seventeen years, dying at the age of sixty-seven, just as he was planning yet another missionary journey!

He was accustomed to sign himself "Apostle of our Lord Jesus Christ for Palestine, Persia, Bokhara, and Balkh", and the red-capped tower and red roof of the church he built at Isle Brewers stands out against the green marshland as much as his vivid personality must have done against the quiet background of his parish.

The River Isle joins the Parret just below beautiful Muchelney, which rises out of the willow-bounded buttercup meadows, with its lovely ancient houses still remote and peaceful.

As its name implies, Muchelney was once an island, and as long ago as 939 the abbey was founded there by King Athelstan. The foundations of the abbey church can be seen in the churchyard of the parish church, neighboured by the beautiful Abbot's House which has survived in an almost perfect state of preservation.

A beautiful little model of the abbey as it looked in the days of its tranquil prosperity was made by evacuee children attending Langport school, under the direction of the Headmaster, and after being shown at the Bath and West Show in the early days of the war, was sent to Muchelney, and adds considerably to the interest of a visit to the Abbot's House. The fourteenth-century Muchelney Breviary, beautifully illuminated, and including a quaint jumble of recipes, "cures", and news, is now in the British Museum.

The parish church has some pre-Reformation tiles from the abbey, and a very curious series of seventeenth-century paintings on the nave roof, of half-length angels of exceeding ugliness, in contemporary costume, surrounded by very solid-looking clouds, and waving texts. The modern cross of Muchelney is on the same base as the original cross, between the church and the fourteenth-century Priest's House —one of the most enchanting houses in Somerset with its deep thatched roof, and the long garden gay with flowers.

IV

There is a road running directly north from Chard to Ilminster, and from there to Taunton, following much the same route as the railway; and another road over the hills, which gives enchanting views before dropping down to the Vale of Taunton.

If we go north, we can make for Broadway, whose name is said to be derived from an ancient track cut through the Forest of Neroche. At Horton Cross, where we rejoin the main road, there is a medieval house, now a farm, and immediately north is Jordans, the birthplace of John Hanning Speke, who was descended from a younger brother of George Speke of White Lackington.

The famous explorer's journals make thrilling reading, and evoke wonder at the courage and perseverance of this determined man, who suffered frequent bouts of semi-blindness, but discovered Lake Tanganyika, explored Lake Victoria Nyanza, and traced the source of the Nile, succeeding in solving the "problem of all the ages".

Crossing many tiny streams, the road comes to Ashill, and runs through the lovely wooded hills of Hatch Beauchamp and West Hatch. The church of Hatch Beauchamp, neighbouring the pleasant manor-house, has a window to the memory of Colonel J. M. R. Chard, V.C., the hero of Rorke's Drift, who died at his brother's rectory at Hatch. West Hatch is an attractive village, but its church is less interesting than that of Hatch Beauchamp. There are some good bench-ends in Thornfalcon church, near by, and from there it is only three and a half miles to Taunton.

v

The roads which runs over the hills from Chard to Taunton passes through Wadeford, a big, scattered village in a valley, which is believed to have derived its name from woad, a plant formerly grown for the dye obtained from it, which was used for dying cloth manufactured at a mill which has since vanished. A Roman pavement, forming part of a villa, was found at Higher Wadeford, and on a hill near by is a curious little temple, brought from the garden of Burton Pynsent.

Combe St. Nicholas has a village green and a towered church with seventeenth-century effigies of the Bonners who once owned Weston manor.

A maze of lanes leads off the main road to Buckland St. Mary, in a lovely situation. The modern and richly decorated church has some curious epitaphs on tombs in the churchyard, including one to John Hill, who was killed in 1858 whilst carting stone for the church, giving an account of the accident, and concluding, "May all carters who read this take warning and never get in their waggons." Another stone is "Sacred to the memory of Betty Trump, who at the early age of 13 was murdered by an unknown hand" in 1823.

Immediately after leaving Buckland St. Mary there are wonderful views as the road skirts the distinctive, tree-crowned height of Castle Neroche, with its great prehistoric camp, and drops down to the Vale of Taunton Deane.

The British camp of Castle Neroche, popularly known as Castle Ratch, was strongly fortified by the Romans and Normans, and is approached by several ancient trackways.

Lastly, on the main road, just before reaching Taunton, is Staple Fitzpane, with its exceptionally beautiful west tower, Norman south door, and seventeenth-century almshouses; and byways to Thurlbear with its remarkable little Norman church, and Stoke St. Mary, charmingly set at the foot of a wooded hill.

VI

The Blackdown Hills, with their little, hidden villages, have roads so intricate it is easy to lose oneself, and impossible to deal with them in an orderly manner, but these villages are so well worth seeing that we will dodge about and find them.

Starting out from Chard by the road which runs directly west before plunging southward over the Devon border to Honiton, we can wander happily to such villages as take our fancy. Close to the Devon border is the sixteenth-century manor-house of Weston, now a farmhouse, and Wambrook, transferred to Somerset in 1896, but a part of Dorset when Sir Simonds D'Ewes lived there in the seventeenth century with his tutor. Sir Simonds, with his wonderful powers of application and insatiable curiosity, has been called the "Beau-ideal of an antiquary". Whitestaunton, farther north, is rather inaccessible, but its small Perpendicular church has several interesting features.

The manor-house dates partly from the fifteenth century, and the foundations of a Roman villa were discovered in the grounds, and beneath an archway is a well, near which there were traces of a Roman shrine. Old workings, believed to be Roman mines, exist in the neighbourhood, and there are barrows and camps in the district.

West Somerset Thatch

The George, Yeovil

Otterford has a hamlet at Bishop's Wood, in the broad defile through which the infant River Otter meanders. The church is two and a half miles away on a hilltop, and although drastically restored, has a Norman font, and interesting brasses to the Combes of Fyfet Court. The registers date from 1558, but large portions were destroyed about 1810 by a churchwarden who was a local shopkeeper, and used the older registers as wrapping paper for his wares!

Due immediately west as the crow flies, but reached by most devious lanes, is Churchstaunton, which was transferred from Devon in 1896. It has a fine Perpendicular church with beautiful window tracery, some good woodwork, and the ancient stocks. Otterhead House takes its name from the River Otter, which rises just above the mansion, and divided the counties of Somerset and Devon until the parish of Churchstaunton was added to Somerset. It was built in the nineteenth century on the site of an ancient farmhouse. From Churchstaunton we can go directly north and strike the road which runs from Castle Neroche along the high ridge of the Blackdowns. Westward of Leigh Hill the greater part of the road marks the boundary between Somerset and Devon, and so we shall come to the Wellington Monument, through enchanting scenery with wide-spreading views, and drop down to Wellington and the Vale of Taunton Deane.

VII

Wellington shares to the full the ability of Somerset towns with few ancient houses to hint at a long history behind their settled modern contentment. It was first mentioned in history when King Alfred bestowed the Manor of Wellington on Asser, the tutor of his children; after which it seems to have followed the even tenor of its ways more or less undisturbed by national events until the fateful years of the Civil War and the Monmouth rebellion. A Court Leet is still held annually in October by the steward of the Lord of the Manor.

It is said the term Wellington Roundheads was proverbial in the West of England for violent fanatics, so possibly it was the local citizenry who stirred up the troops of Lieutenant Eure in 1640, when he absented himself from church and was brutally murdered on suspicion of being a Papist. Sir John Popham's house was seized and garrisoned for Parliament by Colonel Bovet, and was attacked by the Royalists under Sir Richard Grenville, who practically destroyed the house.

The correspondence between Monmouth at Taunton and the Duke of Albemarle at Wellington is an interesting episode in the history of the Rebellion. Following the Battle of Sedgemoor, Judge Jeffreys paid one of his unwelcome visits and left three Wellington men hanging, and others in the pillory for their share in the Rebellion.

The parish church stands beside the main street, and has a beautiful example of medieval carving in the figure of Richard, a fourteenth-century parson of the church, but its most conspicuous feature is the splendid monument to Lord Chief Justice Popham, with his effigy, gorgeous in his judge's robes, his wife by his side, and groups of his relatives about him, all beautifully coloured under a canopy painted with his arms and supported on eight black columns. He built a "large, strong and beautiful house" in Wellington, the site of which is said to be marked by Old Court. As Lord Chief Justice, he presided over the trial of Sir Walter Ralegh and the Guy Fawkes conspirators, and other celebrated cases of the day. Lord Ellesmere, and Coke, spoke of him with admiration, although there were not wanting detractors to accuse him of undue severity and of corruption. He founded and endowed almshouses at Wellington for six men and six women, which have been rebuilt.

Another favourite of James I was John Salkeld, who was presented to the living of Wellington in 1613, having been converted to Protestantism by the King himself. He styled himself "The Royal Convert" and was arrested during the Commonwealth for his strong Royalist sympathies.

Wellington was also the cradle of the Southeys, and the poet, in an autobiographical fragment, traced his family back in the church registers of Wellington to 1696, when his grandfather was baptized, his mother being a Locke, of the same family as the philosopher.

An Act of Parliament enabling a sum not exceeding £100,000 to be paid for manors, lands, and tenements, explains how the Duke of Wellington came to own the manor of Wellington in 1813, but his reason for choosing the title from the town, when created a Duke in 1809, has never been explained, as it appears he did not visit Wellington until 1814.

The Wellington monument was built in 1815, and its triangular shape is said to represent the type of bayonet used at Waterloo. It is 175 feet high, with a spiral staircase in the interior, and is a landmark for many miles around.

Chapter Sixteen: TAUNTON AND THE VALE OF TAUNTON DEANE

Taunton—South through the Vale—East and North—South again through Milverton

TAUNTON is one of the friendliest and most lovable towns in the kingdom, and typically English in its modest, unassuming ways. It has stoutly maintained its right to be the county capital, in the face of the claims of the cathedral city of Wells, and the size and importance of Bath, by its peerless position, like a spider in a web of roads, right in the heart of the county, and unmatched as a centre from which to explore all parts of Somerset.

Taunton's history is bound up with that of its castle, whose foundation by Ine, King of the West Saxons, in 710 was the beginning of the "Town on the Tone"—and a very eventful history it is, full of alarms and excursions, right down to the seventeenth century.

It was in 1497 that Taunton began to display its passion for espousing lost causes, by supporting Perkin Warbeck, who seized the castle one night, and fled the next, having heard that the royal troops had reached Glastonbury. Within a fortnight he was brought back to Taunton, a prisoner, and confessed to Henry VII that he was an impostor.

Taunton's support of the Parliamentary cause in the Civil War appeared to be another fatal move at first, for the defences of the town were totally inadequate, and at the beginning only the castle held out, but when the first siege was raised, Blake improved the defences of the town and castle. When the Royalist forces appeared again, the great Parliamentarian commander swore that rather than capitulate he would eat his boots—and nearly had to do so, for when relieved, two-thirds of the town had been consumed by fire, the thatch had been taken from houses to feed the horses, only two barrels of powder remained, and bread was fourteenpence a pound—a great sum in those days.

After the Restoration the fortifications of Taunton were destroyed and its Charter of Incorporation revoked, as a reprisal for the part it had played in the Civil War. It is thought that the demolition of the Norman keep and the partial filling of the moats dates from this time.

Twenty-three years after this work of destruction, James, Duke of Monmouth made a triumphal entry into Taunton, and was presented by the "Fair Maids of Taunton" with the colours they had worked for him under the direction of their schoolmistress, and the following day he was proclaimed king.

Taunton's most tragic days followed the defeat at Sedgemoor. The privations of the siege had at least been lightened by the heroism of the defenders and enthusiasm for the Parliamentarian cause. The Assizes at Taunton were an exhibition of judicial savagery unequalled until the days of Nazi Germany, and quite unlooked for in the seventeenth century. Naturally, everyone expected the ringleaders to be executed when the Rebellion failed; what no one had anticipated was the wholesale punishments which followed.

There have been modern attempts to whitewash the part Lord Chief Justice Jeffreys played at Taunton and elsewhere after the Rebellion and it is true the initial blame lay with King James, who, contrary to all precedent, declared everyone who had taken part in the Rebellion guilty of high treason, and as such liable to the death penalty—but it is impossible to forgive the ferocious joy the Judge showed in carrying out the King's will.

In 1822 the castle and manor of Taunton were sold by the see of Winchester, thus ending a unique jurisdiction by which Taunton Deane had for many centuries been virtually a palatinate of Winchester in the diocese of Bath and Wells.

The remains of the ancient castle are now the headquarters of the Somersetshire Archaeological Society, which saved them from destruction to house its Library and Museum. The earliest surviving part dates from the twelfth century, but in the main it dates from the Edwardian period, with many traces of reconstructions carried out during the reign of Henry VII. The Great Hall was probably built about 1208, and partly reconstructed in later times, and was used as an Assize Hall until the Shire Hall was opened in 1858. In contrast with the tragic scenes of the "Bloody Assizes" it saw some lighter episodes, after the Assizes were transferred, in connexion with political meetings, particularly that of 1831 when Sydney Smith originated the immortal phrase which inspired countless political cartoons, by comparing opposition to the Reform Bill with Dame Partington's efforts to push away the Atlantic Ocean with a mop.

In the present day to pass under the old gateway of Castle Bow and enter the courtyard is to find a quiet haven from the roar of the busy streets, and pass many happy hours browsing among the wonderful collection of books and relics of Somerset history and archaeology.

When we come to North Street again, we can see two old gabled houses dating from Tudor times, one of which was the old White Hart Inn, where Taunton men and women were hanged by Jeffrey's order from the inn sign, whilst he enjoyed his wine.

The famous towers of Taunton's churches, which are a landmark for miles around, are worthy of the county which seems to have specialized in noble Perpendicular church towers. Both were pronounced unsafe and taken down in the nineteenth century, but happily they were rebuilt in facsimile.

St. Mary Magdalene's tower is 163 feet high. It is crowned with elaborate pinnacles, and has fine carvings in the spandrels above the west door. The spacious interior with its four aisles is richly beautiful. The oldest part of the building is probably the fourteenth-century north aisle, and the nave has a fine oak roof. There are memorials to famous citizens of Taunton, some of whom have had a more than local fame. The gentle, scholarly Joseph Alleine, became curate of St. Mary's in 1654. Beloved by all, his attainments made him the intimate and friend of the founders of the Royal Society, and his writings won the warmest praises of such judges as Richard Baxter, but all this could not save him when the Act of Uniformity was passed, and both he and the Rector, George Newton, were ejected. Joining with the grandfather of John and Samuel Wesley, Alleine continued evangelizing, and suffered so much persecution that he died at the age of thirty-four, "worn out by his labours", and was buried at his own expressed wish in the chancel of his old church. No other Puritan, with the exception of Richard Baxter, has been so affectionately remembered, and his book *An Alarm to the Unconverted*, later republished as the *Sure Guide to Heaven*, became a best seller, and has frequently been reprinted in England and America.

Robert Gray, a Taunton boy who became a wealthy London merchant and a benefactor to his native town, is remembered with a life-size figure and a laudatory rhymed inscription. General Rawling, who was killed in the 1914–18 War, traced the source of the Bramaputra River and explored thousands of miles of unknown Tibet and New Guinea.

Thomas Cranmer, Archbishop of Canterbury, who was burned to death in 1556, was Archdeacon of Taunton from 1525 to 1540.

St. James's church, which dates from the fifteenth century, has a beautifully proportioned interior with an unusually lofty chancel, a magnificent font adorned with twenty-one figures of apostles and ecclesiastics; a pulpit dated 1633 and displaying no less than seven mermaids carved on it; and some modern screens in the chapel which were displayed at the Wembley Exhibition.

The oldest of the Nonconformist churches is the Congregationalist, Paul's Meeting House, which was founded by George Newton when he was ejected with Joseph Alleine from St. Mary's. John Wesley preached at the opening of the Octagon chapel in 1776, and Coleridge frequently walked over from Nether Stowey to preach in the Unitarian chapel.

Taunton has three rows of almshouses, the most picturesque of which are the thatched almshouses now known as St. Margarets, and used by the Somerset Rural Community as an office. The Thomas Gray almshouses were founded in 1635, and those founded by Richard Huish in 1615 for "thirteen poore, needy, maimed, impotent and aged men" were so richly endowed that two hundred and fifty years later he became the "founder" of the Huish Grammar School.

All that remains of Taunton's Augustinian Priory founded in 1151 is the old Priory Barn and some fragments of arches in Canon Street. The delightful Vivary Park is laid out on the site of the monastic fishponds.

Taunton is a noted educational centre, and King's College dates its foundation prior to 1293. It was rebuilt by Bishop Fox in 1522; and under the headmastership of the Rev. James Upton became the largest provincial school in eighteenth-century England. Archbishop Sheldon, who built the Sheldonian Theatre at Oxford, was educated there.

Among many natives of Taunton who have achieved fame were Thomas Savage, who founded Rhode Island in conjunction with William Coddington, and took a leading part in politics and war during the early days of Massachusetts; Edwin Norris, the orientalist, who was one of the earliest decipherers of cuneiform inscriptions; and Alexander William Kinglake, the story of whose early travels is known through the pages of his own *Eothen*. His younger brother, Robert Kinglake, was one of the originators of the Somerset Valhalla of Worthies, in the Shire Hall at Taunton.

II

The fair vale watered by the River Tone is still as fertile and famous as when Michael Drayton asked, "What ear so empty is, that hath not heard the sound of Taunton's fruitful Deane?" and one of the most popular of Somerset's old songs, heard wherever Somerset folk gather together, is *Richard of Taunton Deane*, as dear to Somerset hearts as *Widdicombe Fair* is to the men of Devon.

Some of the villages of the Vale we saw on our journeys from Chard, but there are still many others which will repay a visit, even when, as at Trull, they are so close to Taunton that their population has expanded into rows of council houses. There is still charm left at Trull in the rushing, noisy river in its small gorge with overhanging bushes, in the ancient causeway crossing the narrow, one-arched Ramshorn Bridge; and most of all in the church with its wonderful woodwork. The full-length figures on the amazing pulpit stand right out from the panels like carved toys, and the bench-ends represent a Sunday procession in a small parish church in the sixteenth century.

Some of the epitaphs to children attract "collectors", and near the old stocks under the churchyard yew is the grave of Mrs. Juliana Ewing, daughter of Mrs. Gatty. She began writing when still in the nursery, and her first volume of children's tales was published when she was only twenty-one. She contributed many of her best stories to the magazine founded by her mother, and called *Aunt Judy's Magazine* in allusion to her nickname. Best known among her stories are *The Land of Lost Toys* and *Lob-lie-by-the-Fire*. She was only forty when she died. A cot in Great Ormonde Street hospital, London, to the memory of Mrs. Ewing and her mother, was endowed by juvenile subscribers to *Aunt Judy's Magazine*.

Two miles south of Trull is Pitminster, whose Perpendicular church has some monuments to the Coles family, who owned Barton Grange after the Dissolution. The neighbouring Poundisford Park was a Chase of the Bishops of Winchester, which came into the possession of the Hill family, who built the manor-houses of Poundisford Park and Poundisford Lodge, which are still largely Tudor.

We can return to Taunton by way of Corfe, and Orchard Portman, or by Angersleigh, West Buckland, and Bradford.

Orchard Portman, whose name commemorates the marriage of a Portman with the heiress of the Orchard family, has a small Perpendicular church with a Norman south door, and a curiously shaped font, a carved wooden pulpit and stalls, a brass to Humfredus de Collibus or Colles, dated 1693, and several fine altar tombs to the same family. The ancient manor of the Portman family was demolished about 1845.

Angersleigh, west of Pitminster, has a very small church with a carved oak reading desk and lectern; West Buckland church is partly Norman and partly Perpendicular, and has a curious chancel arch, but its greatest attraction for most is the fine view from the churchyard. The date of the remarkable tower is known by the fact that John Peryn left 3*s*. 4*d*. in 1509 towards the building of the new tower. A lane runs from West Buckland to Gerbestone Manor, enlarged in late Tudor or early Jacobean times, and beautifully restored in 1925.

Northward lies Bradford, with its church on a wooded bank above the Tone, here crossed by a fourteenth-century bridge. There are some Norman remains, an effigy of a knight of the time of Richard II, and the old stocks.

Bishop's Hull, in the immediate neighbourhood of the church, is still an attractive village, but it has proved too near Taunton to escape a great increase of population, and is now joined up with the borough. The church has been extensively restored, but it still retains an elaborate Jacobean tomb with the effigy of one of the Farewell family, whose fine Elizabethan mansion originally served as the court-house of the general court baron of Taunton Deane.

Among those buried at Bishop's Hull is William Crotch, who was a child prodigy. Born at Norwich in July 1775, he taught himself "God Save the King" at the age of two, and was soon able to play other tunes. Dr. Burney read a paper on his accomplishments to the Royal Society, and in 1779 the child came to London with his mother. An advertisement which appeared in October of that year said: "Mrs. Crotch is arrived in town with her son, the Musical Child, who will perform of the organ every day as usual, from one o'clock to three, at Mrs. Hart's, milliner, Piccadilly." He played sitting on his mother's knee. At the age of seven, he could play the violin, as well as the pianoforte and organ, although he had received no regular instruction, but in 1786 he was sent to Cambridge and studied music, and within three years was giving weekly concerts. At fifteen he was appointed organist of Christchurch, four years later he took his Degree as Bachelor of Music, and at the age of twenty-four was Doctor of Music. He was also an artist, poet, and composer. His most lasting success was the oratorio *Palestine*, practically the only oratorio by an English composer which has survived half a century. He went from triumph to triumph and became the first principal of the Royal Academy of Music in 1822. Some time previous to his death he stayed with his son, the Rev. W. R. Crotch, master of Taunton Grammar school, and died suddenly in 1847.

III

East of Taunton are Ruiston and Creech St. Michael, on the edge of the Curry country. Ruiston church has a massive tower, a richly carved font and carved panels from the old rood-screen incorporated in the reredos; and Creech St. Michael, whose fine church tower is the signal for passengers on the main line train to get ready to alight at Taunton, is well worth visiting. The village is set on the Tone, over-looking the marsh, and framed in low, green hills.

IV

The Glastonbury road runs across the moors from Durston, which has only the old tower of its church and its carved bench-ends surviving from the nineteenth-century restoration. There was once a Priory and Preceptory of Mynchin Buckland, or Buckland Sororum in the parish, but it has long vanished. It was the only Priory of Women the Order of St. John of Jerusalem possessed in England.

A lane runs north from Durston through St. Michael Church, a very small parish, with a very small church containing some monuments to the Slade and Bacon families. General Sir John Slade, who was born at Mansel House in 1762, was the father of yet another of Somerset's famous travellers. Adolphus Slade, born in 1804, was a Vice-Admiral in the English Navy and an Admiral in the Turkish Navy. He travelled extensively in eastern Europe and the Near East and wrote numerous interesting accounts of his journeys. During his seventeen years as administrative head of the Turkish fleet he brought it to an unprecedented pitch of efficiency, his period of service including the Crimean War.

It was in the neighbouring parish of North Newton that the famous Alfred Jewel was found in 1693. The original is in the Ashmolean Museum at Oxford, and a copy at the Taunton Museum. Replicas of the jewel form the badge of the Society of Somerset Folk. The jewel was found on the estate of Sir Thomas Wroth, Parliamentarian and author, who had purchased the manors of Newton and Petherton from his cousin.

When Sir Thomas came to Petherton in 1613, he found the minor canons of Wells had built an alehouse and stable out of the stones of the ruined church of Newton for their use when they collected rents and held courts. He rebuilt the church, and it was probably he who furnished it with the magnificent woodwork.

North Petherton, with one of the grandest of all the grand church towers of Somerset, also has some interesting architectural features, and a headless fifteenth-century cross in the churchyard with carving on the socket.

v

North of Taunton is Cheddon Fitzpane, preserving the name of its Norman Lord, and West Monkton, which is named after the monks of Glastonbury, who owned it, and has a Perpendicular church with a lofty tower, and an epitaph to William Kinglake, physician, who died in 1660:

> "Contention's doubtfull
>   Where two champions bee;
>   Thou hast conquered Death,
>   Now Death hath conquered thee."

The parish stocks and whipping-post are under the yews in the churchyard. Thurloxton, half-way between Taunton and Bridgwater, and a little off the main road, has a small church noteworthy for the carved oak screen, which has rests for books attached to it, a fine seventeenth-century oak pulpit, and a west door made from a solid block of wood with the date 1500 over the entrance. Our old friend Parson Woodforde of Ansford came there as curate in 1763, and strikes a modern note in his diary by being unable to find lodging until invited to stay with the squire—but the charge bears no relation to modern prices, for he only paid 1s. 1½d. for stabling for his horse, laundry and all.

Kingston St. Mary, three miles north of Taunton at the southern end of the Quantocks, has a church prettily situated on rising ground above the Bridgwater road.

The Valley of Kingston is celebrated for its cider, and the apple orchards were wassailed until late in the nineteenth century. The Kingston Black Apple, produced by some local peculiarity of the soil, makes the best cider.

VI

It is Norton Fitzwarren's boast that "When Taunton was a furzy down, Norton was a market town"—a proud boast indeed when it is remembered the county town was founded in A.D. 710. Norton Fitzwarren lies under a hill crowned with a thirteen-acre British Camp. The church dates from the fourteenth century, and has a fine screen showing carvings of a ploughman and his team, and some dragons, believed by archaeologists to refer to the local tradition that a fiery dragon used to issue from the hill camp and lay the Vale waste—a tradition which probably has its origin in British raids on the Saxons of the Vale. The south-west corner of the churchyard is a favourite place for gypsy burials.

In the country between Norton and Milverton are Heathfield, Hilfarrance, and Oake, with interesting little churches. Milverton, in a deep combe, was once a place of importance, and had a considerable woollen trade. The town climbs a hillside and has old houses opening on a raised cobbled pavement running up to the church, which has a splendid collection of sixteenth-century carvings. The ancient vicarage is said to have once been the country residence of Cardinal Wolsey.

John of Milverton, who was born in the town in the fifteenth century, became a Carmelite friar, and was chosen English Provincial of the Order at a general chapter at Paris in 1456.

Dr. Thomas Young, who was born at the Bank House in 1773, was a youthful prodigy who went to school at the age of nine, and left at the age of fourteen with a knowledge of Greek, Latin, French, Italian, Hebrew, Persian, and Arabic. He was elected a Fellow of the Royal Society when only twenty-one. His writings and researches covered such a wide area that he contributed no less than sixty-three articles to the *Encyclopaedia Britannica*. His wave theory of light changed the whole science of optics, and his theory of colour vision, revised and elaborated by Helmholtz nearly half a century later, is still the basis of all researches into the subject of colour vision and colour-blindness. He was also the discoverer of the key to ancient Egyptian hieroglyphics, by unravelling the secret of the Rosetta Stone, yet he was a conspicuous example of a prophet not without honour, save only in his own country. Loaded with honours by France, and the friend of all great continental scientists, in England he was considered only a trifler. The great scientist Helmholtz said, "He was one of the most clear-sighted men who have ever lived, but he had the misfortune to be too greatly superior in sagacity to his contemporaries. They gazed at him with astonishment, but could not always follow the bold flights of his intellect."

There are some beautiful manor-houses, now farms, in the neighbourhood of Kittisford, whose church has been restored, but has an unusual wooden arcade and a pulpit with the date 1610 cut twice over, the carver having miscalculated the space the first time. Cothay is one of the best examples of an Early Tudor manor-house in this part of Somerset, and Greenham Manor Farm dates partly from the time of Edward III and partly from the Tudor period.

There is a long climb up to the pleasant old farm of Thorne St. Margaret, and the restored church with its Tudor brass to John Worth:

> "John Worth lies here, and John is grace
> And worth doth virtue sound.
> His virtue praise hath left on Earth,
> His grace hath glory found."

The Perpendicular church of Sampford Arundel, near the Devon border, has a single roof covering the nave and aisle, and a curious sculpture of hands holding a heart; the little church at Runnington retains an outside stairway; and Langford Budville church has a fine battlemented tower. On one of the columns of the south arcade is carved a needle and thread, which has been conjectured to have some connexion with Queen's College, Oxford, where the old custom of presenting a needle and thread to each Fellow and undergraduate in lodgings, under a bequest of the founder, is still maintained every New Year's Day.

A magnificent avenue of limes brings us to Chipley Park, where Locke wrote part of his *Essay Concerning Human Understanding*, whilst staying with the Clarkes; and deep lanes through high rock walls where trees arch overhead lead to Nynehead with its mansion neighboured by the church. The church at Nynehead is full of statuary and tombs to the Sandfords and Clarkes, and has totally unexpected treasures in the blue and white fifteenth-century reliefs by Della Robbia, and a tablet of the Trinity from a chapel in Italy, believed to be by the fifteenth-century sculptor Mino de Fiesole, and given to the church by the Rev. John Sandford in 1830. There are also two quaint epitaphs, one without a name or date:

> "A little book and tapers light
> Did solace me in my last night.
> My taper spent, book closed I late,
> In bed thereon to meditate."

And a pun on the names of Henry Sandford and his wife, whose maiden name was Ashford:

> "Two *Fords* conjoyn'd incorporate
> A husband and his spoused mate,
> Make one fair streame whose very name
> Might give to heraldry a theme.
> But as propense all rivers runne
> Into the ocean whence they come;
> Soe they to earth their tending have,
> Both here concenter in the grave."

The River Tone flows through the beautiful grounds of Nynehead Court, and Wellington is only a mile and a half away to the south.

Chapter Seventeen: THE BRENDON HILLS

Wiveliscombe—The Devon border—The Northern Villages—Dunster.

THE Brendons have a particular fascination for those who love solitude. It is possible to walk for miles, even along the chief roads, without meeting a soul, and their villages are tucked away down some of the loneliest lanes in Somerset.

There is a ten-mile road along the top of the ridge which, once you have climbed up to it, runs at an almost unvarying height of 1,200 feet from Elworthy to Wheddon Cross. It is shut in between high beech hedges, with every break in the foliage giving superb views across the sea to Wales, and inland to Exmoor and the Devon hills and valleys.

The old trackway starts out from Wiveliscombe, a pleasant little market town, set on a green hillside, which has a long history. It was granted by Edward the Confessor "for the good of his soul" to the See of Wells, and detailed records of events in the town are preserved at Wells.

Full details of the training of persons mustered for the Elizabethan "Home Guard" at Wiveliscombe during the Armada scare have been preserved. Apparently they at first suffered from the same disabilities as modern Home Guards, as the training on Sunday afternoons and holidays was done without powder for the shot, owing to the expense. As they improved they were eventually allowed half charges and bullets because some had been found "by reason of the churlishness of their weapons and not being made acquainted therewith by degrees, are ever after so discouraged as either they winke or pull their heades from the place, whereby they take no perfect level, but shoot at random, and are never good shots".

Wiveliscombe had little to do with the Civil War, but three men were hung in the town after the Monmouth Rebellion, and many Wiveliscombe men lost their lives at Sedgemoor.

After the allied forces entered Paris in March 1814, Wiveliscombe held high revel, and "H. Sully Esq. displayed a laughable transparency of Napoleon and the Devil" whilst on other houses there were "many beautiful devices". Even the London newspapers reported the town's junketings on this occasion; *The New Monthly Magazine* for September 1st, 1814 said: "The inhabitants of Wiveliscombe have celebrated the peace in a manner no less spirited than original. . . . Among other curious performances which took place during the actual course of the procession was the manufacture of a coat, through all the processes of weaving, fulling, dying and making, in the space of four hours! . . . the coat . . . was actually worn by Mr. Hancock at dinner. . . ."

Only slight traces remain of the palace built in the fourteenth century by Bishop Drokensford, and the church was rebuilt in 1827. It is said that on the night when it had at length been determined to pull down the old church, a sad knell was sounded by the bells in the tower, strange sounds were heard from the church itself, as if spirits were "wailing for the doom of the habitation in which they had been lodged for so many centuries, and when the door opened a chill blast of misty uncertain solidity issued upon the sexton and masons to their great discomfiture".

Practically all that remains of the ancient church is the monument to Humphrey Wyndham and his wife, who died within two years of each other in the seventeenth century, and are remembered with a long epitaph.

II

A road climbs up from Wiveliscombe near Brompton Ralph, whose church has a fourteenth-century screen restored by an American in memory of his grandfather, who had lived in the parish; and Tolland, a pretty little village set in orchards, with a stream flowing in front of its cottages. Tolland has a tiny church restored in the nineteenth century, but its chief treasure is Gaulden Manor, now a farm, where James Turberville, Bishop of Exeter in the sixteenth century, lived after his deprivation in 1559, when he refused to take the Oath of Supremacy to Queen Elizabeth.

The neighbouring Willet Hill is crowned by a sham tower which is a landmark for many miles around.

Another road into the Brendons from Wiveliscombe gives access to the villages of the southern slopes, which attract chiefly by the charm of their setting in remote, sheltered valleys. Huish Champflower and Chipstable; Waterrow, beside a bridge over the Tone; and Venn Cross, a rural station on the Barnstaple railway, serving a number of villages in Somerset and Devon, are all within easy reach. Among other villages of the borderland of Devon are Stawley, on the Tone, with a small Early English church; Ashbrittle, high on the Brendons above the Tone, and right on the county boundary; Raddington, also on the boundary, with good woodwork in its church; Skilgate, on the lower slopes of Haddon Hill; and Upton, with the tower of the old church still marking the original site, although the church itself has been removed to a more convenient position at Rainsbury, by the cross-roads overlooking a little valley watered by the River Bathern.

Brompton Regis, locally known as King's Brompton, stands on the more cultivated fringe of Exmoor, and the church has a plain tower of the Exmoor type with a seventeenth-century brass to a nineteen years old girl of the Dyke family:

"Reader, it is worth thy pain to know
Who was interred here below.
Here lies good nature, pity, wit,
Though small in volume yet most fairly writ.
She died young, and so oft-times tis seen
The fruit God loves He's pleased to pluck it green."

South of Brompton Regis is Baron's Down, enchantingly set in a district of oak coppices and rhododendron thickets above the valley of the Exe and the ruins of Barlynch Priory.

Northward from Brompton Regis the roads climb up to the old trackway on the summit of the Brendons, and eastward through lonely byways and enchanting scenery to Withiel Florey, a tiny hamlet with a very ancient church; the insignificant and easily missed source of the River Tone; and Ralegh's Cross, now only a broken fragment, to mark the place where the body of Simon de Ralegh, a hero of Agincourt, rested on its way from Devon to Nettlecombe.

III

The exquisite northern slopes of the Brendons, with their woods, overlooking the sea, can be reached from any of the byways running south from the main road between Taunton and Minehead, or the quiet little stations of the branch railway which also serves the Quantock hills for the first part of its lovely route.

If we go by the road, we can branch off just before Norton Fitzwarren is reached to Bishop's Lydeard, with its many thatched cottages, and attractive stone houses with trim gardens.

The church has a marvellous fan-vaulted screen; sixteenth-century bench-ends with Somerset scenes carved on a painted background; and a sixteenth-century brass to Nicholas Grobham and his wife. There is also a glorious Perpendicular tower, and an unrivalled example of a fourteenth-century churchyard cross, with rich sculptures on the socket and shaft, and a modern head, in the form of a crusader's cross which blends admirably with the older work.

Sir John Popham had a mansion here, which was held in the Civil War by Sir Richard Grenville and reduced to ruin, but some almshouses endowed by Sir Richard Grobham in 1616 can still be seen. A deep lane between red rocks, shaded by huge trees, runs up behind Watts House, and there are many charming lanes into the Brendons.

Ash Priors affords the sight comparatively rare in Somerset scenery of a real common, but here, too, there are Somerset lanes, to a typical west Somerset village, with houses of red sandstone or ochre-washed walls, and a small, plain church of the same red sandstone. The village once belonged to the Priory of Taunton, and the sixteenth-century priory is still inhabited. All around are woods and steep lanes, to such charming places as Halse, with its small church, which has a very fine fifteenth-century rood-screen, sixteenth-century Flemish glass brought from Florence by a former rector, and modern bench-ends carved by villagers. There was a branch house of the Knights Hospitallers and a nunnery at Halse, the latter of which is now a farmhouse. The tithe barn has been thatched and is used as a pavilion for the playing fields, there is a centuries-old mill, and a mile away at Stoford another old barn invested with many legends of the Knights Hospitallers.

Fitzhead, west of Halse, has a restored church and churchyard cross neighboured by Fitzhead Court, a fine old mansion with a plaster ceiling decorated with the arms of the Cannon family, who lived there in the reign of Charles II.

Another road runs up from Ash Priors to Elworthy and its prehistoric barrows, and scattered farms, where a road winds down into a lovely valley watered by a tiny brook, past Combe Sydenham House to Monksilver, and other lanes beckon us to Combe Florey, set in a tree- and flower-filled combe just big enough to hold the pretty village.

Combe Florey gets its name from the Floreys, who were the ancient owners of the manor. Combe Florey House dates from the eighteenth century and has an Elizabethan gatehouse, well set on a green hillside, and the Perpendicular church contains some interesting memorials, but Combe Florey's greatest attraction is its association with Sydney Smith, who was rector from 1829 to 1845. His father settled at Bishops Lydeard after he had "bought spoiled and sold" nineteen different places in England, and died there in 1827 at the age of 88, so it was not Sydney Smith's only association with west Somerset. When he settled at Combe Florey, he indulged his cheerful eccentricities to the full. His daughter, Lady Holland, wrote that "he carried his system of furnishing for gaiety even to the dress of his books, which were not brown, dark, dull-looking volumes, but all in the brightest bindings". The open windows "admitted a blaze of sunshine and flowers" and he entertained his friends with gay and ingenious pranks, such as fitting two donkeys with antlers when a guest suggested the view of the paddock would be improved by deer!

With all his brilliant wit, which won for him a European reputation, he was never unkind, and Lord Dudley said, "You have been laughing at me for seven years and have not said a word that I wished unsaid"—and how many wits could claim a like kindliness?

Lydeard St. Lawrence, where Southey's grandfather farmed, has a towered church on a slight rise, and a twisty, narrow, and picturesque street with a raised path on one side. A window in the church commemorates Sir Joseph Trutch, who built the suspension bridge over the Fraser River in British Columbia, and became the first Lieutenant-Governor when the colony was confederated to the Dominion of Canada in 1871.

There was formerly one of the quaintest epitaphs in Somerset on a tombstone in the churchyard, of which a record was made by Mr. A. S. Macmillan in his comprehensive collection of *Somerset Epitaphs*. The stone was to the memory of William Rich who died in the eighteenth century:

> "Beneath this stone in sound repose
> Lies William Rich of Lydeard Close:
> Eight wives he had yet none survive,
> And likewise children eight times five;
> From whom an issue vast did pour
> Of great grand-children five times four.
> Rich born, rich bred, but fate adverse
> His wealth and fortune did reverse.
> He lived and died immensely poor,
> July the 10th aged ninety-four."

Stogumber is a large village which took its name from its Norman Lord. The church has an unusual squint, passing through two piers; a chapel built by Cardinal Beaufort; the tomb of Sir George Sydenham, who fought for Charles I; and a sixteenth-century brass to Margery Wyndham. There is a tradition that Harry Hill's well at Stogumber cured a man of leprosy in the sixteenth century and has borne his name ever since.

There is a pleasant little lane running uphill from Stogumber to drop down to the Monksilver road nearly opposite Combe Sydenham House, the Elizabethan manor-house which was the scene of one of Sir Francis Drake's legendary exploits—the firing of a "cannon-ball" from the tropics to Combe Sydenham, as a sign to his betrothed, Elizabeth Sydenham, that he was still alive! The lady was just setting out to get married to Drake's rival, but returned home to await the redoubtable widower, whom she not only married but survived. The cannon-ball—a meteorite—is preserved at Combe Sydenham to this day, and local tradition further avers that it returns to the house after any attempt to remove it.

The road continues down the glorious combe, with its high, rounded hills, thickly covered with woods of oak and beech which turn to gold in the autumn, to Monksilver, a fascinating little village of thatched cottages clustering round a simple little church with grotesque gargoyles, some ancient glass and much good woodwork. It is down this same valley that the Sir George Sydenham, who lies in Stogumber church, rides every night between midnight and cockcrow, though why his spirit should be so restless is not apparent. It would seem more appropriate, if less picturesque, for the neighbourhood to be haunted by the unknown murderer of Elizabeth Conibeer and her two daughters, commemorated on an eighteenth century tombstone in Monksilver churchyard:

> "Inhuman wretch, whoe'r thou art
> That didst commit this horrid crime
> Repent before thou dost depart
> To meet thy awful Judge Divine."

Williton can be reached either from Monksilver or Stogumber by way of Sampford Brett, which derives its name from the family of Brett, one of whom murdered Thomas à Becket. The church was rebuilt in the Strawberry Hill Gothic style in 1835.

The small town of Williton is like a village in the charm of its old houses covered with flowering creepers, and its thatched cottages. The church was completely rebuilt on the site of a chantry chapel founded by Robert Fitzurse, for the good of the soul of his brother Reginald, another of those concerned in the murder of Thomas à Becket.

A mile west of Williton is Orchard Wyndham, which has been a seat of the Wyndhams since Sir John Wyndham settled there in the sixteenth century. The so-called "Mother Shipton's tomb", extremely difficult to find, has a faked inscription to a Roman child.

Elizabethan Nettlecombe Court is within sight of the charming lane which climbs the Brendons from Washford cross-roads, near the Western Regional wireless station, to Ralegh's Cross on the summit of the hills. The estate was granted to Hugh de Ralegh in the reign of Henry II, and came to the Trevelyans by marriage in the fifteenth century. The tribulations of a teetotaller in the hard-drinking days of the seventeenth century are recounted in a letter written by George Trevelyan, who not only had to pay a fine every time he refused to drink, but had his head knocked against the wall by an exasperated hostess because he "wouldn't drink square like the other gentlemen".

The mansion is neighboured by the church, very thoroughly restored in the nineteenth century, and chiefly remarkable for its chalice and paten, dating from the fifteenth century, and of most beautiful workmanship, which are among the oldest pieces of English plate in existence. The Seven Sacraments font is also famous, and there are some interesting effigies of the Ralegh family.

Washford, delightful though it is with its many thatched cottages and flower-filled gardens, has its crowning glory in Cleeve Abbey, in "The Flowery Vale". The old abbey still stands, in such a splendid state of preservation that the lives of the Cistercians can be imagined, living in peace and quiet in their remote valley, and clinging to the severe rules of their austere order. They took no part in national events, and lived such blameless lives that even the King's Receiver pleaded for them, but that could not save them from the rapacity of the King, and the abbey was handed over to Robert, Earl of Sussex.

Cleeve Abbey was the only Cistercian house in Somerset, and was founded in the twelfth century. So quietly did life flow in the Flowery Vale that although much has been written about the building, little is known of the men who lived there during its four centuries of existence. That they exercised hospitality we know, not only from the inscription still to be seen over the gateway, "This gate shall ever be open to all who enter honestly," but also from the testimony of the King's Receiver, which would certainly not be prejudiced in their favour, that it housed "17 priests of honest life who keep hospitality". There are records of benefactions, chiefly from the Mohuns, and their successors, the Luttrells, of Dunster Castle; and mention of the abbots as local landlords, but that is all.

George Fownes Luttrell bought the manor of Old Cleeve in 1870, and started the careful work of restoration which has brought the abbey buildings to their present state of perfection.

The charming little village of Old Cleeve, mellow with the consciousness of a proud antiquity, lies between the abbey and the sea, with only the tower of its interesting Perpendicular church showing above the trees. It contains an effigy of some unknown person with a cat at his feet.

There is a delightful walk from Washford to Watchet along the disused track of the old Mineral Railway, whose sleepers were taken to France at the beginning of the 1914–18 War. There is a break in the track at Washford, but it can be picked up again on the hillside above, where it runs through Roadwater village to Combe Row. In the nineteenth century, Welsh and Cornish miners were induced to come to the Brendons, and houses sprang up along the old trackway, schools and chapels, too, were built, and for a time the mining was very profitable, but between 1880 and 1890 the price of iron fell rapidly owing to the low cost of importing ore, and the Brendon mines began to fail, the miners gradually left to find other work, and the new villages fell into ruin, until in one man's lifetime all had returned to loneliness and peace, and the wild cherries seeded in the disused pits to make the white spring beauty of the present day. Only the chapel with "Beulah" over the door, near to Ralegh's Cross, remains to tell of the once busy scene.

There is a holy well at Roadwater, in the garden of an old cottage which was once a chapel dedicated to St. Pancras. On the hillsides above are the little lonely villages of Treborough, with a slate-roofed, whitewashed church, in beautiful woodlands near a 30-foot waterfall; Leyland Chapel, which once belonged to Cleeve Abbey; and Luxborough, neighboured by numerous prehistoric barrows, in a wild and lonely corner of the hills.

Withycombe, on the lower slopes of the Brendons, has a stream murmuring past its whitewashed cottages, and a church with a beautiful carved screen, one of the local group of seven probably made at Dunster. There are two fine effigies, one of a civilian dated about 1290 and the other of a lady, probably of the Fitzurse family, about 1300. Sandhill manor-house, built about 1588 and formerly the seat of a branch of the Escott family, is now a farm. It was once the home of Joan Carne, to whom there is a brass in Withycombe church. It is said she was a witch and murdered all her three husbands and that after her death in 1612 the mourners returned after her funeral to find her at home, frying eggs and bacon! Her spirit was eventually "laid" in a neighbouring pond, but as it is said to approach her old home by a "cock-stride" every year, presumably it will be necessary to lay it again some day!

IV

Dunster, which proudly ranks as a town but is smaller, lovelier and more peaceful than many a village, is a perfect feudal survival, dominated by the splendid castle still inhabited by the Luttrells, and complete with ancient inn, yarn-market, parish church, priory ruins, dove-cote, water-mill, and packhorse bridge across the little River Avill.

Sir Henry Maxwell-Lyte has told the story of castle and village in *Dunster and its Lords*, which traces its history from the Conqueror's companion-in-arms, William de Mohun, who built the castle and made it the centre of his great barony, until modern times. It is one of the few castles in the country which have been uninterruptedly inhabited since the Conquest, and only changed hands once, by purchase, in 1375. The widowed Lady Elizabeth Luttrell, bought the reversion of it from Lady de Mohun, widow of Sir John de Mohun, who got the best of the bargain, for she lived nearly thirty years after the receipt of the money, and poor Lady Elizabeth died before she could take possession!

Many of the earlier Luttrells fought in the French wars, and Sir Hugh was Seneschal of Normandy in the fifteenth century, but Dunster, too, saw fighting in the time of Stephen and in the Civil War. It was besieged by Robert Blake, and after a siege of 160 days, was compelled to surrender, although the garrison was allowed to depart with all the honours of War.

The thirteenth-century gateway built by Reginald de Mohun is the only link with the original owners in the beautiful castle of to-day. The great gatehouse was built by Sir Hugh Luttrell in the reign of Henry V, and the greater part of the remainder is Elizabethan, with later alterations which have converted it into a home without losing any of its impressiveness. Among its treasures is an oak staircase carved with hunting scenes, and a room hung with painted Cordova leather showing episodes in the life of Cleopatra and Marc Antony. There is also a fine collection of pictures, but one of its most notable possessions is the muniment-room, with all the documents relating to the affairs of the castle and its owners from the earliest times, beautifully arranged by

William Prynne in 1650, when he was sent to the castle by
Cromwell as a prisoner, hideously branded on both cheeks
and with both ears cut off, through his activities as a seditious
libeller, but with his energetic spirit quite unquenched.

Gallox Hill has the remains of two ancient camps. Conegar
Hill, which faces the castle from the opposite end of the main
street of Dunster, is crowned by an unfinished ornamental
tower built in the seventeenth century by Sir George
Luttrell. It is a landmark for miles around, and is sometimes
mistakenly photographed as Dunster Castle. Many of the
surrounding hills are densely wooded, but others, like Grabbist,
are bright with heather and thick with the low bushes of
whortleberries, or bilberries, locally known as "wurts".

Dunster Castle is the "Stancy Castle" of Hardy's *A Laodician*
and the "Lullington" of Lady Constance Malleson's
Fear in the Heart, and is said to have inspired Mrs. Alexander
to write the hymn *All things Bright and Beautiful*, and it is, of
course, mentioned in Blackmore's *Lorna Doone*, for we are
now on the outskirts of the scenes in which that grand love
story is set.

The road which turns off from Dunster High Street to run
past the curious old building known in modern times as The
Nunnery, but with no recorded history, and up through the
glorious scenery of the valley of the Avill, practically marks
the boundary between the Brendons and the hills of Exmoor,
and eventually finds its way to Dulverton; a long, lonely and
almost incredibly lovely way with never a village between
Timberscombe and Exton, where the River Exe comes
down from the moors.

Chapter Eighteen: EXMOOR AND THE SEA

Exmoor—Dulverton—Simonsbath—Vale of Porlock—Minehead

EXMOOR, the home of the wild red deer, is as legend-haunted as Dartmoor, but its legends have a more cheerful trend, for the moor, vast and lonely as it is, has a wonderfully friendly atmosphere. The wild life is as abundant as it is interesting; it is the only place in the Northern Hemisphere where the wild red deer is still hunted as in the days of the Norman kings; and Exmoor has one great advantage over Dartmoor—it reaches down to the sea.

Books about Exmoor are as many and even more varied than those about Dartmoor, for there is a whole cycle of literature on the wild red deer, including the classic books by Richard Jefferies, the Hon. J. W. Fortescue, and Henry Williamson, and many hunting reminiscences; whilst Blackmore's novel has brought its own flood of fascinating books identifying the sights and scenes in The Land of Lorna Doone. Not so well known, but giving a delightful insight into village life on Exmoor is *The Book of Simple Delights*, written by Walter Raymond, who lived in a cottage at Withypool in the early years of this century, where he was visited by many congenial friends.

All these books make a background, and inspire those who have never been there with a longing to visit Exmoor, with its wild deer, its diminutive wild ponies, and its fascinating wild life generally, but nothing can take the place of the knowledge and love of the moors which comes from exploring on foot, or on horseback, lingering in its enchanting villages. It is a place where no plans should be made, unless they are very elastic ones, for the spirit of the moor cannot be captured by "shock" tactics, much less by rushing about in a car. There are few roads, and even fewer bus routes, but there are charming little inns or lonely, hospitable farms, in which to stay, and a wealth of interest for those who are content to suit their wanderings to the unhurried life of this remote countryside.

The loveliest river valleys of Exmoor, all haunts of anglers, converge near Dulverton, the picturesque little market town on the Barle, which is a great hunting centre with kennels of stag, fox, and otter hounds in the neighbourhood.

South of Dulverton is Brushford, whose church has a chapel designed by Sir Edwin Lutyens, and an altar tomb to Col. Aubrey Herbert, diplomatist, traveller, poet, and linguist, who at one time commanded an Albanian regiment, and who was born at neighbouring Pixton Park, which is set in a great deer park, high on a hillside between the valleys of the Barle and Exe.

We can follow the winding course of the Barle from Dulverton, at first through wooded banks, below the old camp of Mounsey Castle, and the lonely farm of Ashway, the birthplace of Sir George Williams, founder of the Young Men's Christian Association, who received his early education at a dame school in Dulverton; and far below the lonely village of Hawkridge, which is nearly a thousand feet above the old clapper bridge of Tarr Steps across the River Barle. The bridge is 180 feet long with its paved approaches, and was so cunningly built by its prehistoric architects that it has survived the fierce winter floods of countless centuries.

Under the heights of Withypool Common, we pass quiet little Withypool, charmingly set in a wooded hollow, with its old thatched cottages and ancient church, and its bridge across the Barle. Beyond, ever lonelier and wilder, is the way to Simonsbath, in the very heart of the district which John Knight and his son tried to tame.

When Exmoor was disafforested in 1819, John Knight

bought the King's Allotment and other lands adjoining it—a waste country with only one small farm. He and his son Frederick made roads, built houses, and planted shelter belts of trees. They were responsible for the formation of the parish of Exmoor, which is the most extensive in Somerset, and built the church, parsonage, and school. It is true they made many mistakes and had many failures and much they achieved fell into ruin later, but there are still many homesteads and farmlands surviving in the deep valleys intersecting the forest, and the courage, resourcefulness, and energy of father and son in spite of some costly failures, were justified by the social and economic development they made possible in areas of the moor which had been waste time out of mind.

A road runs north from Simonsbath to Brendon Two Gates, where it crosses the Devon boundary and reaches the sea at Lynmouth, but we can keep to the Somerset side, leaving the road near the source of the Exe, to trace the river through its many windings across the desolate moors to Exford, another great centre of stag-hunting and angling. Beyond Exford the river winds under Winsford Hill, on which the ancient stone bearing the name of a kinsman of great British chieftain Caractacus is still standing, to the dear little village of Winsford with its many bridges, and huge trees, and fifteenth-century church, making up a quaint and pretty little haven from the wilder moors. Below Winsford the Exe flows through wooded banks to Exton, and so winds south beside the road to Dulverton and the Devon border.

II

Some of the loveliest villages in Somerset lie between Dunkery Beacon, the highest point on Exmoor, and the sea, so it is a joy to know that the National Trust owns no less

15

than 12,420 acres and leases over a thousand acres more of this glorious district, including Dunkery itself, the wonderful valleys of Horner, Cloutsham, and Sweetworthy, the woodland walks of Selworthy and its entrancing village, and the little villages of Horner and West Luccombe, Allerford, and Brandish Street with their packhorse bridges, Bossington with its famous walnut trees, and many another beauty spot, safeguarded for all time, chiefly through the generosity of Sir Richard Acland.

Nearly all the villages of the district have interesting churches, but that of Selworthy is exceptionally spacious and fine, and the view from the churchyard, across the unspoiled Selworthy Green to Dunkery Beacon, is as famous as countless pictures and photographs can make it. The church has some of the most remarkable Perpendicular work in the country, and the south aisle has a sixteenth-century roof which has been pronounced "perhaps the third finest waggon roof in the west of England"—no small praise for a remote country church. Brasses to the Stenning family, ancient seating, mural monuments and many other examples of beautiful workmanship, go to make up the fascinating whole.

There is also some good fifteenth-century work at Wootton Courtenay church; Tivington has a thatched chapel dating chiefly from the early part of the fifteenth century, with a cottage tacked on to one side at a later date, and Lynch chapel is a perfect example of a small manorial chapel.

Luccombe, enchantingly situated in the very shadow of Dunkery Beacon, also has an ancient church with good woodwork, and interesting monuments, including a mural tablet to the royalist rector, Henry Byam, who was born in the village and was buried there. He raised a troop for the King during the Civil War, in which four of his sons were captains.

Cloutsham Ball, one of the fields of Cloutsham Farm,

above Luccombe, is the scene of the opening meet of the Devon and Somerset Stag-hounds each year. The district is wild and lonely, rich in hanging woods, but so remote that many a West Countryman smiled to read a brilliant account in a London paper of the "streets of the little village crowded with people" attending the opening meet of the season!

III

The beautiful Vale of Porlock, with its level fields in an amphitheatre of beautiful hills, opens on to Porlock Bay, which is nearly five miles across from Hurlestone Point on the east to Gore Point on the west. Southey knew Porlock Vale well, and when weather bound at the Old Ship Inn one day composed a sonnet on the "verdant vale, so fair to sight". It has also been described in Whyte-Melville's *Katerfelto*, and Blackmore's *Lorna Doone*, and in the present day Mr. E. W. Hendy has made his home above the Vale, and described its natural history in his books; and of course every lover of Coleridge has reviled the unwitting "Gentleman from Porlock" who brought *Kublai Khan* to its untimely end.

There are really three Porlocks, but the most famous is the Porlock of the Ship Inn, the many thatched cottages—there is even a thatched bank—and the famous hill with its gradient of one in four. The church, with the truncated tower, is also well-known. It is said the top blew off in a storm in 1700, and the spire was repaired by roofing over—and local tradition further avers that it blew as far as Culbone, where it was utilized to complete their spireless little church! Culbone's spire certainly looks just the right size and shape to a believing eye!

Porlock is only a small town now, but it was a place of importance in far-off times, its fame as a port attracting many raids by the Danes. The Saxon palace and the greater part of Porlock was destroyed by fire. Saxon Harold, the son of

Earl Godwin, landed there in 1052 on his way from Ireland. The encampment in Hawkcombe Valley is said to have been thrown up during his attack. Porlock had an important market for centuries, and was a great haunt of smugglers at one time.

The most beautiful monuments in the church are the effigies of John, fourth Baron Harington, who was killed in the French wars in Henry V's reign, and Elizabeth Courtenay his wife, but the fine modern reredos has an especial interest as a memorial to a seventeenth-century rector Dr. Adam Bellenden, Bishop of Aberdeen and Chancellor there, who came to Porlock in 1642, four years after he had been deposed by the Covenanting Assembly of 1638.

Porlock had another notable rector in the following century when Stephen Hales held the living. This remarkable physiologist and inventor found no knowledge or activities come amiss. He botanized in Cambridgeshire with William Stukeley, was a Fellow of the Royal Society, a trustee of Georgia, actively connected with the foundation of the Society, now known as the Society of Arts, and was one of the eight foreign members of the French Academy of Sciences. The plant *Halesia* was named in his honour, and it is said he originated the idea of placing an inverted egg-cup in pies or tarts to prevent the juice from boiling over.

Pretty little West Porlock, bowered in roses, lies half-way along the two miles from Porlock to Porlock Weir, a typical bit of west Somerset coast scenery, with a tiny harbour and a cluster of picturesque houses and inns pressed under gigantic wooded hills. It was here the famous Porlock Ghost appeared, a week after the interment of "a wicked boaster" called Lucott. Twelve parsons were called upon to lay him in Porlock church, but only one proved bold enough to tackle him, and finally laid the ghost by persuading him to enter a box, which was then hurled into the sea.

A quarter of a mile from Porlock Weir is Ashley Combe,

a summer seat of the Lovelaces, first occupied by Byron's daughter, Ada, who married the Earl of Lovelace. There is a completely enchanting cliff walk through the woods to Culbone, so sheltered by hills that the sun only reaches it for four months of the year. Culbone has long claimed to be the smallest complete church in England, and its claim has now been recognized. Originally Norman or earlier, it is only 33 feet long, with a nave 12 feet 8 inches wide, and a chancel under 10 feet, altered in the fifteenth century.

An old rhyme says:

> "Culbone, Oare, and Stoke Pero
> Three such places you'll seldom hear o'."

whilst another versions finishes "Parishes three, no parson'll go", but to-day, in spite of their remoteness, they are all heard of and visited, not only by the parsons, but by tourists —Culbone for the charm of its quaint little church, Oare for its associations with Lorna Doone and Jan Ridd, who were married there, and Stoke Pero, perhaps the loneliest and least visited, also has a quaint little church and an old farm, and is only a mile from Cloutsham, where crowds enough meet on the opening day of the stag-hunting, if no other time.

The beautiful Culbone Woods continue nearly all the way along the cliff to the Glenthorne Valley which marks the boundary between Somerset and Devon.

On the roadway above is Yenworthy Farm, which dates back to the seventeenth century, where the old flintlock gun is preserved with which Widow Fisher is said to have rebelled a raid by the Doones. There is a climb up from Yenworthy to the road between Porlock and Lynton crossing Countisbury Hill, from which it is easy to reach Oare Church, Malmsmead farm and the Doone valley which Blackmore made world famous with his great romance, and although the waterslide was purely a figment of his imagination, the wild and lovely scenery of lonely hills and valleys would alone be sufficient to justify a visit, even without the spell of the romance he has cast on this enchanting countryside.

IV

Although Minehead has developed into a popular holiday resort, the picturesque old village remains to delight all those who love the little west Somerset cottages with their thatched roofs, flower-decked, whitewashed walls, and queer tall chimneys.

Minehead's church town, with the wide, shallow steps up to St. Michael's church, with its fine Perpendicular tower, has been photographed and painted nearly, if not quite, as frequently as Selworthy Green, and the view from Minehead's church porch is no less striking, and even more widespread, for on a clear day it is possible to see the coast sweeping away to the far-distant height of Brean Down on the north Somerset coast, with all the green and lovely hills of the Brendons and the Quantocks and the heights of Exmoor to give a surpassing beauty to the landscape.

The church is full of ancient and lovely things including an exquisite example of the local series of carved wooden screens; ancient monuments and brasses; and the quaint little seventeenth-century figure of "Jack Hammer" on the rood screen, which formerly stood in the tower and chimed the hours on the old clock. There are several memorials to the Quirke family, and below Church Town are the alms-houses, which have an inscription over the doorway:

> "Robert Qvrcke sonne of James Qvrcke Built this house ano: 1630: and Doth give it to the vse of the poore Of this parish for ever and for better Maintanance doe give my two inner Sellers at the inner end of the key And cvrssed bee that man that shall Convert it to any other vse then to The vse of the poore 1630."

But in 1934 members of the Urban Council boldy decided to defy the curse, close the almshouses and use the income from the charity to build small bungalows on the outskirts of the town to rehouse the tenants. The council were reminded of the curse, but presumably his spirit was in sympathy with the project to modernize the charity, as no ill effects are known to have followed.

The "inner Sellers" mentioned in the inscription still exist in Quay town, that quaint little cluster of slate-roofed whitewashed cottages with gaily painted doors and window frames, clustering round the grey old harbour in the shelter of pine-clad North Hill, which Defoe praised as "the best port, and safest harbour, in all these counties, at least, on this side".

Formerly there was a good deal of trade with Ireland, although it had a setback in the reign of Charles II when the importation of cattle from Ireland was banned. Minehead has a "Cow Charity", derived from the sale of a great number of cattle imported from Ireland in 1669, which were seized and sold, the money being invested for the benefit of the poor. In later times contraband was more successfully dealt with by the smugglers.

Minehead abounds in legends and tales of the supernatural, of which by far the most famous is "The Whistling Ghost", whose fame reached so far that it was recorded by Sir Walter Scott in his notes to *Rokeby*. It was the amiable and popular Mrs. Leakey, who lived at Minehead in 1636, who became the plague of the neighbourhood after her death.

Matters reached such a pitch that in 1637 the Bishop of Bath and Wells actually presided over a Commission to inquire into the question of the alleged apparition, but they eventually reported, "Wee doe believe that there was never any such Apparition at all but that it is an imposture devise and fraud for some particular ends but what they are wee know not."

Two customs believed to date back to pagan times are still maintained in Minehead district: the hobby-horse in Minehead itself, and apple-wassailing in Carhampton. The hobby-horses of Minehead and of Padstow in Cornwall are the only two surviving in England, although there are some in various European countries. Known as "The Sailors' Horse", the Minehead hobby-horse consists of a light, boat-shaped framework of wood, about eight feet in length, concealed with gay houseling painted with coloured circular spots. A man wearing a grotesque tin mask and a tall conical cap decorated with ribbons, supports the framework on his shoulders, and has a long rope tail, which he manipulates with telling effect on those who refuse to contribute to the collection. The horse is accompanied by a drummer and accordion player, who play a traditional tune. It is a comical sight to see the hobby-horse prancing and pirouetting, bowing to those who "pay their way" and fluttering its ribbons and rushing with flailing tail at the recalcitrant.

It is unlucky that the happy holiday-makers who come to Minehead in the summer never have any chance of seeing the hobby-horse, but they have many compensations; Minehead's sands are very wide and golden, and if the sea goes out a long way, there is one of the finest bathing pools in the West Country on the pleasant esplanade. There is glorious sunshine on the sea front with its pretty gardens, and cool shadow in the woods of North Hill, and there is the excitement of the stag-hunting season when the streets are brave with hunting pink, superb horses, and eager hounds.

Although Minehead has steadily grown in popularity, it has remained compact and attractive, with its wide, tree-lined main street leading inland from the sea past the old manor-house to a central square with an old coaching inn, and a statute of Queen Anne, presented to the town in 1718 by Sir Jacob Bancks, who, although a Swede by birth, held a commission as Captain in the English Navy. He married Mary Luttrell, the widow of Francis Luttrell, who, it is said, he rescued from a fire in her town house. He was knighted in 1699, and through the Luttrell influence, he was elected Member of Parliament for Minehead, and represented the town in nine successive Parliaments.

V

Everyone who knows Minehead knows Greenaleigh Farm, in the pine-woods of North Hill overlooking the sea, and in normal times justly famous for its cream teas, but fewer have penetrated the deep glen in which the ruins of the ancient Burgundy chapel lie. Nothing is known of its history, but tradition credits it with being a great resort of smugglers, and a small cave on the shore below is known as the Smugglers' Doom. In early times the coast suffered many raids, and none is mentioned in connexion with Minehead until 1120, when William de Marisco, a notorious pirate, plundered the coast of Wales and Somerset from his refuge on Lundy Island. Piracy flourished so flagrantly in Edward II's reign that the King issued a commission to "punish and suppress the rebels of the Somerset and Gloucester coasts who defie the King and rob his ships carrying provisions to him in Gascony", but all attempts seem to have failed, for piracy was still flourishing until as late as the seventeenth century, after which it seems to have gradually been replaced by smuggling, which reached amazing proportions and here, as elsewhere, smugglers had active co-operation from the local gentry.

On the southern slopes of North Hill, a mile and a half from Minehead, is the pretty little hamlet of Bratton, and the ancient manor-house of Bratton Court, on the site of a much older building. It is especially notable for the use of oak for the mullions and window tracery, in place of the more usual stone. The great gatehouse has its original oak gate, studded with iron.

A curious chamber over this gateway is said to have been used as a study by Henry de Bracton, the famous judge of the reign of Henry III. It is claimed he was born here, although the claim is disputed by Bratton near Okehampton, and Bratton Fleming, near Barnstaple. It is also claimed that the effigy in Minehead church was placed there in his memory by relatives, although he was buried in Exeter Cathedral, of which he had been Chancellor. However much doubt there may be about the details of his life, of his learning and eminence there is none at all. His position in the history of English law is unique, and his treatise *De Legibus et Consuetudinibus Angliae*, the first attempt to treat the whole extent of the law in a systematic and practical manner, had an immediate and lasting influence. Milton quoted from his work in his *Defence of the People of England*.

*Blue Anchor Bay—Watchet—The Seaward Quantocks—The
Western slopes*

ALL the west Somerset coast is backed by ranges of hills, and
everywhere there are rich woods and bright flowers, and an
enduring charm of small, unspoiled villages.

Walking to Blue Anchor along the sands from Minehead
involves a good deal of paddling, and by way of the low-
lying fields necessitates jumping over the many little brooks,
and it is better to go by the train which stops at a station
right on the beach, or by bus to Carhampton, where the
church, all glorious with colour as in medieval times, can be
seen, before taking the winding lane down to Blue Anchor
and the sea.

Carhampton is bowered in apple orchards, and the age-
old custom of wassailing the apple-trees is kept up. On
January 17th, Old Twelfth Night Eve, the farm labourers
and farmers and their friends gather in the orchards and sing
the old wassailing songs, handed down orally for countless
generations, and hang toast soaked in cider from the
branches. Guns are discharged, and a great hubbub is made,
to exorcise the powers of evil and ensure good cider crops.

Blue Anchor has changed but little even in the present day.
A long sea wall, a few houses, and a magnificent camping
site in one of the meadows, are the only addition to the
glorious sweep of sands and fields stretching away past
wooded Conegar Hill and its tower to Minehead—a view
which Turner painted.

There is a scramble, rather than a walk, along the pebbles
and rocks which stretch eastward of Blue Anchor to

Watchet, and for once the road has greater attractions, for there are glorious views of the Brendons the whole way, and a superb view eastward along the coast from the top of Cleeve Hill before dropping down into Watchet.

The older part of Watchet is more like a Cornish fishing village than a west Somerset town—a place of quaint nooks and corners gathered round its little harbour. It shows very little sign of its age, and to those who flash through in a car, even less of its charm, but to those who know and love it, its fascinations are as great and varied as its history is long and eventful.

Time and again the ancient chronicles record that the Danes raided Watchet "and brought great evil in burning and man-slaying", for as early as the tenth century Watchet was worth raiding—it was a prosperous port with its own mint. Coins struck there in the reign of Æthelred II can be seen in Taunton Museum and also in Stockholm Museum. A field beside the road to Williton, known as Battlegore, is the traditional scene of a great fight between the men of Watchet and Williton and the Danish forces in A.D. 918, described in the *Anglo-Saxon Chronicle*. Chatterton, in his "Rowley" poems, describes how Ælla, the Governor of Bristol, fought in this battle.

During the Civil War a Royalist ship was captured by Parliamentarian troopers, when lading in Watchet Harbour.

Watchet gave its name to a shade of light blue often referred to by early writers. It was mentioned by Chaucer in his *Miller's Tale*, and by William Collins in his poem *The Manners;* Tom Coryat, describing the coronation robes of the French King and Queen, mentions "their bootes . . . of watchet velvet . . .", and Charles I wore a waistcoat of watchet blue at his execution. The Oxford dictionary also mentions a watchet fly used by anglers in the eighteenth century.

Watchet was once famous for its laver, which was exported in the eighteenth century to London and other centres as a pickle. A nineteenth century writer on food claimed there was a charm about it which ought to have kept it in the front, as one of the distinctions of English cookery, and it had a revival in London before the 1914–18 War, when it was on sale in London again, and was served at exclusive clubs. There is still a vast quantity of red and green laver to be found on the seaweed-covered rocks at Watchet, so possibly it is destined to come into fashion again. Recent scientific research has shown that laver is rich in iodine, and the *Encyclopaedia of Gastronomy* includes several recipes for laver as an adjunct to roast mutton; a breakfast dish blended with oatmeal and fried like potatoes; or for eating cold as hors d'œuvre or savoury.

In the present day, Watchet's chief industry is its paper mills, which are so hidden away that few visitors realize they are of any great importance, but it is interesting to know that the first shipment of Swedish wood pulp into England after the last war was the 1,200 tons unloaded at Watchet in March 1946.

St. Decuman's church, high on a hill, once served both Watchet and Williton, and is half-way between the two places. Its fine tower is a landmark by sea and land, and it is generally accepted that the "Ancient Mariner" set sail from Watchet "Below the hill, below the kirk, below the light-house top".

The splendid church is the third largest in the district, and has a magnificent series of monuments to the Wyndham family, which include an Elizabethan altar-tomb and canopy, and some unique embossed portrait-brasses. There is also a touching and much-quoted epitaph to Sir Hugh Wyndham, who fought for Charles I, and was but ill-rewarded by Charles II. Yet, with all its historic and architectural interest, it is legend and romance which attract so many visitors to Watchet church, for it was in St. Decuman's that Lady

Florence Wyndham was buried at the end of the sixteenth century, and woke from a trance when the wicked sexton cut her finger in an attempt to steal her rings. The romance lies in its association with *Lorna Doone*, for Lorna's unfortunate mother, who was killed by the Doones on her way to Kentsford Manor, was buried in the churchyard. Many have come to seek the grave and gone away disappointed, for if ever the grave existed, it has long been forgotten.

Close to the church is the Holy Well of St. Decuman, who is said to have come over from Wales on a hurdle—presumably a coracle—and lived as a hermit on the site of the church, until one day, whilst he was praying his head was struck off by a passing pagan. Tradition avers the saint picked up his head and carried it under his arm to the well, where he washed it! Unfortunately, tradition, as usual, is content to leave it at that, and nothing is known of his further proceedings, or what the doubtless very frightened pagan did. By ecclesiastical standards, he should have been converted instantly, but possibly he dropped down dead of sheer fright! Anyway, there is the church to the saint's memory; and on Wells cathedral front, and every other picture or statue to his memory, St. Decuman is shown holding his head in his hand, as testimony to the truth of the legend.

No part of the country is richer in legends and customs which have persisted to the present day than the west Somerset coast, and Watchet is no exception, as we have seen, but its greatest link with the past is the ancient Baron Court which has been held annually in October for over 500 years. The Court meets in the snuggery of the Bell Inn, and after the presentments have been dealt with, appoints a Portreeve for the Borough, an ale taster, stock drover, bailiff, crier and inspectors of weights and measures—all offices without duties nowadays, with the exception of the Portreeve, who collects a royalty on every cargo of coal coming into

Watchet. After all this business has been done the Court adjourns to lunch, which always includes a Michaelmas goose and a steaming bowl of ale punch, made from a recipe that has been a carefully guarded secret of the inn for 300 years or more.

There are charming footpaths and cliff-ways at Watchet, but they must be sought for in the woods of the Warren, or byways from the disused mineral railway track, one of which leads to ancient Kentsford Manor, now a farmhouse, but still attractive with mullioned windows, and a garden of beautiful trees and flowers. It was sold to the Wyndham family by Sir John Luttrell in the reign of Edward VI, and Charles I is reputed to have slept there on his way to Dunster Castle. There is an old chapel close by, and the narrow pack-horse bridge across the brook has a small cross of red Quantock stone in the side.

II

The Quantocks can be reached from Watchet by the coast road through the pretty little hamlet of Doniford, which was for centuries the home of the Huish or Hewish family, one of whom was Alexander Huish, born at Wells about 1594, one of the four correctors of the "Polygot Bible". It was at Doniford that Major-General Dunster-ville—the immortal "Stalky" of Kipling's story—made his home for a number of years between the wars.

The Quantock Hills are perhaps the loveliest, as they are the most famous of Somerset's hill ranges, their exquisite beauty enshrined in the no less exquisite prose of Dorothy Wordsworth's journals and all too brief references in the works of William Wordsworth, Coleridge and Southey. The Wordsworths might have made the Quantocks as great a literary shrine as they eventually created in the Lake District, if their landlord had not taken alarm at their "queer" ways and turned them out after only a year of joyous comradeship in work and friendship.

The hills reach in an unbroken line from West Quantoxhead to Hestercombe, above the Vale of Taunton Deane, with the sea at their northern foot, and an old British trackway running for twelve miles along the top of the ridge—a peerless range to explore on foot, but even more exhilarating for a gallop on horseback on a summer's morning before breakfast.

Great hanging woods on the southern slopes, deep wooded combes on the north, and the famous Holford beeches on the heights above Alfoxden Manor, alternate with bright swathes of ling and heather, which is more plentiful here than anywhere else in Somerset, and with lush meadows and the deep red of ploughed fields or the gold of ripening grain. There is an air of deep peace and contentment, reflected in the placid and unchanging beauty of the little villages and the hearty, friendly hospitality of Quantock folk.

West Quantoxhead, perhaps better known now as St. Audries, from the church and mansion built in the nineteenth century by Sir Alexander Acland Hood, and seat of Lord St. Audries until 1924, when it became a school. The small church and the great mansion, although modern, look extremely picturesque against their background of well-timbered park-land, and the rectory was for many years the home of the Rev. J. R. Vernon, author of *The Harvest of a Quiet Eye*. He is buried in the church of which he was rector for so many years.

East Quantoxhead lies a mile off the main road and near the sea—a perfect grouping of thatched cottages, ancient church, manor-house, and duck-pond. East Quantoxhead was the home of the Luttrells long before they bought Dunster in the fourteenth century, and the present owner can trace his descent back to the first Norman lord—one of the longest tenures on record in England. There is a fifteenth-century tomb in the church to Hugh Luttrell, and a memorial window to Alexander Fownes Luttrell, who was rector of East Quantoxhead for nearly seventy years. He never spent a single night away from home after taking his eldest son to Eton in 1840, and at the time of his death in 1888 was probably the oldest clergyman of the Church of England.

The manor-house was restored and enlarged in 1610 by Sir George Luttrell, but retains a considerable amount of earlier work. There is an Elizabethan cock-pit; latticed windows opening on to the charming old walled garden; and elaborate plaster-work in some of the rooms. A fossilized lamb's heart, stuck over with pins, has hung over the vast fireplace in the kitchen for over two hundred years, as a testimony to the superstition of some long-dead domestic who used it to ward off a witch's curse.

Town's End, an attractive whitewashed house bowered in roses and honeysuckle, stands on the main road beside one of the lanes leading to East Quantoxhead. It was here that Lawrence Irving spent his honeymoon, and Sir Henry Irving captivated the villagers with his charm when on a visit. In 1784 that remarkable person Sarah Biffin, was born in the house. Although born without arms or legs, and never exceeding 37 inches in height, she displayed a talent for painting early in life. She was awarded a prize medal by the Society of Arts in 1821, and her work was patronized by George III, George IV, William IV, Queen Victoria, Prince Albert, and the King of Holland. She died in Liverpool in 1850, and a self-portrait in watercolours hangs in the Liverpool Museum. In 1925 Liverpool paid a tribute to her memory by holding an exhibition of her works, consisting chiefly of very fine miniatures.

Down another charming lane leading to the sea is Kilve, with its church and the ruins of a chantry, which was founded in 1329 and is said to owe its partial destruction by

16

fire to the ignition of smuggled spirits hidden there a hundred years ago. The great attraction of Kilve, for those "in the know" is the glatting—hunting for conger eels with "fish-dogs", and very exciting sport it is. All the coast from Watchet to the Parret abounds in rock pools where conger eels can be found at low tide, and every child spends many happy hours with a long stick and a bucket, searching the seaweed covered rocks for congers, but at Kilve the neap tides bring out men and boys and the specially trained dogs —usually a terrier or spaniel. "Glatts" or congers of from two to five pounds are found, and sometimes larger ones up to twenty pounds weight are captured.

Shortly after leaving Kilve the main road takes a bend to the south to Holford village, Alfoxden Manor, and all the lovely combes in the neighbourhood, with thick woods and prehistoric camps, and the superb views the Wordsworths and their friends loved. Other lanes branch off to Kilton and Lilstock, secluded hamlets right on the coast; to Stringston with its quaint little church topped by a broach spire of red tiles—a rarity in west Somerset; and Dodington, a little village with a small church, and the Elizabethan manor of the Dodingtons, now a farm. The family were seated at Dodington in the twelfth century, and the last male descendant was George Bubb Dodington, Lord Melcombe, whose diary, published after his death, threw a curious light on the lives of eighteenth-century notabilities who had been his intimates.

Further south is another ancient mansion, Fairfield House, on the site of a manor of the Verney family. It was built by Sir Thomas Palmer in the sixteenth century. The Palmers originally came from Wingham in Kent, and some baby clothes preserved at Fairfield House recall the most extraordinary case of triplets known to medical history, when Edward Palmer's wife gave birth to a son on each of three successive Sundays in June 1489. All the boys lived, and were knighted by Henry VIII. Fairfield is now the seat of Lord St. Audries, who is descended from the Palmers in the female line.

East of Fairfield Park is Stogursey, a corruption of its ancient name of Stoke Courcy, whose church has a remarkable series of Norman arches and other interesting features, including some ancient effigies of the Verneys, and a sanctuary ring attached to the base of one of the pillars, for the refuge of evil-doers.

The almshouses founded by Sir William Poulet in the reign of Henry V were rebuilt in the nineteenth century, but retain the old bell which has sounded at six in the morning and six in the evening ever since the foundation, and is locally known as "Ding-Dong Darling".

The neighbourhood of Stoke Courcy teems with interest. There is an ancient mill, still working; a Bronze Age tumulus at Wick; the enchanting little village of Shurston; Fiddington, another delightful village where the earliest spring flowers are found; and diminutive Stolford, on the coast.

Immediately south of Stoke Courcy is Nether Stowey, for ever famous as the home of the Nether Stowey Brotherhood of eighteenth-century poets. Here Coleridge lived and worked in perfect fellowship with his friend Tom Poole, and was visited by many of the celebrities of his day. The whole story of his life and work there, and his friendship with the Wordsworths at Alfoxden, is told in their letters and journals, and has given rise to almost a library of books, but comparatively few have done justice to the great influence on Coleridge's work exercised by that lovable character, Tom Poole, who was born, lived and died at Nether Stowey, but numbered among his closest friends and admirers not only Coleridge, but also the Wedgewoods, John Rickman, Secretary to the Speaker, and Sir Humphrey Davy, who dedicated his last book to Tom Poole "in remembrance of thirty years of continued and faithful friendship". Although the greater part of his life was spent in Stowey, Tom Poole superintended the first regular census ever taken in England, travelled in Europe, and contributed to the *Morning Post* and *The Watchman* on agriculture and economics. His cousin, John Poole, who became Rector of Enmore, was a brilliant scholar, and founded one of the earliest elementary schools in the kingdom at Enmore, which attained such celebrity it was visited by people of all ranks from far and near.

Stowey Female Friendly Society was founded by Tom Poole, and provided with a motto by Coleridge, which has been used ever since.

A very different type of person was born at Nether Stowey over two hundred years before Tom Poole—that widely discussed character, Robert Parsons, the English Jesuit, whose methods were disliked even by Catholics, but whose courage was unquestioned. Another native of Nether Stowey was Sir Edward Walker, the seventeenth-century historian and Garter King-of-Arms, who bought Shakespeare's house, New Place, on the death of Shakespeare's last surviving descendant, and died there in 1677.

Nether Stowey was once a market town, and had an annual cattle fair, but now it is a quiet village drawing people chiefly to see the little cottage, marked by a plaque, in which Coleridge lived, which was preserved for the nation chiefly through the activities of the Rev. William Greswell, the Quantock historian, who was born at Kilve, and buried at Dodington, of which he was rector.

Just outside the village, on the Bridgwater road, is the much-photographed gazebo, and the long wall which hides the fish-ponds of a vanished monastery, and a manor-house begun in the fifteenth century by Lord Audley, who was beheaded for his share in the rebellion of Perkin Warbeck before he could complete it. The stones for the mansion were brought from the ruins of a Norman castle which crowned the neighbouring Castle Hill.

Over Stowey, south of Nether Stowey, is a smaller village whose church has a memorial window by Burne-Jones to the memory of the great Victorian Radical, Henry Labouchère, the first and only Baron Taunton, who built Quantock Lodge in the well-wooded grounds of the hillside above the village. Near by are Marsh Mills, the home of John Poole; enchanting Cockercombe and Seven Wells Combe, Danesborough, or Dowsborough Hill, crowned by a fine tumulus; Aisholt in a pretty little combe; and Holwell Cave with its stalagmites and stalactites.

Near the entrance to one of the combes is the site of Walford's Gibbet, where John Walford of Stowey was hanged in the eighteenth century for the murder of his wife, under tragic circumstances which have often been re-told.

The last of the Quantock "broom squires", who were engaged in making besoms, lived at Over Stowey, and only retired a few years before the last war.

Among the villages of the foothills is Spaxton, which found itself in a blaze of publicity in the middle of the nineteenth century, when Agapemone, or "Abode of Love" was founded at the Four Forks by Brother Prince. An account in *Macmillan's Magazine* said that the community at one time numbered nearly 200, and all those who owned property made it over to Prince, and lived in Agapemone, having all things in common. In his more flourishing days, Prince always appeared in great state, "driving out in a carriage and four, with postillions and outriders, attended by bloodhounds"—no wonder the villagers gossiped and scandalous tales circulated freely! After the death of Prince the colony continued to exist, but on less spectacular lines, and its sensational foundation, although by no means forgotten, is forgiven! Charlinch church has an epitaph to a bygone priest whose death "merits rivers of tears, though the tide were pearls dissolved or crystal liquefied". Near Charlinch is the beautiful old manor-house of Gothelney, once the home of the Bournes, and Blackmore Farm, which has a ruined chapel attached to it.

The main road passes close to Brymore House, the birth-place of John Pym, who led the House of Commons in the early years of the Long Parliament, was one of the Five Members whose arrest Charles I attempted, and has been acclaimed as "the founder of party government in England". North of Brymore House is Cannington Park, said to have been the site of the battle of Cynuit in the days of Alfred the Great.

Although Cannington looks modern, it has had a long history. The manor has been in the possession of the Clifford family for centuries, and a tradition persists locally that "Fair Rosamund", who was beloved by Henry II, was born there, and spent her early youth in the nunnery, of which a fragment still remains. Cannington church has several unusual features, and near by is Gurney Street farm, an old manor-house with a tiny domestic chapel and priest's chamber.

North of Cannington are the flat meadows bordering the tidal estuary of the Parret and the sands of Stert Flats—a lonely region seldom penetrated by strangers, but with its own queer charm of breeze-swept levels, and quaint little villages at Otterhampton, with its ancient little church; Combwich, where there is a ferry across the Parret at certain states of the tide; Stockland Bristol, which derives its name from the fact that it formed part of the endow-ment of Gaunt's Hospital in Bristol; and most remote and quaint of all, the tiny hamlet of Stert, with its fishing nets hung on stakes at the seaward edge of a mile or more of mud flats bare at low water, and reached by the curious sledges peculiar to the mouth of the Parret, and locally called "mud-horses". The Bridgwater pilot cutters usually lie in the river under Stert Point. The curious local type of centreboard open boats are chiefly at Combwich, and are used for reaching nets set on the far side of the channel.

This lonely area abounds in tales of witches, phantom hounds, and headless riders. One phantom rider bestrides a vast pig, and all the tumuli have their tales of pixies and phantoms, many of the stories having their origin in old Scandinavian legends of Thor, Odin, and Frey, which may have been brought by the old Danish invaders.

III

East of Cannington the main road continues through Wembdon, which has an ancient and once famous holy well, to Bridgwater, where it branches south to Taunton, but other roads seek out the villages of the eastern slopes of the Quantocks—Durleigh, with its ancient church, and the old manor-house, now Bower Farm, which dates from 1500, and was a possession of the Seymour family. It disputes with Wulfhall in Wiltshire the honour of being the birthplace of Queen Jane Seymour. The old dove-cote attached to the manor has over 900 nesting niches.

Enmore has a modern "castle", an ancient church, and a unique fifteenth-century churchyard cross. The Rev. E. H. Smith wrote his book on *Quantock Life and Rambles* in the rectory of Enmore, and gives interesting details of the work of his predecessor, John Poole, and other local personalities.

Goathurst has an old church with effigies of Sir Nicholas Halswell, who died in 1633, and his wife and nine children, and a chapel of the Kemeys-Tyntes, who have been seated at the Tudor Halswell House for centuries.

IV

Herstercombe nestles in a picturesque dell on the south flank of the Quantocks, and there is a charming walk up the wooded combe to the summit of the hills.

In the neighbourhood of Hestercombe are Ruborough Camp, a Roman entrenchment enclosing twenty-seven acres, and Broomfield, with its interesting old church neighboured by Fyne Court, home of Andrew Crosse, the philosopher, who carried out many experiments in electricity there. He was regarded as a wizard by many of his neighbours, but Tom Poole, and Sir John Trevelyan of Nettlecombe valued his work at its true worth, and Sir Humphrey Davy, and other scientists, took a keen interest in his experiments.

The road descends through beech woods from Broomfield to Cothelstone Park, and the ancient church has monuments to the Stawells, who were lords of the manor in former times. Only the gateway survives of their old manor-house as a reminder of a grim tale of Jeffreys, who hanged two of Monmouth's followers near this very gate because Lord Stawell had dared to plead for them. It is said that formerly certain tenements were held by payment of a number of bushels of rye annually on Michaelmas Day, the tenants being known as "rye renters". There is a beautiful little Holy Well near the manor-house.

Cothelstone Beacon commands a really glorious panorama of sea and land, although it lacks the height of neighbouring Will's Neck, the highest point of the Quantocks.

Crowcombe is another enchanting village, with thatched cottages, an ancient church with fine, carved bench-ends, a richly sculptured churchyard cross, and a village cross, both dating from the fourteenth century, and a church house, now carefully restored, but once in danger of being lost, according to Richard Jefferies. In his charming essay *Summer in Somerset* he describes how the building was occupied by two different people, and when the occupant of the upper floor proposed to share the cost of repairs with the occupant of the ground floor, the latter said he thought of pulling his part down!

The entrance gates of Crowcombe Court, the ancient home of the Carews, are between the church and church house.

West of Crowcombe, on the road to Stogumber, is the ancient Heddon Oak, so famous that it is actually marked on the Ordnance Survey. It is said to be haunted by the ghosts of some of Monmouth's followers who were hanged from its branches.

Crowcombe is the starting-point for the beautiful walk up Will's Neck to the Triscombe Stone, so diminutive that it is hard for the stranger to find, but famous as the scene for the opening meet of the Quantock Staghounds, and as a wishing stone, but in any case well worth finding for the superb view.

Beyond Crowcombe village is Halsway Manor, said to have been a hunting-lodge of Cardinal Beaufort, and Bicknoller, an attractive village with an interesting church which was once a chapelry of Stogumber. It has some quaint epitaphs, including one in the churchyard to members of the family of Bartholomew Safford, a Presbyterian minister from 1646 to 1662:

> "Three Saffords out of view
> Mabel, Mary, Bartholomew
> Bartholomew Saffords flesh and bone
> His wife, his sister and his son
> Mabel became for worms a bait
> December 9th in forty-eight
> Mary was fitted for the bier
> On March 4th that same year
> Death on Bartholomew did fixe
> On March the 2nd forty-six
> Wife sister brother father dear
> Christ's minister and pastor here".

On the hill above Bicknoller is Trendle Ring, an almost circular camp which, unlike the many other camps crowning the hills of the Quantocks, is pitched on a steep slope. There is a delightful road over the shoulder of the Quantocks to St. Audries through the deep wooded glen of Weacombe with its tiny lake.

INDEX